WRITTEN OUT OF HISTORY:
Our Jewish Foremothers
A Book for All Seasons and Reasons . . .

- Included on the Jewish Welfare Board Jewish Book Council list of "Recommended Books for Bar/Bat Mitzvah". . . .

- Selected for the catalog of the National Women's History Month promotion for use in schools in the USA during March each year. . . .

- Recommended as a gift book for seasonal holidays by NEW DIRECTIONS FOR WOMEN . . . .

- Selected by many seminaries and universities in the USA as a supplementary course text since 1979 . . . .

Praised by reviewers, both popular and academic:

"Among the 'classics' of feminist writing about Jewish women are...(other books cited) and *Written Out of History* . ."
> Feminist Collections Bulletin, v. 4, no. 2, Winter 1983
> University of Wisconsin Library System

"Anyone interested in knowing about the accomplishments of Jewish women must read the lovely book, *Written Out of History* by Sondra Henry and Emily Taitz."
> Rifka Haut, in *Judaica Book News*, Winter 1983-84.

". . . the pages are brightened by women of all kinds of valor. . . this book. . . can lead all of us who know too little about Jewish women in history to begin to fill the vast gap in our knowledge."
> Morris U. Schappes, Editor, *Jewish Currents*

"I teach a course on women in Jewish history where this book is a required text and has proved to be a valuable source of information for my students. . . it is a fine book and there was a clear need for it."
> Norma Joseph, Dept. of Religion,
> Concordia University, Montreal.

Send for complete list of BIBLIO PRESS titles about/by/for Jewish women published since 1979, to, PO Box 4271, Sunnyside, NY 11104

Third Edition 1988

Sondra Henry
and
Emily Taitz

Written Out Of History:
Our Jewish Foremothers

BP
BIBLIO PRESS
Sunnyside, NY

Dedicated to our daughters and sons,
the inheritors of a great heritage.

Scott, Patricia, Gordon,
Daniel, Tamar, Miriam, Ariel

Copyright © Sondra Henry and Emily Taitz
Third Edition 1988
Biblio Press, Sunnyside, NY
ISBN 0-930395-06-9
Library of Congress Catalog Card No. 87-063559

This book was a 1986 Selection of the Bnai Brith Jewish Book Club
(1983 Second Edition Revised)
ISBN 0-9602036-8-0
Library of Congress Catalog Card No. 82-074284

First edition 1978
Bloch Publishing Co., New York, NY
ISBN 0-8197-0454-7
Library of Congress Catalog Card No. 77-99195

Cover photos: l. to r. top row: Ernestine Rose, Rosa Sonneschein,
Golda Meir. Bottom: Rebecca Gratz, Sadie American,
Rebekah Kohut, Rose Schneiderman.

Printed in the United States of America

This book was typeset in 12/13 Baskerville.

Cover design: SGW Associates, NYC.

Acknowledgments

We would like to thank the many people who have helped us to make this book a reality. Special appreciation is due to Frances Harris, a valuable research assistant, and Eva Yarett, Temple Israel Great Neck librarian, who helped locate books and articles; also to the dedicated librarians Dina Abramowicz of YIVO, Anna Kleban and Susan Young then of the Jewish Theological Seminary, and Dr. Israel O. Lehman of the Hebrew Union College in Cincinnati, who helped obtain copies of rare documents and manuscripts.

Our gratitude must go to the late Dr. S.D. Goitein of the Institute of Advanced Studies in Princeton, who responded to our letters and questions. His books provided us with essential information not available elsewhere.

Edya Arzt of the National Women's League of Conservative Judaism encouraged us at a most crucial time. Her recommendations helped us to achieve publication.

We thank our translators: Joseph Adler and William Ungar (Yiddish), Aliza Arzt (Arabic), Elisa Blankstein and Isaac Taitz (Hebrew), Linda Davidson and Vladimir Rus (Italian), Alice Morawetz (German). Because of their faith in our project, they gave generously of their time and talents, and often worked with poor or incomplete copies of old manuscripts, or hazy microfilm.

We received much valuable assistance from Rabbi Carl Wolkin who encouraged us from the inception of our plan, as well as from Rabbi Mordecai Waxman, Dr. Ruth Waxman, Rabbi Emanuel Zapinsky, Eva Sussman, Rabbi Shlomo Balter, Rabbi David Feldman, Laura Braverman, Willa Morris, Rosalyn Ullman, President of Temple Israel Sisterhood, and many others who provided us with valuable information and help.

Our sincere thanks go to the editors Lisa Besdin, Rachel Muchnick and David Szonyi whose constructive criticism with our original draft helped us clarify our own thinking. Thanks also to our typist Susan Forman whose cooperation helped to achieve a successful manuscript.

Thanks to Dr. Martin Cooper and Dr. Irving Levitas for their helpful suggestions; to Elizabeth Friedman for sharing her knowledge with us; and to Doris B. Gold for invaluable editorial assistance. Every effort was made to credit copyrighted material, but if omissions have occurred, corrections will appear in future editions.

Thanks also to:

The Jewish Publication Society of America for permission to reprint excerpts from Franz Kobler, *A Treasury of Jewish Letters;* David Philipson, *Letters of Rebecca Gratz;* Cecil Roth, *House of Nasi: Donna Gracia; The Holy Scriptures, According to the Masoretic Text.* Cecil Roth; *House of Nasi: The Duke of Naxos.*

KTAV Publishing House, Inc., for permission to quote and reprint excerpts from Israel Zinberg, *A History of Jewish Literature* (translated and edited by Bernard Martin).

Frederick Ungar Publishing Co., Inc., for permission to reprint excerpts from the Will of Frau Frumet (Fani) Wolf from Franz Kobler (ed.) *Her Children Call Her Blessed.*

Thomas Yoseloff for permission to reprint excerpts from *The Memoirs of Glückel of Hameln,* (translated and edited by Beth-Zion Abrahams).

Hadassah Magazine for permission to reprint excerpts from
S.D. Goitein, "New Revelations from the Cairo Geniza",
Hadassah Magazine, October, 1973.

Rabbinical Assembly for permission to reprint excerpts from
S.D. Goitein, "The Jewish Family in The Days of Moses
Maimonidies", *Conservative Judaism,* Fall, 1974.

The Swallow Press for permission to reprint excerpts from
Nathaniel Kravitz, *3000 Years of Hebrew Literature.*

The authors wish to express their grateful appreciation
to the following for permission to reproduce material from
these collections:

Hebrew Union College—Jewish Institute of Religion, Cincinnati, for
excerpt from the *Letter* in Hebrew of the *Rebbitzin Mizrachi.*

Jewish Theological Seminary and Library for permission to
reproduce *Meneket Rivka,* Title Page; Daily Prayer Manuscript,
handwritten by "Bat Meshullamim"; Prayer book, printed in
Dessau, 1696, Verse by *Ella,* 9 years old; *De Rebecca Polona,* Gustavo
Zeltner, cover page.

Bibliotheque Nationale, Paris for permission to reproduce
photograph of *Kizzur Mordecai,* handwritten by *Frommet of Arwyll*
(1454).

The Historical Society of Pennsylvania, for permission to reproduce
Rebecca Gratz, photo of Malbone miniature, from Leach's
Philadelphia Portraits.

Jewish Museum, for permission to use photograph of Torah Ark curtain, executed by *Leah Ottolenghi,* 16th cent.

American Jewish Archives, for permission to use portraits of selected
American Jewish women.

Contents

Preface   xiii

I.   A TRADITION OF CHANGE—AN
      OVERVIEW   1

II. THE FIRST JEWISH HEROINES—
      BIBLICAL WOMEN 15

III. BURIED TREASURES OF EGYPT AND
       GREECE 30

       1. *Mibtahiah* 30
       2. *Sambathe, the Jewish Sibyl* 38

IV. DAUGHTERS OF THE LAW—THE
       WOMEN OF THE TALMUD ... 44

       1. *Ima Shalom* 48
       2. *Beruriah* 54

V. POETS AND WARRIORS—OASES IN
      THE DESERT 59

       1. *Sarah* 62
       2. *Kahinah* 65
       3. *Kasmunah* 68

VI.   STOREHOUSE OF JEWISH WRITINGS
      —THE CAIRO GENIZA 71

VII. SISTERS IN EXILE—1000 to 1600 C.E.   83

      1. *Women scholars, prayer leaders,*
         martyrs, businesswomen 83
      2. *Rebecca Tiktiner* 92
      3. *Anxious Letters* 102
      4. *Rebbetzin Mizrachi* 108

VIII. SCRIBES AND PRINTERS 114

IX.   LIBERATED WOMEN, RENAISSANCE
      STYLE 123

      1. *Devora Ascarelli* 127
      2. *Sara Coppia Sullam* 130

X.   WOMEN OF INFLUENCE 136

      1. *Benvenida Abrabanel* 137
      2. *Dona Gracia Nasi* 139
      3. *Anna the Hebrew* 143
      4. *Esther Kiera* 146
      5. *Esperanza Malchi* 150

XI.   VOICES FROM THE GHETTO 152

      1. *The Prague Letters* 152
      2. *Glückel of Hameln* 165

XII. ONE STEP AHEAD—HASIDIC
      WOMEN 175

XIII.   THE THREE PORTALS 184

    1. *Sarah Bat Tovim and others* 184
    2. *Frau Frumet Wolf* 197
    3. *Judith Montefiore* 201
    4. *Rachel Morpurgo* 204

XIV.   OPENING DOORS: WOMEN
      AHEAD OF THEIR TIME 212

    1. *Rebecca Gratz* 218
    2. *Penina Moise* 224
    3. *Grace Aguilar* 229
    4. *Emma Lazarus* 236
    5. *Rebekah Kohut* 243

XV.   FROM FOREMOTHERS TO FUTURE
      LEADERS 249

    BACKNOTES 266

    BIBLIOGRAPHY 293

    INDEX 299

Index to Illustrations

Manuscript of *Meneket Rivka* by Rebecca Tiktiner,
Cracow, 1618 96

Ernestine Rose, suffragist, 19th century 98

Manuscript *De Rebecca Polona* by Gustavo Zeltner,
1719 101

Letter of *Rebbitzin* Mizrachi, in Hebrew 111

Kizzur Mordechai, Inscription by Frommet of
Arwyller, 1454, scribe 116

Prayer book, with Yiddish verse by printer's
daughter, Ella of Dessau, age 9 years, 1696 120

Torah Ark curtain by Leah Ottolenghi 125

Cover of manuscript of the Hebrew prayer,
Adon Olam, woman seated at writing table 133

Italian transliteration of Hebrew prayer *Adon Olam,*
by Illie bat Menachem, Meshullam family 134

Last page, manuscript of *Adon Olam* indicating the
writer to be an educated Italian Jewish woman .. 135

Twentieth century Jewish women cited in
chapter XV ....Center Spread

Lillian D. Wald, 20th century social worker 174

Rebecca Gratz, photo of Malbone miniature,
from Leach's Philadelphia Portraits. 222

Preface

"A woman of valor, who can find?
Her worth is far above rubies."

PROVERBS 31:1

Contrary to the ancient byword, we have not found the woman of valor to be so rare. But in the annals of Jewish history, she did remain hidden, ignored, and thus unknown to most of us. When we first began our journey through Jewish history, we discovered that the Jewish woman was almost invisible; virtually "written out."

Our search for historical documentation about Jewish women began with the Hebrew Bible; with the Matriarchs, Hannah and Deborah. But after Biblical literature, there was a vast gap in most books until the 19th century, when women such as Emma Lazarus, Henrietta Szold, and Golda Meir appear.

When we started our research in 1976, we searched for footnotes and minor bibliographic items to point the way to individual women. Although they were not easily discovered, we persisted, feeling sure there were many women who had contributed to the richness of Jewish life. The thought haunted us.

Slowly, we found other figures of note. Beruriah, scholar of the Talmudic era (2nd century C.E.) appeared first. She was followed by Deborah Ascarelli and Sara Coppia Sullam, Italian-Jewish Renaissance poets (15th and 16th centuries); and Gluckl of Hameln, who wrote her memoirs in the 17th century. These led to the discovery of still others.

While we searched for our Jewish foremothers, we learned more about Jewish history and Jewish Law. We discovered that many of the limitations and restrictions on women's role which became accepted in the Jewish society of Eastern Europe, were not necessarily the strictures of Jewish Law, but evidence of prevailing social attitudes. There seemed to be a real confusion between what the Law said, and what contemporary Jews assumed it said. As one Jewish historian has commented:

> Custom became master, and custom is a tyrant. Custom survives the circumstances which give it birth, and because the retention of it is based on sentiment it is not amenable to the assault of reason.[1]

As our search continued, we discovered Rebecca Tiktiner (died c. 1550), Benvenida Abrabanel (died 1560), and Eva Bacharach (1580-1651) who, despite prevailing restrictions, became serious scholars. Gracia Nasi (c. 1510-1565) was known to be a great philanthropist, a designation usually reserved for men.

Dipping far back into the past, the Aramaic papyri of the Elephantine colony revealed information on Mibtahiah, a forceful Jewish woman from the 5th century B.C.E. From documents of the Middle Ages, preserved in the Cairo *geniza*, we found evidence of active professional women, whose rights had been assured in their marriage contracts.

Women wrote many of the letters from the Prague Ghetto in 1619, revealing fragments of their daily lives. In the printing centers of Europe, beginning in the 1500's, women set type for Bibles and prayer books, and printed their own works as well.

From an emerging wealth of letters, court proceedings, marriage contracts *(ketubot)* and memoirs, women were revealed as property owners, traders, traveling merchants, doctors, teachers, scribes, printers, writers, poets, even ritual meat slaughterers, *rebbes,* and experts on Jewish Law.

It was this newly collected evidence about Jewish women that we gathered into the first edition of 1978, *(Written Out of History: A Hidden Legacy of Jewish Women Revealed Through Their Writings and Letters)* hoping to provide what was missing from other histories for the general reader.

A continuing examination of Jewish women (their personal, familial, vocational and communal lives) has confirmed our initial findings and revealed a multi-faceted role for women. They were traditionally responsible for the home and hearth, for the major Sabbath preparations and the laws of *kashrut*. But in addition, they sometimes performed the commandments *(mitzvot)* even when not required to do so. Many of their activities often belied later impressions of submissiveness. Occasionally an individual woman did challenge conventional societal rules and became a leader, a social activist, or a fighter for the rights of others.

During the past ten years Jewish women have come to learn more about their history and the history of women in general. Women's studies are now part of scholarly fields, becoming established in many universities as a legitimate discipline. The economic, social and religious activities of women are today seen as a fruitful research area. Sociologists, anthropologists, historians and students of literature have examined their subject matter from a woman's point of view, and have made valuable contributions to their fields.

Yet in spite of this increased interest in Jewish women and their activities, another work with a broad historical approach has not yet appeared to replace this volume. For the interested layperson who wants a general introduction to the "world of our mothers," *Written Out of History* still seems the only popular source.

In this new edition, as in the previous two, we did not propose to present an encyclopedic work on the subject. Many historical figures, especially those from more recent times who have single biographies, are not included here. Rather, we have tried to summarize available information about the role of women in Jewish history and to highlight some of their lives.

While our first edition was limited to women who left specific writings of their own, this edition includes others who have not. In the last chapter we have journeyed again into the past and added new information about women which has come to light in recent years. For the most part, these are women whose lives differed from the basic stereotypes or who were examples of a pattern in a specific time or place.

In the new section, we have also included women who lived and worked in the 20th century and who laid the groundwork for many aspects of modern life. Jewish labor leaders, early Jewish feminists and the first women rabbis have rightly become part of Jewish women's history, as have women scholars who have made important contributions to the field. However, these do not replace the earlier "women of valor" but are added to their ranks.

Letters and comments from readers have affirmed that this book, in its own way, has become a ground-breaking work. We feel pride in having helped some women to find their own lost history and their place in Jewish tradition. It is our fervent hope that it may continue to do so.

Sarah bat Tovim, the singer of psalms, said: "Every wise woman builds her house." The women in the pages that follow have given us the foundation. It is their legacy on which we build.

I

A Tradition of
Change—An Overview

"Strength and dignity are her clothing"
PROVERBS 31:25

People often discuss the Jewish woman's "traditional" role as opposed to the role she might desire
now or in the future. A dig into the past, however,
reveals a myriad of different roles, depending on
which country, which era, or which historian we
choose. One of the purposes of this book is to point
out that the role of women throughout history has
been varied, dynamic, and important. Like the men
whose deeds fill the pages of Jewish history books, the
women, too, covered the broadest spectrum of activities.

Often the ideas that men held about women were
more stereotyped and limited than the actual roles of
the women warranted. The following representative
view of the nineteenth century described women
idealistically, if naively, and is a good example of this
limited outlook toward the female sex.

Inspired devotion of strength and life to Judaism was
as natural with a Jewess as quiet, unostentatious
activity in her home. No need, therefore, to make
mention of act or name.[1]

This observation might have been true of certain
women, but was surely not universal enough to be-

come the accepted norm. Yet ideas like the above accounted for the fact that so many outstanding women were ignored or bypassed by historians. People tend to overlook things they do not expect, or are not educated to accept. So, by simple omission, it was implied that women were dedicated, if passive, "homebodies." They were proud of their work in keeping and building a Jewish home, and satisfied with the role of helpmeet—a role commonly believed to be the only one to which a Jewish woman ever aspired, and which automatically excluded any other.

Despite the constant attempt to stereotype women, however, there were always some who did not fit into the mold. For those women there was another interpretation of woman's role, and other guides to follow. Along with the strict and narrow view of woman as helpmeet, was another philosophy, sometimes hidden but always there. It started with Sarah, the first "mother in Israel," and continued growing. It was the idea that woman could be strong and righteous and equal. She stood side by side with men and made decisions with him, like Sarah did when she told Abraham to send Hagar and Ishmael away (Gen. 21: 1-14). Sometimes she made decisions *for* him like Deborah the prophetess did when she sent Barak to fight (Judges 4). She ruled over nations as did Queen Salome Alexandra when she reigned in Judah for seven years, giving the Jews the only peaceful years they enjoyed during the time of the Hasmoneans (1st century B.C.E.). Much later, she studied Torah like Beruriah did in the second century C.E., and became a scholar like Samuel ben Ali's daughter (12th century) and Jacob Mizrachi's wife (16th century). She could even put on phylacteries *(tefillin)* and prayer shawl *(tallith)* and pray like the men if she wanted, and there were those who did.[2]

Are these things permissible for women? Many people believe they are not. It is worthwhile to return to the source material for Jewish law and custom—the Bible and the Talmud—and briefly review what it actually does say about women.

The Bible says very little about women's specific rights; rather it makes assumptions based on what was the accepted custom at a given time. The Talmud outlines women's rights in areas such as marriage relationships and makes certain role divisions between the two sexes. These divisions do not always imply inequality, but one can infer a delegation of function. In general, the rabbis viewed women as intellectually inferior, "lightminded", and extremely sexually and physically oriented, hence a constant lure and temptation to men.[3]

Biblical society was polygamous, and laws about women and marriage were based on the assumption that it would remain so. Obtaining a divorce *(get)* was permitted according to Biblical law and simply involved the man giving the woman a bill of divorcement (Deut. 24: 1-4). A discussion of what happens if a woman should want a divorce and the husband not want it, simply never came up in Biblical writings. The ruling as stated was further elaborated by Talmudic law, and became the only way a divorce could be granted (i.e., the writing of a divorce by the husband). Whether this was the original intent of Biblical opinion on divorce must unfortunately remain unknown.

Adultery is another issue discussed originally in the Bible and elaborated and interpreted in the Talmud. The Bible claims that adultery occurs when a woman *who is married,* is sexually intimate with another man—any man (Lev. 20:10). The man is not considered to have committed the sin of adultery unless the woman is another man's wife. So, if a married man had an intimate relationship with an unmarried woman, he was required either to marry her (if she gave her consent) or to pay damages to her father for the loss of her virginity (Deut. 23: 28-29). Since the society was polygamous, it was a simple matter for him to marry, even if he already had several wives. Only when the woman was already married was this not possible. A definition of adultery, therefore, was dependent on the status of the woman and not at all on the "faithfulness" of the man.

Perhaps these regulations were logical in a society where men could have many wives, but when this custom had passed, the rulings concerning adultery still remained in force as before. A man, on the slightest suspicion of unfaithfulness on his wife's part, could bring her to the rabbinic court to undergo a shameful ordeal involving the drinking of "bitter water" (water which was mixed with dust from the Tabernacle floor, and into which the Priestly words of admonition to the woman [regarding unfaithfulness] have been washed off from a scroll) in order to prove her virtue (Num. 5: 11-31). Her husband's virtue was never tested by such methods.

Polygamy was not officially abolished until the beginning of the eleventh century when Rabbi Gershom of Mayence (Germany) ruled that the Biblical law permitting it was to be suspended for one thousand years. This *takkanah* (ruling) was accepted by Ashkenazi Jews but not the Sephardim. Although secular law in most countries prevents it, Sephardic Jews still believe polygamy to be permissable and they practiced it in isolated areas into the twentieth century.[4]

Inheritance is another issue where the Biblical Law is based on an assumption: inheritance goes from father to son. To allow a woman to inherit land when she ultimately married and left her home to live with

her husband, did not fit the social custom. The issue
of a woman inheriting property came up only once in
the Bible, when the various tribes were being allotted
their portions in the Promised Land. In this case, a
man, Zelophehad, had died in the desert and had no
sons (Num. 27: 1-11). His daughters petitioned for his
portion to be given to them, "so it may not be lost
from the tribe." Moses' ruling favored the daughters
and the tribe. The land remained part of the tribe's
portion and the young women were then specifically
ordered not to marry anyone outside their tribe so
that the land would never be lost from the tribe's
holdings. This was the basis of the ruling. Had there
been one surviving son, the question would never
have arisen, but as it was, this ruling set a precedent.
The rabbis may have been aware of the inherent un-
fairness of this law when it operated outside the tribal
system of land holdings, but they could not change
Biblical Law. They did, however, make many allow-
ances for daughters—one of which was a dowry—to
try to alleviate the obvious injustices in this area.[5] As
Jews became less and less tied to the land, it was not
uncommon for daughters to be given part of the inheritance through a specific will or other written request despite the accepted procedure of Biblical and
Talmudic times.[6]

Another aspect of Jewish law which has caused
women much difficulty in the area of ritual equality is
the ruling concerning laws of purity *(niddah).* It states
very clearly in the Bible (Lev. 12-15) exactly when a
person is considered ritually impure. (The word
impure—in Hebrew, *ta-may*—has no associations with
cleanliness or dirt as we understand it, and should not
be interpreted as such. It is a word that implies only a
fitness to approach God and/or partake of certain
ritual obligations). Those things which constitute im-

purity include: contact with a dead person or animal, the appearance of an open or running sore associated with certain skin diseases, a discharge of pus or semen, and the time of menstruation. If any one of these would occur, the person affected had to remove himself from the community for a week, or until the condition disappeared, and then ritually purify him/ herself in a body of water *(mikveh)*. During the time of the impurity, the person was not allowed to come in contact with any other member of the community nor to approach the Holy of Holies, which was the specific dwelling place of God.

These rather simple and perhaps even primitive principles of purity have been interpreted in many ways and often misunderstood. By no means are they the basis for the currently accepted understanding among the Orthodox Jewish community that women may not be called to the Torah for an *aliyah* (the honor of going up to the ark and saying a special prayer when the Torah is read).[7] The denial of the privilege of *aliyah* to women is based on the idea of sexual distraction, and, in the Talmud, on the principle of *kavod ha-tsibbur* (honor of the community)—a principle which implied that the calling up of women to read Torah might cause the congregants to infer a lack of education or committment on the part of the men.[8] Laws of purity are not involved in this ruling.

It is perhaps simplistic to point out that there were no Torah scrolls, nor any synagogues at the time the Biblical laws were first developed. Synagogues were first established during and after the Babylonian exile. Moreover, a passage in the Talmud clearly states that the Torah, being in itself a holy object, is not affected by any condition of purity or impurity that may exist in the person who comes in contact with it.[9]

Separation of men and women was originally initiated in the period of the Second Temple, to avoid unnecessary social interaction during the holy rituals. However, there is evidence that the strict and consistent separation of the sexes in the synagogue was not common practice until the thirteenth century and then it reflected the social separation common in general society.[10] Despite these facts, it is a widely assumed notion that woman's menstrual cycle has somehow made her unclean. And this in spite of the fact that Jewish law openly holds the commandment: "be fruitful and multiply" to be one of the most significant *mitzvot* (commandments) (Gen. 1:22) and that without the woman's menstrual cycle, the observance of this *mitzvah* would not be possible.

So we come finally to the *mitzvot* (commandments), the essence of an observant Jewish life. The Bible states that the *mitzvot* are the laws of God and they must be taught to one's children (Deut. 6:8). Written in the original Hebrew—a language which has no neuter word for children, but only words for sons or daughters—the verse reads: "You will teach it to your sons." For those who came later and were exposed to societies where women were openly considered inferior, this verse was an invitation to an interpretation excluding women from all learning. This exclusion created an even more severe limitation on women than is immediately apparent. Torah study, through the course of many centuries, became the most respected and valued occupation a Jew could engage in. Since women, by definition, had no obligation to be taught or to learn or teach, they were automatically barred from that group of persons who ranked highest in the community. There were, of course, those who taught their daughters, either because they had no sons or because they believed the commandment referred to all children.[11] If one searches, one can find a differing rabbinic viewpoint in favor of teaching women.[12] But the doubt always existed for some.

Then there was the obvious reality of life: woman was tied down with children; bearing, nursing, and caring for them. She might be answering to the needs of infants and children for most of her adult life. What would be more logical and humane than that she be excused from all the *positive commandments that have to be performed at a specific time?*[13] Consequently, she was excused—but not prohibited—from observing the commandments. It was widely understood that if a woman chose, she could take upon herself these additional obligations. Even in the darkest periods of Jewish history, there were those who stood out as holy women, learned and wise beyond what anyone expected of them, such as Dulcie of Worms who was martyred in the Crusades, (1213) or Jacob Mizrachi's wife (16th century), who humbled herself begging for money to support her yeshiva.

It has been suggested by several noted scholars that in spite of the restrictions placed on women within Talmudic Law, woman's role was not always limited.[14] Women led full lives in the middle ages in places like Egypt and in Mediterranean communities, and participated in all aspects of Jewish society from trade and politics, to philanthropy and scholarship. Religious leadership and formal rabbinic study were perhaps the only areas where they met any resistance. Maimonides (1135-1204), one of the most prominent Jewish philosophers and thinkers was very influential in imposing restrictions on women, which subsequently became a part of normative Judaism. His assertion that women not be appointed to any communal office is still accepted today in many places.[15] There are Jews who believe that Maimonides re-introduced or reinforced the anti-feminist attitudes that had been scattered throughout the Talmud.

The opposing Biblical trends: one which considered a woman a "peripheral Jew" in a subsidiary role to a man, and one which considered her an equal, continued beyond the Biblical period to the Talmudic period and beyond. Rabbi Eliezer ben Hyrcanus said: "woman's place is at the spinning wheel."[16] Rabbi Meir respected and encouraged his wife's learning and valued her example. We have statements warning men not to gossip with women, who are "lightminded," not capable of study, and even too unreliable to serve as witnesses in court.[17] On the other hand, we also find men being commanded to honor their wives more than themselves, and to listen to the advice of their wives.[18] Later, we have men like Samuel ben Ali who trained his own daughter to teach students at the academy in Baghdad, and we have Maimonides who felt that women should be restricted and even suggested that wife-beating (for certain offenses) was permissible.[19]

A recent book points out that the overwhelming feelings of the Talmudic rabbis were against the equality of women and that the excuse of exempting them on the pretext of household chores, was not sufficient reason for their exclusion from the obligations of performing certain *mitzvot*.[20] It makes the point that the lack of obligation eventually amounted to a prohibition for women. While all this is true, there are instances of women throughout Jewish history who did accept the obligations of Jewish Law and were considered to be learned and outstanding, even in the eyes of men. Beruriah, the scholarly wife of Rabbi

Meir, may be an exception (as this author insists). Every woman who did something noteworthy and left her footprints in our history, however lightly, may be an exception. Taken together however, they are a credit not only to woman's ability and strength, but to the ability of Jewish Law to be flexible enough to accept them in spite of all prejudices and ideas to the contrary.

There almost always were women who stood out as models for the next generation. In their time, they were known and respected by Jews of both sexes. In order to broaden our concepts of Jewish history, today's Jews need to hear and learn about them as well.

Women are presently seeking the right to be called to the Torah and to be recognized as equals under Jewish law: to have equal right to perform *mitzvot*, to initiate a divorce, to serve as a witness in a Jewish court, to be counted in a minyan (a group of ten required for a prayer service), and even to change the liturgy from "God of our fathers" to "God of our ancestors."[21] Yet missing from their arguments is a series of precedents which are not readily available.

We should know about Mibtahiah, a Jewish woman in the fifth century B.C.E. who *had* the right (along with all other Jewish women—even slaves) to be divorced without her husband's consent, and Beruriah, wife of Rabbi Meir, who put on tefillin each morning and studied three hundred laws each day. Important as well, are women like Wuhsha, in the eleventh century, who served as witnesses in the Jewish courts despite the Talmudic law to the contrary, and the learned women of the Middle Ages and beyond who preached and interpreted for their own congregations of women, upstairs, behind the *mehitza* (screen separating the women's section from the rest of the synagogue). They wrote their own beautiful prayers

calling on the "God of their Ancestors" and beseech-
ing Sarah, Rebecca, Leah, and Rachel, the *mothers* of
Israel, for help. We should be familiar with Hannah
Rachel Werbermacher, the mystical woman rabbi of
the Hassidim who lived in Poland in the 1800's. It is
important to look back and find them, and discover in
the process, more about ourselves and our history.

Who are all the women in these pages? Many were
outstanding in their achievements. Others made
memorable contributions to Judaism. Some are like
footnotes to history; they represent a trend, or an
attitude, or a way of living. Women like Dona Gracia
Nasi, Rebecca Tiktiner, Sarah Bat Tovim, and so
many, many more, should be remembered and
studied as important figures in Jewish history. Others
were chosen because they alone, by some quirk of
fate, were preserved through their writings and letters. Still others are mentioned because they tell us a
special story that should be known. Persons like the
captive woman in Egypt who pleads for help from the
Jewish community, personify a whole world of troubles, courage, and loyalty within Judaism. Women like
Esperanza Malchi who (in 1599) corresponded with
royalty, held a special kind of hidden power which
often they themselves did not recognize. Each woman
has a story to tell in the saga of Jewish life. Each one
presents us with another small part of the varied
picture of Jewish women's history.

We have tried to consider each woman in the
context of her time, avoiding the temptation of
imposing twentieth century views on another era.
They were not "oppressed" in the sense that we use
the term, in the context of the 1970's feminist
movement. For the most part, they did not even feel
oppressed. As far as we know, women did not often
question a role which, like the Biblical woman of

valor, placed them in the home as guardians of their households.

Before the modern age recognized the individual citizenship of each person, the Jew could only exist within his or her close, cohesive community at whose center lay the only institution which did not limit women—the home. The wife and mother (and there was no alternative life style to being a wife and mother) held an honored and important place there. There were many outlets for her interests and energies—sometimes more than she could handle. Earning a living was not only a man's job, but a family enterprise. So, women and even female children, often shared in every conceivable profession in which a husband might engage. Where the man devoted himself to study, the woman was often the principal breadwinner in the family.

Preparing food was an indispensable and important part of daily living, and Jewish living. Sabbath, festivals, and rules of *Kashrut* (dietary laws) were all a real concern. Laws of family purity, including regular immersion in the *mikveh* after each menstrual period, were important. Men too, went to the *mikveh*. They were also liable to impurities, not only from women, but from their own bodily functions or from everyday living experiences. So the woman who became an expert in laws of *Kashrut* (as did Rashi's daughters in the twelfth century) or in laws of purity, was studying rituals and customs that were important to the entire community, and not just to herself.

Within the scope of the Jewish community there was room for the learned woman as well as for the woman who had never learned how to read. Women poets, writers, and printers expressed themselves and contributed to Jewish life as much as the women who stayed home and baked the Sabbath *challot* (bread) and taught their children the *alef-bet* (alphabet). The Jewish community needed them all.

It would be incorrect to imply that Jewish women chafed under the yoke of oppression from men. Yet it would be equally wrong to imply that they never rebelled or fought for more rights, either in the ritual or in the working world. Even in the Middle Ages when secular laws in Europe considered women the wards of their husbands, the Jewish woman found new opportunities to advance herself. Venturing into the world of trade and finance (occupations of increasing importance in the expanding societies of Europe and Asia), she often became financially independent and was able to have a greater voice in the Jewish community. Women agitated for the removal of restrictions in the performance of religious precepts and won society's approval to practice commandments from which they were exempt. They began to recline at the seder table along with men, to observe the Fast of the First Born on the day before Passover, and to say the blessing on the *Etrog* and *Lulav* on Sukkot, even though these were timebound *mitzvot* and were not required of them.[22]

Women in the earliest Jewish settlements in England earned the right, by their proficiency and importance in business matters, to be independent witnesses and to borrow and lend money under their own names. These instances are by no means unique.

Where society generally favored the Jewish community, such as in medieval Egypt or Renaissance Italy, or in England and America in the 1800's, women received greater freedom and more rights. Where the Jew was oppressed and poor, in places like the Arab lands after the fall of the Ottoman Empire, or in Europe in the early Middle Ages, the Jewish woman likewise enjoyed fewer advantages. Wherever

Jews lived, they were influenced by those around
them. So Mrs. Mizrachi, who lived in Kurdistan, an
area between northern Turkey and Iran, said she was
well-born and did not go out alone; while Glückel, a
Jewish woman from Germany worked as a trader of
pearls and went on business trips from one city to
another, braving the dangers of highwaymen and local
wars. Each time and place allowed women different
advantages and disadvantages. Some places and times
stressed the inclination towards women's rights, which
had always been part of the Jewish heritage. Other
times and places emphasized the auxiliary role of
women.

Judaism is a tradition that began thousands of years
ago. From its beginning it has been changing, and it
continues to do so. We can find models of an enlightened attitude or a rigid one, instances of loyalty and
strength, piety and understanding. We can also find
cases of women who were illiterate, or unworthy, or
who performed evil deeds. The scope of their activities
is a study in contrasts. Differences between women
like Ima Shalom, an aristocrat of the rabbinic era, and
Kahinah, a warrior of the seventh century, could not
be more pronounced. Women like Esther Kiera, a
Turkish-Jewish politician of the 1600's and Devora
Ascarelli, a Renaissance poet, represent different
worlds. Yet they are all part of the rich heritage of
Jewish women. We can select Sarah or Deborah, or
one of the many Rebeccas, Rachels, or Esthers whose
words and deeds are contained in these pages. Or we
can choose them all, remembering that they represent
hundreds of others whose words and deeds have been
lost, neglected by others, and forgotten in the passage
of time.

II

The First Jewish Heroines

"... The rulers ceased in Israel, they ceased,
Until that thou didst arise, Deborah,
That thou didst arise a mother in Israel."

JUDGES 5:7

The women whose stories are told in the pages of
the Bible are as different from each other as the
women of today—as different as they have always
been throughout history. Some are heroines, others
are just shadows flitting through the back pages of
early history with barely a mention of their names.
The stories of the Bible show no lack of outstanding
female characters. In the second chapter of Genesis,
the very first book, a woman is introduced into the
Biblical narrative in the character of Eve.

Eve is indeed an extraordinary woman. A great deal
of discussion has been devoted to her and to her sin
of eating the forbidden fruit of the Tree of Knowledge. In so doing, Eve became the first human being
to commit a definitive act based on her own thinking.
It was she, and not Adam, who made the first choice
in the Garden of Eden—and she decided in favor of
knowledge over obedience.[1]

The next woman who comes to our attention as a
decisive factor in Jewish history is Sarah, considered
to be the first mother of the Hebrews. Thanks to recent archeological discoveries, much more is understood about Sarah now than was previously understood.

Sarah (or Sarai, as she was originally called) grew
up north of Canaan (the area which became Israel) in

a country dominated by the Hurrians, a part of the
Mitanni kingdom. She migrated south with her husband Abraham, and their household. Sarah had no
children, but despite this obvious lack she was 'safe' in
her marriage with Abraham. As was the custom with
all the well-born women of Haran, a center of the
Hurrian society, Sarah's marriage contract protected
her from divorce even if the marriage was childless.[2]
It also gave her several options. One of these options
was to give her husband her own personal slave as a
concubine. The child resulting from this union was to
be considered her child. The marriage contract also
guaranteed that any child born to Sarah subsequently,
would have the rights of inheritance—the right of the
first-born.[3]

In fact, Sarah exercised these options. She presented her personal handmaiden Hagar, an Egyptian,
to Abraham.[4] The son Hagar bore was called Ishmael.
Many years later, when Isaac was born to Sarah, she
came to regret the earlier decision. Hagar had become
arrogant and hostile to her mistress Sarah, and
Ishmael, headstrong and wild, taunted her own young
son. Sarah decided to send Hagar and Ishmael away
into the desert.[5]

Sarah's treatment of Hagar is often criticized by
readers who judge biblical events by today's standards
of morality. In the context of her world however,
Sarah was acting in the best interests of her family,
and protecting Isaac from the detrimental influence
of a pagan half-brother whose ways were foreign to
her own.

The practices of the Hurrians were unique in their
age. They were part of a civilization of the ancient
Middle East that recognized women as individuals
with specific guaranteed rights. The Babylonians,
while granting certain wives more rights than con-

cubines,[6] nevertheless considered women to be property,[7] as did the Canaanites. Later on, the Greeks did little to improve on that primitive notion. In the "advanced" Athenian society, a woman was still considered to be the inferior of a man in every respect, fit only to serve him and bear his children.

In this context, the Hurrians were ahead of their time. Although their culture has long passed on, they left their mark on Jewish civilization. It was from them that Sarah probably took her conception of herself as a woman who was capable of independent action. She was neither afraid to say what she wanted nor to act on it. Moreover, even God supported her decisions,[8] advising Abraham to listen to all that Sarah said, because his seed would continue in Isaac, not in Ishmael.

When the time came for Isaac to marry, Abraham's servant Eliezer was sent back to Haran to seek out a wife for him. He found Rebecca, but she was not sent to him without first asking for her consent. Her brother went to her and said: "Wilt thou go with this man?" Rebecca answered: "I will go."[9] In the time of the patriarchs and matriarchs (2100-1500 B.C.E.), this practice was hardly accepted procedure. Girls were betrothed at an early age by their fathers or other male relatives and their own agreement was not sought. This short passage in the Bible concerning Rebecca, set a standard which some societies have not yet reached today.

Leaving her family's household in Padan-Aram to join her new husband, Rebecca took with her the same ideas of her basic worth as an individual and as a woman, that Sarah had learned. Early in her married life, Rebecca also had direct communication with God, who spoke to her during her pregnancy. When she "inquired of the Lord" concerning the children who struggled even in her womb, God answered:

Two nations are in thy womb,
And two peoples shall be separated from thy bowels.
And the one people shall be stronger than the other
people;
And the elder shall serve the younger.[10]

It is on the strength of this message from God that
Rebecca made the decision to go against Isaac's wishes
in order to ensure that Jacob, the younger, received
the rights of the first-born son.[11]

In advising Jacob to go to her blind and dying husband disguised as his brother Esau, Rebecca is often
accused of being manipulative (a shortcoming commonly attributed to women). However, it is important
to remember that Rebecca, like Sarah, was acting
within her legal and societal prerogatives. In the country of her origins, it was not an automatic procedure
for the oldest child to receive the inheritance according to the rights of the first-born. It was possible for
this privilege to be bestowed on the most capable son
instead.[12] Since Isaac was old and no longer as per-
ceptive as he had once been, and since Rebecca had
received the word of God concerning her sons, she
may have felt that the decision was hers to make. In
choosing Jacob, she, like Sarah before her, became a
mother in Israel.

When Jacob became old enough to marry, he also
journeyed to Padan-Aram, the home of his mother
and grandmother, to seek a wife. He found not one,
but two—Leah and Rachel.

Of the two sisters, Rachel was the more beloved, but
Leah was the more prolific. She first gave birth to
four sons while Rachel was barren. Rachel chose to
exercise the same prerogative as Sarah had. She too

gave Jacob her handmaid Bilhah, saying: "Go in unto
her; that she may bear upon my knees, and I also may
be builded up through her."[13] Bilhah had two sons,
but it was Rachel's own children, Joseph and Benjamin, born much later, who were their father's favor-
ites.

As we can see, the mothers of Israel—Sarah, Rebecca, Leah and Rachel—brought a conception of independence and strength which was passed down to
the Jewish people. The influence of the early Babylonian culture was also there, making an equally strong
imprint on early Israelite society. The two strains together form the many-faceted impressions of women
found among the pages of the Bible.

Leaping over several centuries of ancient history, we
find ourselves with the Israelites in Egypt. Among the
people who were enslaved by the Pharaoh was a family of the tribe of Levi. They had two sons, Aaron and
Moses, and a daughter Miriam. Of the three, Miriam
was by far the more active and charismatic. She was
instrumental in saving her brother Moses from the
Pharaoh's harsh decree to kill all male children born to
the Hebrews.[14] Hiding in the bulrushes near the river
where her baby brother was set afloat in a tiny ark,
Miriam watched Moses' rescue by the Pharaoh's
daughter and arranged for her own mother to be his
nurse. Despite the fact that Moses, upon returning to
his people as a leader, chose Aaron as his chief assistant, Miriam still emerged as an important figure. It
was she who led the women of Israel in praise of God,
after the Israelites had safely crossed the Red Sea.

And Miriam the prophetess, the sister of Aaron, took
a timbrel in her hand; and all the women went out
after her, with timbrels and with dances. And Miriam

sang unto them, Sing ye to the Lord, for He is highly exalted; The horse and his rider hath He thrown into the sea.[15]

During the wandering in the desert, it was told that Miriam was followed by a well which supplied the Israelites with fresh water.[16] This legend may indicate that she had a talent for finding water—a most valuable asset for a desert people.

The most interesting and puzzling story pertaining to Miriam occurred during the wandering of the children of Israel in the desert. Suddenly there was a challenge to Moses' judgment led by his own siblings, Aaron and Miriam.[17] The issue at hand was Moses' marriage to a Kushite woman (a non-Israelite from the African land of Kush). In answer to the challenge, God chastised both Miriam and Aaron for slandering their brother. As a punishment, Miriam was stricken with leprosy—a skin disease which was considered "unclean" so that its bearer had to live outside the camp and not approach anyone for seven days. When Aaron and then Moses, pleaded with God to forgive Miriam, she was healed. Nevertheless, as a punishment, she had to live outside the camp for the prescribed period, while Aaron did not receive any punishment.

Why was the punishment visited only on Miriam? The text of the Bible, in its use of the feminine singular verb for speaking (*va-t-'daber*) implies that only Miriam spoke out against her brother and Aaron merely listened.[18] She may generally have been more outspoken and critical of Moses than her acquiescent brother Aaron, who had his own sphere of influence in the priesthood.

Despite this small lapse however, Miriam is considered to be one of the three most important people who led the Jews out of Egypt and guided them in those early years.[19] She died in Kadesh, which was in the Wilderness of Zin, during the first month of the fortieth year of the wandering.[20] Referred to as a prophetess and a guide to the women of Israel, she remains one of the more popular figures of the Bible.

Hannah was another Biblical woman who, through her children, changed the course of history. Two things are especially noteworthy about Hannah's life: first, that she was the mother of Samuel, the great prophet who anointed both Saul and David as Kings of Israel, and second, that her prayer to God is one of the longest passages in the Bible attributed to a woman.

The Biblical account tells us more about Hannah. She was married to a man named Elkanah, and shared him with another wife, Penina.[21] Penina had many children, but Hannah was childless, which made her very unhappy. The love that Elkanah had for her was small compensation for this obvious failing in her marriage. Children were considered a gift from God and the main purpose of the union of husband and wife. Hannah could hardly overlook the fact that God had failed to bless her in this way.

There are several parallels between the story of Hannah's life and the story of Rachel. Both were the more beloved of two wives and both were barren. Rachel's prerogative of giving her handmaid to her husband to bear children in her name, was no longer practiced in Israel. Hannah's only recourse was to pray to God. This she did with such fervency, that she was thought by the High Priest to be drunk and not able to control herself. A thousand years later, her prayer became an example of sincerity and devotion that was held up as a paradigm by the rabbis of the Talmud.[22]

Hannah promised that if a son were born to her, she would dedicate his life to God.[23] Her prayer was answered and Samuel was born. No sooner was he weaned than she brought him to the High Priest to reaffirm her vow. It was at that time that she recited her beautiful and moving praise to God, who had granted her a son, thus giving her what she most desired.

Samuel remained at the Temple and was a prophet of God all his life. He is one of the great figures of Biblical history. Hannah continued her life with Elkanah and bore three more sons and two daughters.

Although Hannah's prayer to God is in thanks for a personal request for a son, her words transcend personal and individual feelings. In the following powerful and sincere lines, she praises God who "killeth and maketh alive".

> And Hannah prayed, and said:
> My heart exulteth in the Lord,
> My horn is exalted in the Lord;
> My mouth is enlarged over mine enemies;
> Because I rejoice in Thy salvation.
> There is none holy as the Lord;
> For there is none beside Thee;
> Neither is there any rock like our God.
> Multiply not exceeding proud talk;
> Let not arrogancy come out of your mouth;
> For the Lord is a God of knowledge,

And by Him actions are weighed.
The bows of the mighty men are broken,
And they that stumbled are girded with strength.
They that were full have hired out themselves for bread;
And they that were hungry have ceased;
While the barren hath borne seven,
She that had many children hath languished.

The Lord killeth, and maketh alive;
He bringeth down to the grave, and bringeth up.
The Lord maketh poor, and maketh rich;
He bringeth low, He also lifteth up.
He raiseth up the poor out of the dust,
He lifteth up the needy from the dung-hill,
To make them sit with princes,
And inherit the throne of glory;
For the pillars of the earth are the Lord's,
And He hath set the world upon them.

He will keep the feet of His holy ones,
But the wicked shall be put to silence in darkness;
For not by strength shall man prevail.
They that strive with the Lord shall be broken to pieces;
Against them will He thunder in heaven;
The Lord will judge the ends of the earth;
And He will give strength unto His king,
And exalt the horn of His anointed.[23]

There are many women in the Bible in addition to those mentioned: Huldah, the prophetess who was consulted by King Josiah;[24] Ruth, a figure beloved by Jews and non-Jews alike, who was a faithful convert to Jewish life and the ancestor of King David;[25] and Esther, queen of Persia who saved the Jews from

Haman's evil plot of destruction.[26] Yet one woman
towers above them all — Deborah the Prophetess.

Deborah stands alone among the other great
heroines of the Bible. Sarah, Rebecca, Leah and
Rachel are remembered and revered as mothers and
wives, and as women who carried out the will of God.
Miriam was also a leader and prophetess, but she led
only the women of Israel. Esther, the heroic queen,
saved the Jews—but under the direction of her cousin,
Mordecai. Deborah was a judge, a leader and unifier
of all Israel, a prophetess, a warrior, and a passionate
believer in Israel's ultimate victory.

In the early years of the nation of Israel, the people
were divided into tribes, each with its own territory.
They could hardly have been called a united people.
The Canaanites took every advantage to attack the
tribes separately and had apparently succeeded in dis-
organizing daily life to the extent that the Israelites
could not travel on the roads. It was under these tur-
bulent conditions that Deborah lived.

> Now Deborah the Prophetess, the wife of Lappidoth,
> she judged Israel at that time.[27]

This simple statement indicated that Deborah had
been noticed and singled out for her wisdom. The
people of all the tribes came to her with their problems and disputes and she judged them according to
the Law of Moses.

Seeing the disunity among her people and the problems they had with the Canaanite king Jabin and his
army, Deborah called Barak to her and instructed him
according to the command of God. He was to take an
army of ten thousand men up to Mount Tabor and
fight against Sisera, the captain of the Canaanite
force:

And she sent and called Barak the son of Abinoam
out of Kedesh-naphtali and said unto him: Hath not
the Lord, the God of Israel, commanded saying: Go
and draw toward Mount Tabor and take with thee ten
thousand men of the children of Naphtali and of the
children of Zebulun. And I will draw unto thee to the
brook of Kishon, Sisera the captain of Jabin's army,
with his chariots and his multitude; and I will deliver
him into thy hand.
And Barak said unto her: "If thou wilt go with me,
then I will go; but if thou wilt not go with me, I will
not go." And she said: "I will surely go with thee:
notwithstanding the journey that thou takest shall not
be for thy honour, for the Lord will give Sisera over
into the hand of a woman.[28]

Deborah's words proved true. It was not Barak who
ultimately killed Sisera. It was a woman named Ya-el.
Ya-el was not an Israelite, but a woman of the Kenite
tribe, a group that was allied with Israel. She saw Sisera running from the defeat of his army, and invited
him into her tent. She gave him milk to drink, offered
him a place to rest, and when he lay down to sleep,
she pounded a tent peg into his head and killed him.
With this deed, Ya-el sealed the victory of Israel over
the Canaanites.[29]
A thousand or more years later, men considered
women to be the weaker sex, and women began to believe it themselves. The daring of Ya-el and the decisive actions of Deborah, belie this accepted myth.
After the victory, Deborah and Barak sang a song
praising God and retelling all the events of the battle.
It has been preserved in the Bible as Deborah's Song
of Victory, written supposedly by the prophetess herself. The only other women who can lay claim to the
honor of an original prayer or hymn in the Bible, are

Huldah, whose prophesies were given in the time of
King Josiah of Judah, and Hannah.

Although the Bible discussed all these women with
impartiality and respect for their accomplishments, it
was not uncommon for later Biblical commentators to
reinterpret their virtues in an attempt to fit these
women into current stereotypes. So we have a
statement made by a rabbinic source which says:

> Eminence is not for women; two eminent women are
> mentioned in the Bible, Deborah and Huldah, and
> both proved to be of a proud disposition. . . . .This
> unpleasant feature of their character is indicated by
> their ugly names. [30]

Deborah has overcome all this. Her deeds bear
ample witness even today, to the kind of person she
was. The victory of the Israelites over the Canaanites
is considered to be one of the decisive battles of the
world, one which settled the destiny of the area for all
time.[31] Deborah is considered to be the one person
who by force of her personality and strong patriotism,
managed to unite the tribes into a nation which has
endured until today.

Deborah's Song of Victory is a forceful narrative
outlining all the events in the war against the Canaanites: the terrorizing of the populace by Jabin's army
and the unwillingness of the tribes to fight against the
Canaanite enemy. Deborah's army was organized and
the battle began. "Then did the horsehoofs stamp,"
said Deborah in her vivid description of the battle.
The poem also described Ya-el's bravery and—a most
unusual touch for a victory song—the concern of Sisera's mother for a son that did not return from battle.

Then sang Deborah and Barak the son of Abinoam on
that day, saying:
When men let grow their hair in Israel,
When the people offer themselves willingly,
Bless ye the Lord.
Hear, O ye kings; give ear, O ye princes;
I, unto the Lord will I sing;
I will sing praise to the Lord, the God of Israel.

Lord, when Thou didst go forth out of Seir,
When Thou didst march out of the field of Edom,
The earth trembled, the heavens also dropped,
Yea, the clouds dropped water.
The mountains quaked at the presence of the Lord,
Even yon Sinai at the presence of the Lord, the God of Israel.
In the days of Shamgar the son of Anath,
In the days of Yael, the highways ceased,
And the travellers walked through byways.
The rulers ceased in Israel, they ceased,
Until that thou didst arise, Deborah,
That thou didst arise a mother in Israel.
They chose new gods;
Then was war in the gates;
Was there a shield or spear seen
Among forty thousand in Israel?
My heart is toward the governors of Israel
That offered themselves willingly among the people.
Bless ye the Lord.
Ye that ride on white asses,
Ye that sit on rich cloths,
And ye that walk by the way, tell of it;
Louder than the voice of archers, by the watering-troughs!
There shall they rehearse the righteous acts of the Lord,

Even the righteous acts of His rulers in Israel.
Then the people of the Lord went down to the gates.

Awake, awake, Deborah;
Awake, awake, utter a song;
Arise, Barak, and lead thy captivity captive, thou son of
Abinoam.
Then made He a remnant to have dominion over the no-
bles and the people;
The Lord made me have dominion over the mighty.
. . . . .And the princes of Issachar were with Deborah;
As was Issachar, so was Barak;
Into the valley they rushed forth at his feet.
Among the divisions of Reuben
There were great resolves of heart.
Why sattest thou among the sheepfolds,
To hear the pipings for the flocks? . . . . .

. . . . .Then fought the kings of Canaan,
In Taanach by the waters of Megiddo;
They took no gain of money.
They fought from heaven,
The stars in their courses fought against Sisera.
The brook Kishon swept them away,
That ancient brook, the brook Kishon.
O my soul, tread them down with strength.
Then did the horsehoofs stamp
By reason of the prancings, the prancings of their mighty
ones.
. . . . . Blessed above women shall Yael be,
The wife of Heber the Kenite,
Above women in the tent shall she be blessed.
Water he asked, milk she gave him;
In a lordly bowl she brough him curd.

Her hand she put to the tent-pin,
And her right hand to the workmen's hammer;
And with the hammer she smote Sisera, she smote through
his head,
Yea, she pierced and struck through his temples.
At her feet he sunk, he fell, he lay;
At her feet he sunk, he fell;
Where he sunk, there he fell down dead.

Through the window she looked forth, and peered,
The mother of Sisera, through the lattice;
'Why is his chariot so long in coming?
Why tarry the wheels of his chariots?'
The wisest of her princesses answer her,
Yea, she returneth answer to herself:
Are they not finding, are they not dividing the spoil?

.....So perish all Thine enemies, O Lord;
But they that love Him be as the sun when he goeth forth
in his might.
And the land had rest forty years.[32]

III

Buried Treasures of Egypt and Greece

"She considereth a field and buyeth it;
With the fruit of her hand she planteth a vineyard."

PROVERBS 35:16

Mibtahiah

When those first archeologists unrolled the ancient papyrus scrolls of the Elephantine community, they were opening up clues to the existence of an entire Jewish settlement that had once been lost. They were also opening up vistas of possibilities in the development of Jewish law pertaining to women. The life of Mibtahiah, a Jewish woman who lived in the fifth century B.C.E., shows us what form Jewish society could—indeed, once did—take.[1] Lending money in her own name, even after her marriage, owning property, arranging a marriage contract that carefully safeguarded her property rights, having, without question, the right to divorce: all these were once accepted procedures in the life of a Jewish woman in Elephantine, Egypt.[2]

Isaiah had passed from the scene some two hundred years earlier. His prophecy of the destruction of Judea and the Holy Temple had been fulfilled. In 597 B.C.E., the first group of Jewish exiles, together with their King Jehoiachin, had been led into captivity in Babylonia. Less than ten years after that,

Jerusalem, the Temple, and all of the fortified cities of Judea lay in ruins.[3]

Many other Jews were led into Babylonia after that first exile—but not all. Some, fleeing from the war and destruction that surrounded them, found their way south, to Egypt.

It is not certain whether the community at Elephantine (also referred to as Syene, or "Yeb the Fortress")[4] began then, or whether these new arrivals served to augment a small military group who had been there before. The exact origins of Elephantine are unknown, but by the last quarter of the sixth century, a large and developed Jewish community was settled there.

When the Babylonian empire fell to the Persian King Cyrus, in the year 536 B.C.E., the Jews hailed it as Divine intervention, with good reason. One of Cyrus' earliest decrees gave the Israelites a chance to rebuild their homeland. Because the Jews in Babylonia, like those in Elephantine, were also flourishing, only a small band of Babylonian Jews responded to this opportunity. They returned and began the work of rebuilding the Temple. But King Cyrus died and the Temple in Jerusalem had still not been completed.

In 525 B.C.E., Cyrus' son, Cambyses, became king, and marched down to conquer Egypt and further enlarge his empire. There, in the southern part of the Nile on an island called Elephantine, he found a complete community of Jews, with their own thriving temple, in which they made regular sacrifices to the God of the Hebrews.[5] Because of past Persian intervention on behalf of their fellow Israelites in Jerusalem, they were well disposed towards these conquerers. From that time, Elephantine became a Persian military colony and remained a Persian stronghold in Egypt even after the rest of the country had become independent.

It was in this period of Persian rule that Mibtahiah lived. She was born in 476 B.C.E., fifty years after the Persians had come to Elephantine, and was a member of a prominent family who owned property and slaves. She was not a heroine in the tradition of Deborah. Her accomplishments remained unnoticed by her descendants until more than two thousand years had elapsed.

In 1901, a series of scrolls from the ancient Elephantine colony were discovered by diggers near Aswan, Egypt,[6] and through them, Mibtahiah was reborn. She may be the earliest *Jewish* woman to become known through original documents. The Elephantine papyrii concerning Mibtahiah and her family were in excellent condition when they were found. Some of the seals had never even been broken. From these papyrii we can learn many details of life in Elephantine in the fifth century, as well as facts about the life of Mibtahiah herself. In view of future occurrences in Judaism, her life makes an interesting comparison to the lives of women in later times and places.

The Bible says little about divorce except that it is permitted, and that the husband must write a bill of divorcement for his wife (Deut. 24: 1-2). Several hundred years after Mibtahiah lived, rabbis would interpret this to mean that a woman had no right to divorce her husband without his consent. Only a man could grant a divorce decree to his wife, whereas she could be released from the marriage by her husband's whim. ("If he find something unseemly in her.") In her time, however, Mibtahiah had an equal right to divorce along with her husband. Indeed, all women in Elephantine enjoyed this privilege, even women who were slaves at the time of their marriage.[7]

The law of inheritance was another rule which, from Biblical times, did not favor women. The Bible maintained the right of inheritance only for sons. Daughters did not inherit from their fathers. This law was somewhat ameliorated with Moses' judgment pertaining to the daughters of Zelophehad (Num. 27: 1-11). According to the established law of Israel, if there were no sons, the father's property passed to the nearest male relative. Zelophehad's daughters made a request to Moses that since their father had no sons when he died, they should get their father's inheritance rather than have it go to strangers and be lost from the tribe's portion. Moses granted their petition with the stipulation that they must then marry within the tribe. (Num. 36: 1-12). The daughters of Zelophehad thus became the first Hebrew women to inherit property in their own names. Yet, had there been even one son, they would have received nothing. This law, limiting a woman's inheritance, was also carried over into more modern times, well after tribal restrictions no longer applied.

Mibtahiah may have been an only daughter, with no brothers to inherit. But whatever her status within her family, she received much property from her father, Mahseiah, who put no limit on whom she might marry. A total of seven original papyri were found pertaining to Mibtahiah. These included her marriage contracts and divorce documents, deeds from her father officially giving her specific properties, papers regarding a loan she gave her father, and documents pertaining to her will. All of them were written in Aramaic, which was the language in common use both in Israel and in Elephantine. They show clearly the amount of property she owned and the care with which it was legally protected.

Mibtahiah married three times, twice to non-Jews.

This practice of intermarriage, although officially forbidden to Jews, was very common in Diaspora communities as well as in the Jewish nation itself. Mibtahiah's first husband was a Jew, her second a gentile,
and her third, a gentile who subsequently converted.
(This is deduced from the fact that his name, originally As-Hor, an Egyptian name, was changed to
Nathan after the marriage.)[8] In each case, specific
provisions for divorce were written into the marriage
contracts and were included in deeds and agreements
of property.

Mibtahiah's first two marriages ended, either by
death or divorce. Her third marriage to As-Hor/
Nathan produced two sons who ultimately inherited
all her property at her death.

This prosperous woman was not an exception in
her day. From lists of contributors to the Jewish
Temple in Elephantine, it is clear that many women
were financially independent and made regular contributions under their own names.

When Mibtahiah married, being a woman of means,
she provided her own dowry. She herself was a party
to the contract which included provisions for divorce
and property settlements.

Both Mibtahiah and the Elephantine colony existed
outside of the mainstream of Jewish life. The Jews in
the rebuilt kingdom of Judea, and in Babylonia, may
have looked down on these provincial Jews and their
'different' practices, i.e. their insistence on their own
temple and perhaps even their attitude towards women. Yet the citizens of Elephantine considered themselves Jews and maintained a close tie to the Jewish
government in Jerusalem.

The two opposing attitudes that existed towards
Jewish women in the Bible—the one regarding women
as inferior, the other regarding her as strong and

equal—clearly became separated in Elephantine, where the egalitarian trend prevailed." Mibtahiah's papers and documents show this clearly.

Mibtahiah is important for the information she gave us about the life of a Jewish woman in that period, the degree of power she could attain, her freedom, and recognition as an independent person in her world.

The following is excerpted from Mibtahiah's marriage contract with As-Hor (later known as Nathan), her third husband. It spells out exactly what would happen in case of divorce initiated by either party, and it clearly shows their equality under that law.

I came to thy house for thee to give me thy daughter, Mibtahiah, to wife; she is my wife and I am her husband from this day and forever. . . . I have delivered into the hand of Mibtahiah as money for an (outfit), 1 kebhes, 2 shekels royal standard. . . . I have delivered into her hand 1 garment of wool, new, embroidered, dyed on both sides, 8 cubits long by 5, worth the sum of 2 kebhes, 8 shekels, royal standard; 1 closely woven shawl, new. . . . 1 mirror of bronze. . . . 1 tray of bronze, 2 cups of bronze, (etc.). . . .

If tomorrow (or) any later day Mibtahiah shall stand up in the congregation and shall say: I divorce As-Hor, my husband, the price of divorce shall be on her head; she shall return to the scales and she shall weigh for As-Hor the sum of 5 shekels 2d. and all which I have delivered into her hand she shall give back . . . and she shall go away whithersoever she will, and no suit or process (shall lie). If tomorrow or any

later day As-Hor shall stand up in the congregation
and say: I divorce my (wife) Mibtahiah, her marriage
settlement shall be forfeited, and all I have delivered
into her hand, she shall give back . . . and she shall go
away whithersoever she will. . . . And if he shall rise up
against Mibtahiah to drive her away from the house of
As-Hor and his goods and his chattels, he shall pay
her the sum of 20 kebhes, and (the terms of) this deed
shall hold good for her; and I shall have no power to
say I have another wife than Mibtahiah and other
children than the children which Mibtahiah shall bear
to me. . . . .[10]

The following deed was given to Mibtahiah by her
father as payment for a loan which he could not repay. One of the things he stipulates is that he no
longer has any power over this property. She may
give it to whomever she likes.

On the 3rd of Chisleu, that is the 10th day of the
month Mesore . . . said Mahseiah, the son of
Yedoniah . . . to Mibtahiah his daughter, saying: I
have given thee the house which Meshullam . . . gave
me for its price, and wrote a deed for me in regard to
it, and I have given it to Mibtahiah my daughter in return for the goods which she gave me. . . . I took them
in exchange, and did not find money and goods to
pay thee. Therefore I have given thee this house in
return for those thy goods. . . . and I have given thee
the original deed which was written for me by the said
Meshullam respecting it. This house I have given to
thee, and have renounced all claim to it; it is thine,
and thy children's after thee, and to whom(soever
thou desire) thou mayest give it. I shall have no
power, I and my children, and my descendants, and

any one else, to institute against thee suit or process
on account of this house which I have given thee. . . .[11]

When a divorce was completed, papers, such as the
one shown below, were executed relieving the parties
from further financial responsibility. The following is
a "deed of quittance" which was written to Mibtahiah
by her second husband, the builder Pi. In exchange
for certain money and goods that Mibtahiah gives
him, he agrees to renounce any claim on her.

On the 13th of Ab, that is the 19th day of Pachons
. . . . said Pi the son of Pahi. . . . to Mibtahiah, the
daughter of Mahseiah. . . . at the court of the Hebrews
in Syene: Let us make a division as regards the money
and grain and clothing and bronze and iron, all the
goods and chattels, and a quittance I will give. Then
an oath has been imposed upon thee . . . and my heart
is content with this oath which thou hast made to me
in regard to these goods, and I renounce my claim on
thee from this day and for ever. I shall have no power
to raise against thee suit or process, against thee or
son or daughter of thine on account of these goods in
regard to which thou hast sworn to me. . . .[12]

Sambathe, The Jewish Sibyl

"Strength and dignity are her clothing;
And she laugheth at the time to come.
She openeth her mouth with wisdom;
And the law of kindness is on her tongue."

PROVERBS 31: 25-26

Prophecy was a respected calling for Jews from Biblical times onward. Although the prophets of the Bible—people who claimed direct communication with God, and could foretell the future—were the most famous and revered, they were by no means the only ones. The prophetic tradition had its origins in the earliest history of Israel, and continued well after the Babylonian exile. The diaspora communities also had their share of prophets and prophetesses, and women continued to take part in this time-honoured pursuit following the example of their Biblical sisters. Among them was Sambathe (or Sabbe), the Jewish-Greek Sibyl of Alexandria.

Sibyl is the Greek word for prophetess, and the prophesies of the many Greek sibyls—called the Sibylline Oracles[1]—were a popular form of epic literature of the Hellenic age, during the first century B.C.E.

This was a time of upheaval and change in the world. Alexander the Great had already conquered and passed on, leaving in his wake a Hellenized empire which included Palestine and Egypt. Jews had come to Egypt in great numbers during the reign of Ptolemy I, who ruled there in the third century B.C.E., and they thrived throughout the country. Many had become thoroughly Hellenized because of the influence of the surrounding Greek culture.[2]

In Judea, meanwhile, the Seleucid-Hellenist empire[3] had taken control and the very same assimilation that plagued the Jews in Egypt, divided the Jews even within Jerusalem itself. This basic disagreement among the Jews, along with the anti-Jewish decrees of the Seleucid king, Antiochus, resulted in the Macabbean revolt and the shortlived independence of Judea under the Hasmoneans. Yet even with independence, the Hellenization process of the Jews did not stop.

By the first century B.C.E., the Golden Age of Greek culture was slowly fading and Rome was stirring and expanding towards the height of her power. Hellenism however, was still strong in Alexandria and the other cities of Egypt. It offered a temptation to Jews and indeed greatly influenced even those who remained faithful to Judaism.

In general the Diaspora community in Alexandria did well under Greek rule. Although there was extensive assimilation of Jews, many Greeks were influenced by the high morals of Jewish culture and religion which compared favorably with the immoral behavior of the Greek gods. However, tension between the two cultures also existed and sometimes resulted in a genuine hatred for the Jews by those who practiced Greek and Egyptian religious customs.[4] In this era, (20 B.C.E. to 50 C.E.) when Philo, one of the most famous of the Jewish-Greek spokesmen and philosophers, was writing his "explanations" of Jewish beliefs,[5] Sambathe, the Jewish Sibyl, also lived and wrote.

Sambathe's writing was in the style of Greek epic poetry. Her prophecies were written in Greek, but her subject was the greatness and the majesty of Jewish culture and religion. She was a passionate partisan of the Jewish people and prophesied the coming of the Messiah and the downfall of paganism. Perhaps this is why her work was preserved by the Christians and is available for us today.

Almost nothing is known about Sambathe's personal life. Unlike Mibtahiah, whose life was preserved through papers and legal documents, nothing remains of Sambathe except her writing. Perhaps for this reason it has been suggested by some historians, that the author may have been a man writing under the guise of a woman in order to profit from the Sibylline oracle's popularity as a literary genre. Although it is a possibility, this is no more possible than the opposite thesis—that some of the great prophets, known only by their writings, were women. Taking into consideration the doubts surrounding much of ancient literature, we have chosen to accept Sambathe's femininity.

In the following poem, Sambathe alludes to the origin of the Jews from the hereditary line of Abraham who came down from Ur of the Chaldees (Gen. 11:31). She points out that Jews do not practice magic or believe in signs from nature, or astrology. These practices were common among the Hellenized Jews, to whom her words were most certainly directed, as well as the Greeks and Egyptians who lived in Alexandria. Sambathe also refers to Biblical precepts such as helping the widow and the orphan, and the biblical practice of gleaning—leaving the corners of the fields of grain uncut so that the poor might come and gather them (Lev. 19:9-10 and Deut. 24:19-21). As in all her work, she reasserts the unity of God, whom she refers to by the term "Heavenly."

There Is A City

There is a city, Chaldean Ur,
Whence come the race of most upright men,
Who are ever right-minded and their works good,
They are neither concerned for the sun's course,
Nor the moon's, nor for monstrosities on earth,
Nor for satisfaction from ocean's depths,
Nor for signs of sneezing and the augury from birds;
Nor for soothsaying, nor sorcery, nor incantations!
Nor for deceitful follies of ventriloquists.

They do not, Chaldean fashion, astrologize,
Nor watch the stars. . . .
But they are concerned about rightness and virtue.
Their measures are just both in field and city.
They do not steal from each other by night,
Nor drive off herds of oxen and sheep and goats.
Nor does neighbor remove his neighbor's landmarks.
Nor does the wealthy man vex the poor one
Nor oppress widows, but such rather assists them,
Providing them always with grain, wine and oil;
Always a blessing to those in want among them

He gives back part of his harvest to the needy people,
For 'the Heavenly' made the earth common to all. . . .[6]

The rest of the poem summarizes the history of Israel in glowing terms and prophesies about the destiny of all the countries of the Hellenic world, ending
with this pointed appeal to the Jews:

Oh, Hellas! why do you rely on men.
Who cannot avoid the fate of death?
Why do you offer gifts in vain to the dead and sacrifices to
idols?
Who had led your soul astray thus?
Who had talked you into deserting the great God?
Oh, stand in awe before the name of the Father of all crea-
tures.[7]

   The selection below is the only excerpt of Sambathe's work which makes any allusions at all to herself or to her personal origins. She suggests her relationship to the Jews through kinship with Noah, and
through him "to whom the entire future was revealed" (possibly Abraham). This may have been her
own way of subtly establishing her Jewish identity to
her readers. There were many sibyls who wrote this
type of poetic oracle. Others may have been Jewish,
but Sambathe is the only one whose name and Jewish
identity are confirmed by scholars of her work.

. . . That, is how I predict—I, driven by the sting of ecstasy,
I left the high towers of Assyrian Babylon
In order to announce the fire that was sent down to Hellas,
About the wrath of God, and in order to reveal the divine
secrets to mortals.
The people of Hellas will say that I hail from Eritrea, and
   that I have no shame;
Others will say that I am that Sibylla,
The daughter of Cicero and Gnostes and call me a wild liar.
But when all that will take place, you will remember me,
And no one will call me the wild, but the great prophetess
   of God.
For when the world was covered with water and only one
   righteous man remained.

Who drifted along the torrents in a wooden ark,
Together with animals and birds, to replenish the earth
  again—
I was the daughter-in-law then.
I was born of the blood of him,
Who had survived the primeval,
And to whom the entire future was revealed.
All this should be revealed truly through my lips.[8]

IV

Daughters of the Law

"Her children rise up and call her blessed;
Her husband also and he praiseth her."

PROVERBS 31:28

There are two women, Ima Shalom and Beruriah, whose names, words and deeds have come down to us through the source of the Talmud. In order to understand them and what they were saying, it is helpful to have some understanding of the Talmud itself, how it was written, and in what kind of world these women found themselves.

Let us go back in time to the academies of Babylonia and Judea during the first centuries before and after the Common Era. The scholars sit on benches discussing the Law. Surrounding them are pupils from all over the world—young Jews who have come to learn from the masters. The rabbis each give an opinion on a point of law, and one comment leads to another. A scholar is reminded of a story that illustrates his point. Then another remembers another story. Each one speaks in turn.

Sometimes the stories lead away from the original subject. There are jokes and tales of past experiences. There are anecdotes relating how one may have proved a relevant point of law to a disbeliever. The students and disciples listen and record it all, some in their memories, others in writing. Occasionally they add their own opinions and stories. Or one of the rabbis' learned wives may bring an experience to this open forum. More often it is the rabbis who give the examples of their wives' experiences or wise sayings.

So the discussion goes on. Each word is in the service of God. These are not dusty old men in dusty rooms. Their opinions are often controversial and their ideas are dynamic and sometimes revolutionary. They are idealistic and above all, they have faith that what they are doing is important. The faith of these scholars and sages, and the accumulated wisdom of these academies, make up the Talmud.

The entire Talmud consists of two main works—Mishna and Gemarra.[2] The Mishna is a codification and commentary on all the laws contained in the Bible. Its compilation was begun during the first century B.C.E. Then Judah HaNasi, Patriarch of Judea, and a renowned philosopher and scholar, completed the work sometime during the end of the second century C.E. He divided it into six orders, each containing many different books and each book dealing with a different topic. There are sixty three books in the Mishna—the accumulated discussion of three hundred years. After Judah HaNasi's final codification, the Mishna was closed.

It soon became necessary to explain and interpret the laws in the light of new problems arising in a changing society. The new explanations and discussions came to be called the Gemarra. The Gemarra was written down several hundred years after the Mishna, and is basically an extensive analysis of all the laws of the Mishna along with commentary, stories, examples and wise sayings. The Tosefta and Baraita are records of conversations previously held by the rabbis but not included in the original Mishna.[3]

There are two separate Gemarras, one compiled in Babylonia and one in Jerusalem. Both of these are discussing the same Mishna, but the Babylonian Talmud is usually considered the more comprehensive and authoritative of the two.

During the lifetimes of the great rabbis mentioned in the Mishna and the Gemarra, Palestine—the Roman name for Judea—was ruled by Rome and its appointed patriarchs. Babylonia was part of the Persian Empire and the Jews there had an autonomous community headed by an exilarch. The rabbis in these communities were a very select group. They were not the titular rulers of the Jewish people, but rather the spiritual leaders whose learning and faithfulness to the Law made them examples for all Jews to follow. They were the first to establish learning as an ideal in itself—an activity which brought the Jewish people closer to God.[4] Each small point of the Law that they discussed may seem like an obscure exercise today, but at that time it was far more. It was a pursuit that developed the mind and made something holy of the intellect and the thought processes. In addition, it helped the Jews to continue living under Jewish law even though there was no Jewish government to enforce it.

All of man's and woman's activities and functions were holy, the sages said, therefore nothing was too profane or too unimportant to come under the rule of the Law. Everything from the Ten Commandments down to the smallest word or seemingly trivial phrase was discussed. All bodily functions and the rules surrounding care of the body, sexual habits of men and women, childbirth, and menstruation were talked about in minute detail. Because the Talmud is basically a record of the conversations of all those who participated at the Academies in Babylonia and Palestine, many different people were involved and many different opinions were recorded.

The rabbis were not without humor, either. Interspersed with the wise sayings and learned opinions are funny stories such as the comment of Beruriah to a traveller searching for Lydda,[5] and stories of rhetorical victories over those who brazenly challenged the religious faith and logic of the scholars.

The Talmud is a great work. Its survival through centuries of Jewish life is a credit to the scholarship, wisdom and flexibility of these early rabbis. It is first and foremost a book written by men. Few women contributed to it because of the generally lower status of women in those times, and the feeling among many of the rabbis that as a group, women were inferior to men. Women's "lightmindedness"[6] is often invoked as a reason for her status, or as an example of her lack of ability to deal with serious matters of Law.

Because of this, Ima Shalom and Beruriah, two women whose words are quoted in the Talmud, are especially noteworthy and outstanding. Surely they were not the only wise women who lived during the Rabbinic period. Others are mentioned within the pages of the Talmud as examples of cleverness, clear thinking, or righteous living.[7] But through their words and reputations, Ima Shalom and Beruriah stand out in manifesting the wisdom, scholarship, devotion, and wit that existed among many of the women of their time.

Ima Shalom

Rabbi Eliezer ben Hyrcanus is well known as the Talmudic scholar with the most negative things to say about women. It is he who is quoted as saying: "He who teaches his daughter the Law teaches her frivolity."[8] He also said: "Better the Torah be burned than to be studied by women.[9] And he disposed of it by claiming: "Woman's place is at the spinning wheel."[10]

Perhaps all these statements tell us more about this illustrious rabbi's marriage relationship than he himself would have cared to divulge. He was married to Ima Shalom, one of the few women known to us from the Talmud itself.

Ima Shalom was born in Palestine in 50 C.E., twenty years before the destruction of the second Temple. This was a time of crisis for the Jewish people and for the world. Rome had conquered all of Europe and the Middle East. Jesus had been crucified and his followers were forming their own cults. The Sanhedrin, the main governing body of the Jews in Palestine, had moved to Yavneh after the destruction of Jerusalem. One of the best known and admired of the rabbinic scholars, Rabban Gamaliel, became its head. He and his sister, Ima Shalom, were the children of Simon ben Gamaliel, a descendant of Hillel. Ima Shalom married Rabbi Eliezer ben Hyrcanus, head of the academy at Lydda.

Being surrounded by such illustrious men, Ima Shalom could not help but improve an already remarkable intellect. Rather than take a quiet place at the spinning wheel, she was known to be constantly interfering in the men's discussions.

Although her name means 'mother peace', her reputation is ironically, quite the opposite. She was apparently irascible as well as clever, and her habit of outsmarting others might well have aggravated her husband. Stories concerning her bluntness of speech and actions are found scattered throughout the Talmud. They are stories remembered after the fact, for Ima Shalom lived long before the Mishna was codified and many hundreds of years more had passed before the *Amoraim* (the learned men whose discussions make up the Gemarra) lived. Yet, despite the passage of time, she was not forgotten.

The conflict of opinion between her husband, Eliezer ben Hyrcanus, and her brother Gamaliel, which resulted in Eliezer's excommunication, must have been a difficult burden for Ima Shalom to bear.[11] From the little we know of her, she appears to have borne it with dignity. She remained with her husband, yet worked for her brother's safety, as the story (below) from the book of Baba Metzia (59b) illustrates.

Considering the many stories that describe her sharp mind, it is puzzling that the Encyclopedia Judaica makes no reference to her intelligence at all.[12] It simply identifies her as the sister of R. Gamaliel of Yavneh, then proceeds to describe in detail the lawsuit she had instituted against him, as well as several other family disputes. For those who study the Talmud, however, Ima Shalom reveals a strong character with the courage of her convictions.

The following story about Ima Shalom illustrates the esteem in which she was held by the rabbis of her time.

In verse 20a of the Gemarra Nederim (Vows), the

Rabbis speak of sexual relations, and offer the conten-
tion that a child is born deaf when his parents converse during cohabitation, and blind if the parents
look at "that place". The explanation of the word
"converse" is at the core of the ensuing segment of
the Gemarra, presented by Rabbi Johanan ben
Dahabai.

Rabbi Johanan ben Dahabai holds a dissenting view,
and uses the Ima Shalom story to prove that the Rabbis are mistaken. In so doing, he introduces an interesting play on words:

Nederim (Vows) 20b
Ima Shalom was asked: Why are thy children so exceedingly beautiful? She replied: (Because) he (my
husband) 'converses' with me neither at the beginning
or at the end of the night, but (only) at midnight; and
when he 'converses' he uncovers a handbreadth and
covers a handbreadth, and is as though he were com-
pelled by a demon. And when I asked him: What is
the reason for this (for choosing midnight) he replied,
So that I may not think of another woman, lest my
children be as bastards.

Ima Shalom, in the interests of polite language, uses
the word "converse" *(m'sa-per* in Hebrew) as a discreet
euphemism for describing her sexual relations with
her husband. Rabbi Johanan seizes on this story as
proof that to converse (in the literal sense) during
cohabitation does *not* cause defects in the children, as
proved by Ima Shalom's "exceedingly beautiful"
offspring.

The Rabbis, however, reject this "proof" concluding
that even if Ima Shalom actually did verbally converse

with her husband ("when I asked him: What is the reason for this . . ." etc.), it was nevertheless a conversation pertaining directly to *conjugal* matters, and not merely a discussion about general matters. Ima Shalom's words can therefore not be used to negate the Rabbis' original contentions regarding conversations during cohabitation.

The fact that renowned Talmudic scholars utilized Ima Shalom's words to prove and/or disprove their scholarly contentions emphasizes the respect which Ima Shalom commanded in rabbinic circles. Here was an example of a wise and righteous woman who provided the women of her time with an excellent example.

The following passage concerns the excommunication of Rabbi Eliezer (husband of Ima Shalom) by her brother, Rabbi Gamaliel. The excommunication was extremely controversial because it was partly politically motivated and was a result of Rabbi Eliezer's conservatism, which caused him to disagree with several Sanhedrin rulings.

The allusion to Rabbi Eliezer's "falling on his face" refers to a custom prevalent at that time. The Jew fell on his face and recited personal prayers or pleas to God after the regular recital of the eighteen benedictions of the morning prayer. Ima Shalom feared that her husband might pour out his grief and feeling of injury in his prayer to God and that God would heed him and punish Gamaliel.[13] For this reason she made her husband, Rabbi Eliezer, pledge not to recite the penitential prayers, so that her brother would be safe. One day, she was called out of the room during his prayers and he did indeed fall on his face and pray to

God. According to the story included here, her fears
were justified and her brother, in fact, died.

Ima Shalom's suggestion at the end that "all gates
are locked excepting the gates of wounded feelings"
implies her understanding that hurt feelings do not
heal easily and that God listens to the appeals of those
who have been wronged.

Baba Metzia (Middle Gate) 59b
Ima Shalom was R. Eliezer's wife, and sister to R.
Gamaliel. From the time of this incident onwards [i.e.,
R. Eliezer's excommunication] she did not permit him
to fall on his face.
Now a certain day happened to be New Moon, but she
mistook a full month for a defective one. [i.e., on certain days the prayers were not recited]
Others say, a poor man came and stood at the door
and she took out some bread to him. On her return
she found him fallen on his face. "Arise!" she cried to
him. "Thou hast slain my brother!"
In the meanwhile an announcement was made that he
had died. "Whence did thou know it?" he questioned
her. "I have this tradition from my father's house,"
Ima Shalom answered: "All gates are locked, excepting the gates of wounded feelings."

A well known legend about Ima Shalom's brother,
Rabban Gamaliel, illustrates the cleverness and wit of
another woman. Although the words in this Talmudic
story from Sanhendrin 39a are frequently attributed to
Ima Shalom, they actually refer to an Emperor's
daughter.

Sanhedrin 39a

The Emperor once said to Rabban Gamaliel:
"Your God is a thief, for He stole a rib from Adam."
The Emperor's daughter said to him: "Leave him to
me and I will answer him." Then she said (to the
Emperor): "Last night a robber broke into my house
and carried away some silver vessels, leaving gold
ones in their place."
The Emperor exclaimed: "I wish such a robber visited
my house every night."
"This is what happened to Adam," said she. "God took
a rib from him and gave him a wife in its place."
The Emperor argued further: "God should not have
put him to sleep to steal his rib."
His daughter's reply to this was to have some raw
meat brought. She placed it under her armpit, then
took it out and invited him to eat it.
"I find it loathsome," he said.
Triumphantly she said: "Even so would Eve have been
to Adam had she been taken from him openly."

Beruriah

Rabbi Simlai came before Rabbi Johanan (and) requested of him: "Let the Master teach me the Book of Geneologies." After much reluctance on the part of Rabbi Johanan, he consented. "Let us learn it in three months", Rabbi Simlai proposed. (Thereupon) Rabbi Johanan took a clod and threw it at him saying: "If Beruriah, wife of Rabbi Meir (and) daughter of Rabbi Hanina ben Teradion, who studied three hundred laws from three hundred teachers in a day could nevertheless not do her duty [i.e. do justice to this book] in three years, yet you propose [to do it] in three months!"

This anecdote, taken directly from the Talmud (Pesachim 62b), tells us a great deal about Beruriah. Living within the community of learned rabbis, she was nevertheless held up as an example of dedication and knowledge to these rabbis and their pupils. And Beruriah, unlike Ima Shalom, is well known as a woman of valor in Talmudic times.

Beruriah lived in the second century, during the revolt of Bar Kochba (132-135 C.E.), the final attempt of the Jews to free themselves from Roman rule. Her wisdom and righteousness were legendary even in her own time and she is the only woman in Talmudic literature whose views were considered seriously by the scholars.[14] Stories related about her great knowledge were often preceded by the phrase: "Rightly did Beruriah say . . ."

Beruriah was also a teacher in the academy—a situation which was certainly highly unusual.[15] Her philosophy of learning is made clear by a brief story in Eruvim 53b. It tells of Beruriah rebuking a student for learning in an undertone. Her remark:

Is it not written: 'Ordered in all things and sure?' If
it is ordered in your two hundred and forty eight
limbs, it will be sure, otherwise it will not be sure.

This quotation reflects the general attitude that
memorization was aided by the voice and the body, as
well as by the mind.

Perhaps it was Beruriah's gentle nature which
caused her husband to show more respect for women
in general. Rabbi Meir held his wife in the greatest esteem, and unlike Rabbi Eliezer, his colleague of the past,
he had a more tolerant attitude towards women's participation in studies, allowing them to attend his lectures.[16]

Beruriah's own feelings about the rabbinic attitude
towards women are well illustrated by the story of her
conversation with Rabbi Jose. Here, (Eruvim 53b) she
subtly and deftly pokes fun at the men who held prejudices against her sex:

Rabbi Jose the Galilean was once on a journey when
he met Beruriah.
"By what road," he asked her, "do we go to Lydda?"
"Foolish Galilean," she replied, "did not the sages say
this: 'Engage not in much talk with women?' You
should have asked: 'By which to Lydda?'"

In view of all the stories about Beruriah's nobility
and thoughtfulness as well as her wit and wisdom, it is
even more puzzling to read about the bitter legend
that clouds the end of her life. This legend tells us
that in an effort to prove to her that the prejudices
against women were not unfounded, and in order to
test her, Rabbi Meir secretly arranged for her seduc-
tion by one of his pupils. When Beruriah felt herself

tempted by the advances of the pupil, she killed herself in realization of her weakness.

The story is disturbing for several reasons, not the
least being the lack of censure of Rabbi Meir and the
other man. Having set a trap for a righteous woman
that led to her death, they seem to have escaped any
punishment. Rabbi Meir is said to have fled,
brokenhearted, to Babylonia after her death.[17] Rashi,
the famous 11th century Biblical commentator, elaborated on this story, giving it more credence as a result.
One may well wonder what purpose the denigration
of Beruriah served for those who chose to repeat this
story and to believe it.

The most famous story concerning Beruriah is that
relating to the death of her two sons. They died suddenly on the Sabbath, and Beruriah withheld the news
from her husband so as not to disturb his Sabbath
peace. By her action she illustrated not only the concern of a good wife, but also her realization that her
emotional strength was greater than that of her husband.[18] After Havdalah, the ceremony marking the
end of Sabbath, Beruriah said to Rabbi Meir:

Midrash Proverbs 30, 10
Some time ago I was entrusted by a friend with some
jewels for safekeeping and now he wants them back.
Shall I return them?
Of course, answered Rabbi Meir, the jewels must be
returned.
Beruriah then took him to where their dead sons were
lying. When he collapsed and cried she gently reminded him: "Did you not say we must return to the
owner the precious jewels he entrusted to us? The
Lord has given the Lord has taken away. Blessed be
the name of the Lord."

The quotation: "Hate the sin, not the sinner," which is the law discussed below, is often attributed to St. Augustine, who lived two centuries after Beruriah. This opinion was accepted by the rabbis and is an inherent part of Judaism today.

Berachot (Blessings) 10a
There were once some highwaymen in the neighborhood of Rabbi Meir who caused him a great deal of trouble. Rabbi Meir accordingly prayed that they should die.
His wife, Beruriah, said to him: "How do you make out [that such a prayer should be permitted]? Because it is written: 'Let *Hatta'im* (sins) cease?'
Is it written *hot'im* (sinners)? It is written *Hatta'im!* Further, look at the end of the verse: 'and let the wicked men be no more.'
Since the sins will cease there will be no more wicked men! Rather pray for them that they should repent, and there will be no more wicked." He did pray for them, and they repented.

Here is another story illustrating Beruriah's sharp mind and her ability to rebuke anyone whom she felt did not hold the Torah in the proper respect. Many instances of this kind of challenge and repartee are found within the pages of the Talmud. The anecdote also suggests that a verse should be read carefully and in its entirety before its full significance can be grasped.

Berachot (Blessings) 10a Beruriah was once asked: "It is written: 'Sing O barren, thou that dids't not bear.' Because she did not bear is she to sing?" She replied to him: "You fool! Look at the end of the verse, where it is written: 'For the children of the desolate shall be more than the children of the married wife, saith the Lord.' But what then is the meaning of a 'barren who did not bear?' Sing, O community of Israel, who resemblest a barren women, for not having born children like you for Gehenna!

V

Poets and Warriors: Oases in a Desert

"She girdeth her loins with strength.
And maketh strong her arms."

PROVERBS 31:17

The Talmud exemplified the high level of Jewish learning in the first centuries of the Common Era, but it was not the only development in Jewish life. Not so removed from the academies of Babylonia and Jerusalem, Jewish life had an altogether different quality than that of Talmudic study.

In the vast deserts of Saudi Arabia and across Egypt to the Atlas Mountains of North Africa, lived many wandering and semi-nomadic tribes. Long before Mohammed's birth, these tribes worshipped their tribal gods, obeyed the laws of desert hospitality that Abraham and Sarah had followed, and waged wars against each other. Living among these people, and undifferentiated from them except by their religious beliefs and practices, were groups of Jews. Like the Arabians and North Africans, these Jews were also divided into tribes, each with their own name and leader.

In Saudi Arabia, these tribes were known by Arabic names such as Banu (*b'nai*) Nadhir, Banu Quraiza, Banu Bachdal, or Banu Kainuka. In the South, they intermingled with the Bedouins, but in the North, they had an autonomous commonwealth with fortified castles and cities.[1]

Where did the Jews originate? One theory, held by the Jewish tribes themselves, speculates that they were descendants of a group of Jews who had fought against the Amalekites under Joshua's command and remained in Saudi Arabia. Other legends say they immigrated during the reign of King David, or were the descendants of traders who had an outpost in Southern Arabia to facilitate trade with Africa through the Red Sea.[2] Some historians say they did not arrive in the Arabian Peninsula until after the destruction of the Temple and the exile to Babylonia. Perhaps they came as part of an outpost of the Babylonian army.[3] Despite the varied theories, there is agreement on the fact that Jews arrived very early in recorded history, thrived, and remained powerful for many centuries.

Although not learned in Bible and certainly not in Talmud, the Jewish tribes followed the rules of the Sabbath and feast days carefully, even refusing to unsheath their daggers on the day of rest. They used the Hebrew calendar and were known among the tribes of Saudi Arabia as "the People of the Book" because of their literacy, their attachment to Scriptures, and their generally higher level of learning.[4]

Poetry ranked high among the skills of the Arabian tribes and, along with warfare, was one of the most esteemed of occupations. Like their neighbors, the Jews excelled in both, and many Jewish poets wrote Arabic poetry.

Jewish women in Arabia, especially in Yemen, cleverly used the poetic form for commenting on the events of the day. They could recite Hebrew quotations and Jewish stories from memory, and extemporaneously compose their own creations, combining classical poetry with love songs and political commentary.[5] One such woman poet was

Sham'ah Shabazi, daughter of the poet Shalom Shabazi. She wrote religious poetry and became a legend to Yemenites, many of whom made pilgrimages to her grave.[6] Most of the work of women like Sham'ah was part of the oral tradition of Yemenite women, of which much has been lost over the years.

In 500 C.E., around the time of the Talmud's completion, the Jews formed a powerful and respected group of tribes and were active proselytizers among the Arabs. At one point, they even succeeded in converting the Yemenite King, Abu Karib, and his entire army to Judaism.[7]

Later, doubt was cast on Karib's sincerity as a Jew, but his younger son, Zurak Dhu Nuwas, who ruled after him (520-530 C.E.), was beyond doubt an observant Jew. He even adopted a Hebrew name, Yusuf (Joseph), and attacked a settlement of Byzantine Christians in retaliation for the persecution of Jews in the Byzantine Empire. This zealousness proved to be his downfall. His kingdom was attacked by Ethiopian Christians, and conquered. Yusuf killed himself in true warrior fashion by riding his horse off a cliff.

After Yusuf Zurak Dhu Nuwas' death, the Jewish Kingdom of Yemen disappeared. Many individual Jews remained however—some proselytes, others descendants of Israelites—and cast their lot with the Jewish tribes.

Sarah

Sarah was a Yemenite Jew of whom little is known. There is even question as to whether she descended from Jews or from those early Yemenite converts.[8] She lived long after the fall of the Jewish kingdom, during the time of Mohammed, (570-632 C.E.), and is reputed to have waged guerilla warfare against the self-styled prophet. Eventually Sarah was murdered by a Muslim agent.[9] It is her poetry, however, which has brought her the little fame she has. Sarah wrote a poem eulogizing a Jewish tribe of Southern Arabia called the Banu (B'nai) Quraiza.

B'nai Quraiza, like so many of the other Jewish-Arabian tribes, was once influential and strong. However, when the Jewish kingdom of Yemen was conquered by the Ethiopians, its prestige declined. Rival tribes noted the weakened condition of the Quraiza tribe and sought to conquer it. Abu Jubail, King of the Ghasassin Kingdom (a Christian tribe), not wanting an armed showdown with the skillful Quraiza warriors, conceived of a plot to weaken it. With the assistance of other tribes, Abu Jubail built a large structure for the collection of water at Du Hurud, a spot not far from Medina. Commanding his soldiers to conceal themselves there, he then called the leaders of the B'nai Quraiza to appear before him.[10] Thinking they were being called to receive honors or tribute, the chiefs came alone, without an army.[11] As each one entered the camp, the hidden soldiers killed him.

This plot, although it did not destroy the B'nai Quraiza as an entity, did weaken it sufficiently so that the tribe could be easily conquered by the Awsa-ites and the Chazrajian tribesmen. The actual destruction of the B'nai Quraiza was left for Mohammed himself, who fought against it in February and March of 627 C.E., almost one hundred years later. When the Quraiza lost the battle against Mohammed's army, they asked permission to leave the country. Mohammed refused and ordered them taken to a market place in Medina to be killed. All the leaders and most of the men were slaughtered and thrown into a pit. This event is referred to in the Koran (chap. 33 p. 344-45 of Sale's edition) as the victory of Mohammed over "those who have received the Scriptures" and the place where they were killed is still called "The Market of the Quraiza". As for the women of the B'nai Quraiza, most were traded for weapons.[12]

Was Sarah, the writer of the eulogy, also a member of this tribe, choosing to recall their past history at the time of their final destruction? Or had she simply heard of the event and sympathized with her fellow Jews? Whatever the inspiration for this moving poem, and despite the fact that only a fragment remains, it serves as a rare memorial to a once proud and strong Jewish tribe.

Arabic poetry, unlike western forms, was based on an intricate system of rhyme, meter and syllable length which is very difficult to maintain in translation. Nevertheless, Sarah's feelings of loss and sadness over this great people who have been "obliterated by the wind" comes through. Her poem can apply to many other situations where Jewish loss was "so grave" as to "embitter for its people the pure water". Placed in a twentieth century context, Sarah's poem still has meaning for us.

By my life, there is a people not long in Du Hurud, obliterated by the wind.
Men of Quraiza destroyed by Chazraji swords and lances,
We have lost, and our loss is so grave, it embitters for its
   people the pure water,
And had they been foreseeing, a teeming host would have
   reached there before them. [13]

Translated from Arabic
by Aliza Arzt

Kahinah

Far from the deserts of Arabia, in the Atlas Mountains of North Africa among the native Berber peoples, other Jewish tribes were living. Like their brothers and sisters in Arabia, the Jews could trace their origins back to earliest times: the Babylonian exile or before. Living like the indigenous Berber tribes of the Maghreb (the mountain and coastal plain of North Africa), the Jews were semi-nomadic farmers and warriors and often exerted a powerful influence on the neighboring peoples.

One of the strongest of these tribes, the one which dominated almost all of the area, was the Jewish tribe known as Kahinah (possibly from the Hebrew *Kohan.*)[14] Its leader was known as the most powerful chieftan in Ifrikya (North Africa). She was a woman, and her full title was Kahinah Dahiyah Bint Thabitah ibn Tifan.[15] Known as Dahiyah Kahinah or simply Kahinah (or Kahiyah), she was a strong leader, and was also known as a prophetess who could fortell the future. It was against her that Hassan ibn al-Nu'man, an Arab prince of Egypt, directed his attack.

Prince Hassan, in his battle to win North Africa for the Muslims, had already destroyed Carthage in 687, and was told that if he could destroy the tribe of the Princess Kahinah, he would have all of Ifrikya in his control.

Kahinah succeeded in uniting many groups, both Jewish and Christian, in the fight against the Muslim army. She herself led a large force of Berber and Jewish tribesmen as well as the remnants of the Byzantine army, and gained a victory over the Arabs, who were forced to retreat from the Atlas Mountains.

This victory made Kahinah the virtual queen of the
whole Maghreb region of North Africa. She ruled
over the area for five years—the only time in its history when this area was united under one leader until
the time of French rule in the twentieth century.[16]
Unfortunately, Kahinah's strength proved to be her
downfall.

Prince Hassan was unwilling to accept defeat easily.
Muslim power was spreading and the followers of
Mohammed were gaining strength. After five years,
they were ready for another attack on Dahiyah
Kahinah. Kahinah's forces, partly as a result of her
harsh rule and partly as a result of the active missionary work of the Muslims, had been weakened. Fearing defeat, Kahinah took a calculated risk. She ordered all the Berber cities to be destroyed in the hope
that the Arabs would not want to bother fighting for a
wasteland. She lost the gamble when the Arabs persisted in their siege. Dahiyah Kahinah was killed in
battle near a well which is still called *Bir al Kahinah*
(well of Kahinah) in her memory.[17]

Dahiyah Kahinah does not fit the stereotype of the
Jewish woman today. Nor was she typical of the
women of her own time. Strong and brave, with the
ability to lead, she served her people in the way she
knew best, and united them as no other leader could.
When she died, she commanded her two sons to sur-
render and they were offered a place in the Arab ar-
mies. Eventually they converted to Islam as did most
of the Berber tribes. Scattered groups of Jews, the descendants of Kahinah's people, could still be found in
the Atlas mountains until 1948 when they were resettled in modern-day Israel.

As for Kahinah herself, she does not hold an
honored place in the hearts of North Africa's Jews,
who remember her more for her cruelty than for her

bravery. Whether or not her bloodthirsty reputation is
completely justified, it is nevertheless preserved in an
old ballad which tells about Kahinah (Kahiya) and her
terrible deeds.

> "O! Sons of Yeshurun!
> Do not forget your persecutors
> The Chaldeans, Caesar, Hadrian and Kahiya—
> That accursed woman, more cruel than all the
>   others together
> She gave our virgins to her warriors,
> She washed her feet in the blood of our children.
> God created her to make us atone for our sins,
> But God hates those who make His people suffer.
> Give me back my children
> So that they can mourn me.
> I left them
> In the hands of Kahiya."[18]

Sarah and Kahinah, in choosing poetry and warfare
as their means of self-expression, were choosing activities of high value to their people. Although poetry
was by far the more accepted calling, Kahinah was not
alone among women in choosing the ways of violence.
Deborah the prophetess was involved in warfare, as
were other Biblical women such as Ya-el, who murdered the Canaanite general, Sisera (Judges 5), and
Judith, who cut off the head of Holofernes (Old Testament Apocrypha). In Saudi Arabia, it was a Jewish
woman, Zaynab, coerced into Mohammed's harem
from the defeated tribe of Khaibur, who attempted
(but failed) to poison the prophet in revenge for his
having killed her people.[19] Kahinah followed in their
path.

Kasmunah

When the Muslims had conquered all of North Africa, their next stop was Spain. In 711 C.E., they crossed the straits of Gibraltar and easily overcame the Christian Visigoths who were ruling there. Numbered among the Muslim soldiers who conquered Spain was one of Kahinah's sons.[20]

The Spanish Jews had been severely oppressed by the Catholics, and for them the conquest was a liberation. Many who had converted, returned now to Judaism and started to build up what became the strongest Jewish community ever to exist on the European continent.

In 711, the rebuilding of Jewish culture in Spain began, and within three hundred years, the community boasted such outstanding scholars as Hasdai ibn Shaprut, physician, diplomat and Talmudist (925-975), and Samuel ibn Naghdela, advisor to the King of Granada and leader of the Jews (993-1056).

By contact with the Muslim-Arabic culture, poetry was also encouraged and it flourished among the Jews. Kasmunah, another Jewish woman who spoke in an Arabic voice, was a gentle Andalusian poet who was influenced by the Arabic poetic tradition. Living in the eleventh or twelfth centuries, an era of poetic giants like Solomon ibn Gabirol, Moses ibn Ezra, and Judah HaLevi, Kasmunah's quiet contribution has almost been passed over. However, two of her original poems, written in Arabic, can still be found in a collection entitled *Al-Makkari*.[21]

Beyond the barest minimum, the story of Kasmunah's life remains unknown. She lived in Andalusia, a section of Southern Spain. Her father, Ishmael, was also a poet and gave her early training in that skill, by composing two lines of a poem and having her complete them with another rhyming couplet.[22] Her work suggests a gentle and melancholy temperament and a feeling of closeness with nature.

In her soft poetic style, Kasmunah is far in both spirit and time, from Sarah, the Arabian poet, or Kahinah, the Berber warrior. Yet Kasmunah represents a civilization that nourished all three women. This civilization blended and developed the best of Arabic, Jewish, and Mediterranean cultures.

By the close of the 12th century, the Muslim kingdom of Spain was irrevocably divided. Wars broke out among different factions of Muslims, and the Christians saw their chance to regain a foothold. By 1212, only the kingdom of Granada remained part of the once vast Islamic holdings. The empire that had nurtured Sarah, Kahinah, and Kasmunah, as well as some of the greatest philosophers and writers ever to pass through Jewish history, was beginning to fade.

This first fragment of Kasmunah's writing appears to be part of a poem mourning her fleeting youth and the lack of a husband ("a nameless 'him'"). In choosing this theme, she shows herself to be in tune with many generations of women who felt themselves incomplete outside of marriage. Although she was probably very young when this verse was written, there are no records to show whether Kasmunah ever married.

A vine I see, and though 'tis time to glean,
No hand is stretched forth yet to cull the fruit.
And so my youth does pass in sorrow keen,
A nameless 'him' my eyes in vain salute. [23]

Another poem by Kasmunah is the following beautiful verse in which she addresses a pet gazelle, an animal that she herself raised.[24] Here also, the words lend themselves to an interpretation suggesting a lonely woman who is unmarried. Marriage was the normal procedure among all Jewish communities, and it was considered an obligation of parents to arrange for their children's marriages. Nevertheless, lacking further information about this poet, we can only guess whether her feelings stemmed from a permanent situation which she was powerless to change, or were merely an indication of adolescent loneliness.

In only thee, my timid, fleet gazelle,
Dark-eyed, too, I seek my counterpart;
We both live lone, without companion dwell,
Accepting fate's decree with patient heart. [25]

VI

Storehouse of Jewish Writings—The Cairo Geniza

"She is like the merchant-ships;
She bringeth her food from afar.
She riseth also while it is yet night,
And giveth food to her household."

PROVERBS 31: 14-15

Geniza means hiding place. The Cairo Geniza was a hidden storehouse of vast dimensions that is only beginning to reveal its treasures. Scholars believe it will eventually teach us the way of life of the entire medieval Mediterranean Jewish community.

Such a storehouse developed because it was (and remains) Jewish practice never to deliberately destroy any document, book, or letter which might contain the name of God. The custom was to store these papers until they could be properly buried in the ground. As a result of this custom, thousands of letters and books were brought to the synagogue and accumulated in anticipation of burial.

Fostat, Egypt, was an ancient town not far from modern day Cairo. It had once been a center of Jewish life, and the storage area for their documents had been the lumber room of the ancient Ezra synagogue.[1] This lumber room, or Geniza, was rediscovered in 1752, still full of the holy documents which had been forgotten for centuries.

From that time until the 1890's, little was done about the discovery. The piles of papers, letters, fragments of holy writings, and crumbling legal documents remained in the storehouse room. Occasionally a traveller would enter and take out one or two pieces of material and they would find their way into the marketplace.

The real importance of the Geniza was first realized by Solomon Schechter, the famous Jewish theologian and Talmudist, who was a lecturer in Rabbinics at Cambridge University in England.[2] He was shown two ancient hand-written sheets by Agnes Lewis and Margaret Gibson, English sisters who were travellers and collectors. He was able to identify one of them as a centuries-old fragment of the Hebrew text of Ecclesiastes, and this ultimately led to a decision by Schechter to travel to Cairo. There, he received permission from the heads of the Jewish community to bring almost the entire contents of the nearby Fostat synagogue back to England. Only then was the serious study of this treasure undertaken.[3]

Solomon Schechter began the analysis of the Geniza, but his work was interrupted when he was called to head the Jewish Theological Seminary in New York. Other prominent scholars continued in this enterprise. Jacob Mann (in the 1930's)[4] and S.D. Goitein (in the 1960's until today)[5] are among the most important of these. Their commentaries on Geniza documents and letters added tremendously to our knowledge of the medieval Mediterranean community. One of the most surprising discoveries to come out of these studies was that of the significant position that women held in Mediterranean society—a position long unrecognized by Jewish historians.

Important events in history filled the several hundred years (900-1200 C.E.) covered by the Geniza records, and there were letters and papers that shed light on many of them.

The Karaites, a sect that was noted for its belief in the literal observance of Biblical law, and which rejected the Oral Law which ultimately was recorded in the Talmud, had already left the mainstream of the Jewish people. Their rejection of the Oral Law, beginning in the early ninth century, had created a bitter rift that was never healed.[6] Documents relating to individual Karaites and their active community in Egypt were found in the Geniza.

Also at this time, the vital Jewish community in Babylonia was in decline after the death of its last great leader, Saadia Gaon. Spurred on by the dissolution of the unified Islamic empire and economic difficulties throughout the East, migration to European lands was increasing.

The Jews in Spain were ushering in a Golden Age of culture and philosophy without parallel in Jewish history. This Golden Age lasted for five hundred years and ended with the Inquisition of the fifteenth century. Before it was over, it had fostered some of the greatest thinkers and poets that the Jewish people ever produced. The great scholar and diplomat, Hasdai ibn Shaprut, the Talmudist, Isaac Alfasi and the famous Hebrew poets, Solomon ibn Gabirol and Judah HaLevi, all came from Spain and influenced Spanish-Moslem civilization as well as Jewish culture.

As far east as Egypt, the influence of these great men was felt. The Egyptian Jews of Fostat knew of these outstanding people. United by a common language (Arabic) as well as a common religion and faith, they were able to share the richness of the writings and ideas of these Jewish thinkers.

In France and Germany, Jewish learning was also on the rise. Rabbenu Gershom of Mayence (Germany)[7] was the beloved leader of central European

Jewry. He had studied in the great academies of Babylonia before their prominence had declined. It was his wisdom and understanding which built up the spirit of learning and the love of Jewish law among the Jews in his area, and which, more than one hundred years later, was to influence Rashi, the famed Biblical commentator.[8] Rabbenu Gershom's *takkanot* (regulations) prohibiting polygamy, and requiring the woman's agreement to divorce, had far-reaching effects on Judaism.[9]

Jews were involved in trading during this period, and an active interchange existed through travel as well as letters. Maimonides had come to Egypt from Spain and in the latter part of the twelfth century (1180) was writing his *Mishneh Torah*,[10] a commentary on Jewish law which was destined to influence all of Jewish life for centuries to come.

For the most part, Islamic society in the Mediterranean was cultured, active, competitive, and educated. Jews in this area and elsewhere under Moslem rule thrived despite the disabilities of heavy taxes, restrictive rules, and even special clothing which were imposed on them. The first decree forcing the Jews to wear a yellow patch on their clothing was initiated under Moslem rule in 850 and was enforced more or less strictly, depending on the individual ruler.[11] This innovation spread to other countries as well, and in 1215, the Church Council imposed the wearing of a badge on all European Jews living under Catholic rule.[12]

Despite these problems, Jewish life in Egypt and the surrounding North African countries was dynamic and prosperous. It was far removed from the rumblings of the first Crusades which caused the deaths of thousands of Jews throughout Central Europe and

Palestine. Occasionally, a captive or other unfortunate would find his or her way to Egypt and would serve as a reminder of a common insecurity, for Egypt was a center and a crossroad of Jewish life.

The documents of the Cairo Geniza reveal that women were particularly active participants in the Jewish community of Egypt and the entire surrounding territory from the ninth to the thirteenth centuries. Letters were found—many written by women—referring to life in Iraq, Tunisia, Palestine, Libya, and Kairouan. These letters indicate that, in addition to their household chores, women often worked outside the home.[13] It was stated in the marriage contract whether a wife's earnings belonged to her, to her husband, or were to be used for clothing.

Women engaged in varied and interesting occupations. They might have been "bridecombers"—women who helped with the elaborate dressing and combing of the bride. Or they might have been midwives, doctors, teachers in girls' schools, undertakers, or textile merchants. Women often worked as textile brokers, visiting the homes of other women to buy and sell their wares, or trading the material in bazaars.

The bazaars of medieval Egypt were centers for all types of trading and purchases. The many working women often resorted to the bazaar for freshly cooked foods of all kinds when they could not afford to keep a servant and lacked the necessary time to prepare.

It was not uncommon for women to be learned. Despite Maimonides' disapproval,[14] there are examples of exceptional women working as scribes. There is even a case, documented in the Geniza, of a woman whom many believed was the Messiah. She is known to us today only as the daughter of Joseph.

An old letter, written several years after the fact,[15]

tells us that there was a period of trouble between the Jews and the Muslim rulers over taxation. At this time, an attempt was made to reactivate the rules concerning the special clothing that Jews were required to wear in Baghdad. As a result of this dispute, the entire male Jewish population (probably numbering no more than two or three hundred) was imprisoned.

It was at this time that the daughter of Joseph, a young woman just married, saw a vision of the prophet Elijah. The appearance of Elijah has always been accepted as the forerunner of the Messiah. The Jewish community became convinced that she was their redeemer. The Caliph, after threatening to have her burned, had a change of heart. He himself had a dream which he accepted as proof that she was indeed the Messiah, and as a result he ordered the release of the Jewish men and a special dispensation that they be relieved from certain taxes.

After this event, the daughter of Joseph fades into oblivion. The only document that remains as witness to her existence is the letter sent from Baghdad to Fostat, Egypt, written on the back of an old deed. From this we know that she was considered by many to be a messiah of the Jews. She is mentioned as such in the article on "Messiahs" in the *Encyclopedia Judaica*.

The daughter of Joseph was certainly an exception, but there are not too many self-proclaimed messiahs among either sex. Women, however, did appear in court, and commonly made their own wills, dedicated Torah scrolls, contributed large sums of money to charity, and headed committees for building and repairing synagogues.

Wuhsha is an exceptional example of the freedom and power that could be achieved by a woman in this Mediterranean society.[16] She was a respected businesswoman as well as the daughter of a banker and granddaughter of a *Rosh Kahal* (head of the Jewish community). As a broker and banker, she made loans against valuable objects offered as security. She appeared in the Jewish court in 1098 (this despite the fact that the Talmud says women are not fit witnesses in a court of law) and was apparently well enough known by the local dignitaries so that she did not have to prove her identity.

Her controversial behavior regarding her personal life often shocked the community. When her marriage to Hassun (a Jew who was not properly divorced) caused problems, she hastened to gather proof establishing him legally as the father of her child, not hesitating to confide in important and prominent citizens to accomplish this.

Wuhsha's will reveals the prestige and wealth to which a Jewish woman could aspire in eleventh century Egypt. It provides for an exhorbitantly expensive funeral. When it was read, immediately after her death, it no doubt greatly impressed the community which had frowned upon many of her acts. While traditional Jewish funerals tended to be simple, Wuhsha requested "cantors who will walk behind [the] coffin, each one [to be paid] according to his rank and excellence."

She left very large sums to charity and many bequests for religious purposes, including even the synagogue from which she was once expelled on Yom Kippur.

Wuhsha's marriage to the Jew, Hassun, was performed before a Moslem notary, perhaps because
Hassun had a wife who would not agree to a divorce.
This civil marriage was not approved by the rabbis,
and Wuhsha also lived to regret it. She stated her attitude toward Hassun, the father of her child, clearly
in her will, in which she stipulated that "he shall not
get a penny."

As to the education of her only son, she specified a
proper Jewish upbringing:

> The *melamed* (teacher), Rabbi Moses, shall be taken to
> (my son) and shall teach him the Bible and the prayer
> book to the degree it is appropriate that he should
> know them. The teacher shall be given a blanket and a
> sleeping carpet so that he can stay with him. He shall
> receive from the boy's estate every week five
> dirhams. [17]

Wuhsha was determined to establish the status and
rights of her son, Abu Saad, under Jewish law. A
document in Judeo-Arabic, with the depositions of
two witnesses, was found in the Geniza.[18] It establishes
the fact that Abu Saad, Wuhsha's son, was the child of
a non-religious, but otherwise legal relationship which
should not bar him from a future Jewish marriage. This
document established Abu Saad's legitimacy, as his
mother Wuhsha had intended.

Even where the women were not as powerful as
Wuhsha, individual letters often showed them to be
well-educated, and often, deeply and sincerely religious. According to the dictates of Jewish law, they were
concerned with their children's education and proper
upbringing in Jewish values.[19] This concern was certainly not limited to male children. In a letter from a

dying young mother, addressed to her sister in Fostat, and found in the Geniza, we read the following words:

> My most urgent request to you, if God the Exalted indeed decrees my death, is to take care of my little daughter and make efforts to give her an education, although I know well that I am asking you for something unreasonable, as there is not enough money for maintenance, let alone for education. However, she had a model in our mother, the saint. [20]

These letters and excerpts, as well as those which follow, were all written by women (possibly with the help of a scribe) and reflect the life of the period. In general, they tend to show the timelessness of human emotions—concern for children, love of parents, and longing for husbands, sisters and brothers—much more than the more restrained letters written by men. In addition, these letters reveal the variety of activities that many early Jewish communities offered to women, who, in return, added much to the social and economic life of the Jewish world.

This letter is from a woman living in Kairouan, a center of trade and scholarship in North Africa about forty miles from the site of ancient Carthage. The woman belongs to a scholarly merchant family, and she wrote to her brother who was away on business.

From her correspondence, we can see that this woman was the head of a large, extended family. She sends her brother regards on behalf of all his brothers, nieces and nephews, and details the news about his own wife and children. She advises him about bringing gifts to family and friends.

Most interesting of all is the item about the birth of a daughter, born to her brother Abu-l-Fadi. It would seem that this sister-matriarch of the eleventh century was given the honor of naming the children in the family. She says: "another girl was born and I called her by the name of my mother—Surura." This role is a most surprising one for those of us who are mainly familiar with the nuclear patriarchal family. It is not, however, necessarily surprising in an eleventh century community in Kairouan. It is also interesting to note that even though she, a woman, has the honored place in the family, she nevertheless alludes several times to the fact that a son is more desirable. "May I see a son of yours in the near future," she says, and later: "May God give you what will make you proud." This was probably due to the fact that the son carried on the family name.

The letter clearly shows this woman's prestigious position, and the language indicates that she accepts her power with ease and naturalness. She gives no apology for her sisterly advice, nor does she relate anything about the family that might indicate their discontent with her decisions. At the end of her letter, she notes approvingly: "I took notice of all the nice things you said about Isaac (a younger brother)."

This sister's loving concern and responsibility for her brother and all their family come through very clearly. It is an example such as this family letter from a faraway place and time, that helps us fill in the gaps in the long and varied history of Jewish women.

. . . . Now, what you wish to know, dear brother: your family is in the best of circumstances. Najiya is as you

like her to be and more than that, and so is Maulat.
May God fulfill all the hopes you have for them and
may He let me see a son of yours in the very near future . . .
Najiya never ceases to speak about you—may God
unite you with her and fulfill your hopes for her—but
Maulat is prettier than Najiya. Dear brother, although
you need not be reminded, send (your children) all
that is fit for them and likewise to their mother.
To [your brother] Abu-l-Fadi—may God preserve
him—another girl was born, and I called her by the
name of my mother, Surura (Happy). May she come
into a happy and blessed home and may the two [girls]
be happy and blessed and may God give you and him
whatever will make you proud [i.e. sons]. Abu l-Surur
(Isaac) became a father and called his son Barhun
[Abraham]—may God keep him alive and let his father
witness his wedding. It was a very joyful occasion, such
as we hope to have with you soon. Bring an appropriate present for him [the newborn], a prayer book or
a part of the Bible.
Best wishes from me. Najiya and Maulat and her
mother send you their greetings. I took notice of all
the nice things you said about Isaac [a younger
brother].May you be always happy with Maulat and
Najiya. And peace.[21]

The brutality of the Crusades resulted in many captives who were held for ransom. Since it was considered a *mitzvah* (commandment) to redeem captives
(Baba Batra 8a, 8b and 21a), the Jewish community
regularly raised money for this cause, and no captive
was ever left unransomed. In addition, the poor could
also appeal to the community for help.[22]
During public worship, while the men assembled in
the synagogue's main hall and the women gathered in

the gallery above, public appeals were frequently
made. An individual could request (in writing), with
the synagogue authorities' permission, the right to ask
the community for assistance. Often the person asking
the community for help would appear while her letter
was being read.

This is the appeal of a woman who had been captured by the Crusaders and later ransomed, and is
now requesting help for herself and her child.

Thus says the Lord: "Do justice and deeds of charity,
for my salvation is near to come and my charity to be
revealed." (Isaiah 56:1) "Blessed are those who do justice and deeds of charity at all times." (Psalms 106:3)
I hereby inform the holy congregation—may God en-
hance its splendor—that I am a woman who was taken
captive in the Land of Israel. I arrived here a week
from Sunbat and have no proper clothing, no blankets
and no sleeping carpet. With me is my little boy and I
have no means of sustenance. I now beseech You the
Exalted, and beseech the congregation—may you be
blessed—to do what is proper to be done with any
wayfarer. The Holy One, may He be praised, will
repay you many times and by your help so that you
may never be driven from your home. And may He
bring the Redemption in your days. Amen.[23]

VII

Sisters in Exile

"Many daughters have done valiantly,
But thou excellest them all."
PROVERBS 31:29

The Crusades. The Settlement of Jews in Poland. The expulsion from England. The Black Plague. Expulsion from France. The Inquisition. Expulsion from Spain. The discovery of America. All these events tumble over each other for our attention. Each one is another instance of catastrophe or good fortune in the recounting of Jewish history.

The first Crusade of 1096 was the beginning of a long series of persecutions suffered by the Jews. Originally organized by the Church as a sincere religious attempt to reconquer Palestine for Christianity, the Crusades soon became, in addition, a method to rid Europe of any persons who did not agree with Church dogma. The Jews were the most obvious of these non-conformists and thousands were slaughtered by Crusaders, as well as by various orders of knights who firmly believed themselves to be in the service of God. Women as well as men were martyred in this way.

Less than one hundred years later, in 1147, a second Crusade was launched with much the same results to Jewish communities—destruction, impoverishment, death and martyrdom.

By the time of the third Crusade, in 1190, the Jews knew what to expect, but protection was next to impossible. No sooner had Richard the Lion-Hearted departed England at the head of an army of Knights and Crusaders, then those left behind began attacking the Jewish communities. The massacre at York was the culmination of one such mob action, and was another step leading to the actual expulsion of all Jews from England in 1290.

In many ways, the Crusades established the tone of the Christian attitude towards Jews in the Middle Ages. Church members were taught to consider Jews as different and evil—people to be shunned and punished. Consequently, when the Plague (also called the Black Death) spread through Europe in the four-teenth century, killing thousands of people, it seemed logical to blame the Jews and to kill them or drive them away.

As the usefulness of the Jews waned, and Church pressures increased, Jews were expelled from one country after another. Sixteen years after being forced to leave England, they were forced out of the Prov-ence, a region in Southern France where a thriving Jewish community had existed for centuries, and fi-nally out of all of France, for the second time, in 1394. (They had previously been expelled from France, by the ruler Philip Augustus in 1182.) These expulsions were merely a prelude to the largest and most tragic one, the order issued by King Ferdinand and Queen Isabella in 1492 expelling the Jewish people from Spain.

All these hardships caused Jewish suffering, but at the same time, they also created a community with inner strength and organization. Education in Jewish law was emphasized more than ever. Charity, always a Jewish obligation, became even more important to help poor Jews and those who had to be resettled. As is al-ways the case when education is stressed, the benefits filtered down from the top through the general population. Women, although not always specifically included in the educational process, were also affected positively. They too became scholars and teachers, printers and writers.

The Jews of the Eastern Roman Empire (Byzantium) were not systematically driven out as they were in Western Europe, but the pressure of repeated persecution led them further away from Constantinople, the Byzantine capital, to the provinces of Eastern Europe, the Balkans, and Southern Russia. Places like Baghdad and Egypt, where the population was still predominantly Moslem, remained relatively secure, and Jews continued living there under laws that, if not liberal, at least were not overly harsh.

It was against this backdrop of persecution and wandering that a bright spot appeared in the dark Jewish landscape. It appeared in the form of an invitation from King Boleslav, ruler of the province of Greater Poland. King Boleslav asked Jews to come to Poland under the protection of the crown, to help build up a new middle class and bring Poland into the world of trade. Thus, in 1264, a new haven was created for homeless Jews and a new source of Jewish culture arose.

Behind these events and dates were real people—working, struggling, learning, and in their own small ways, changing the course of history. Many were caught up in the insecurities of the times and became its victims, but others stood out and used the world and what it offered for their own advancement and for the advancement of their people. In the midst of Jewish suffering and an overall instability, some women nevertheless succeeded financially, intellectually, or socially—in overcoming the limits that medieval life imposed on them.

Jewish women in the Middle Ages were emancipated to the extent that they conducted independent businesses and used the money at their own discretion.[1] More than a few of the charitable contributions and funds for the printing of books and maintenance of synagogues, were the direct result of the generosity of individual women.

This was also a period when women, reared in a society where Jewish Law was central and esteemed, demanded many of the privileges of that Law. They sought to exercise the right to observe positive commandments—something traditionally limited to men—and even demanded to be called to the Torah. These demands were well received and women were granted many honors heretofore denied to them.[2]

One woman who was held in high esteem in the Middle Ages was a noted teacher at the Talmudic academy in Baghdad where her father, Samuel, was the *Gaon* (lit. "the Genius," the Jewish spiritual leader). During the twelfth century, Samuel ben Ali, a contemporary and rival of Maimonides, ran the academy and ruled over the surrounding Jewish communities. His views on women's participation in Jewish life were much more liberal than those of his more famous colleague. While Maimonides disapproved of women participating in most aspects of religious life, ben Ali believed the opposite. His daughter, referred to only as Bat HaLevi (daughter of the Levite), had been educated by him in Bible and Talmud. She was known for her beauty as well as her scholarship. For this reason, she lectured the students at the Baghdad academy either from behind a screen or from an adjoining room, so that the young men would not be distracted from the Law by her lovely appearance.[3]

A traveller of the 12th century passing through Baghdad, wrote of Bat HaLevi:

She is expert in Scripture and Talmud. She gives instruction in Scripture to young men through a window. She herself is within the building, whilst the disciples are below outside and do not see her. [4]

Other noted women scholars of the same period
were Miriam Shapira Luria, who lectured in rabbinics
and Talmud in Italy in the 13th century,[5] and Dulcie
of Worms.[6] Dulcie was known to have held public discourses on the Sabbath. Hard working, and the sole
support of her husband and children, she died a martyr's death with her two daughters in 1213. Some say
the three were killed by two knights of the Cross. She
was mourned as:

A singer of hymns and prayers, a speaker of supplications, a declarer of *'Pittum HaKetoret'* and the Ten
Commandments. [7]

Dulcie may have been one of the first of a group of
women known in the Yiddish speaking world as the
firzogerins or foresayers. These women led the women's congregation in the balcony of the synagogue
while the men prayed below.[8] They had to be learned
enough to read aloud and to translate the prayers from
the Hebrew to the vernacular for those congregants
who did not know Hebrew. Many of them wrote their
own prayers or supplications (called *techinot*) for
the women's congregation. These were written in
Yiddish and usually concerned themselves with personal feelings and prayers for families or communities. Such prayers often were addressed specifically to
the Mothers of Israel: Sarah, Rebecca, Leah, and
Rachel.

The better known of these women foresayers were
famous for their beautiful *techinot*. *Marat* Guta,

daughter of Rabbi Nathan, is said to have: "prayed for the women in her lovely prayers."[9] Rebecca Tiktiner was one of the most learned of the *firzogerins*. She lived in the first half of the sixteenth century (died 1550) and was known as a woman preacher.

The family of Rashi, the famous Biblical commentator who lived in France (1040—1105), was blessed with many daughters and granddaughters. Rashi's three daughters, Yocheved, Miriam, and Rachel, were all learned. Rachel (also known as Bellejeune) was credited with having written a responsa on a question of Talmudic Law when her father was sick. It was a reply to Rabbi Abraham Cohen of Mayence.[10]

Rashi's daughters, it was said, put on *tefillin* (phylacteries) every morning in accordance with the commandment (Deut. 6:4-9).[11] His granddaughters, Alwina, Hannah, and Miriam were reputed authorities on dietary laws. This line of French-Jewish scholarship unfortunately ended with the expulsion of the Jews from France.

England was not known as a center of Jewish scholarship, but until the expulsion of the Jews in 1290, women and men thrived in the business world. Documents exist showing that many women were active as money lenders. Among them were: Belia of Bedford, Mirabel of Gloucester (who was a partner with her daughter and granddaughter), Henne of York, Avigay of London, and Belassez of Oxford.[12]

One of the most powerful of these English businesswomen was Licoricia of Winchester. She enjoyed a good relationship with King Henry III and his court, probably because they depended on her for loans. She handled large sums, regularly made loans to the royal family and their associates, and dealt, at times, with the largest Jewish banks of her day. The protection of the King helped her avoid heavy fines and even imprisonment for some of her more complicated business transactions.[13]

Jewish women in medieval England owned property in their own names and acted independently in business. They also dealt with the Jewish rabbinical court wherever that body held jurisdiction over English Jews. In all these areas they were continuing the tradition of freedom (within the limits of Jewish Law) and participation in economic life, that existed in many communities where Jews lived and prospered.

Poland and the area east of the Rhine River was slowly becoming a place of prosperity from the time of King Boleslav's invitation to the Jews in 1264. Despite ghettos, special taxes, and restrictions on owning land, Jews found ways to live and to succeed.

The ancient cities of Prague and Cracow had become Jewish printing centers by the late 1500's. Rebecca Tiktiner's book was printed in both of these cities in 1609 and 1618 respectively. It is the first book ever printed that was written in Yiddish by a woman.[14]

Following in Rebecca's footsteps were many other learned women. Some published their works while others remained unknown outside their immediate circle, or had only enough distinction to have their names preserved in a footnote. Names like *Sarah, Serlin* and *Hebel,* included in lists of women doctors from the Middle Ages, suggest that Jewish women also played a role in the science of the day. Still other doctors included in license records are listed as Jewish women but without mention of their names.[15] One woman, referred to only as Maria Hebrea, about whom little is known save that she was Jewish, stands out in the area of science and medicine for having discovered hydrochloric acid. [16]

In the field of Jewish letters there were also women such as Hannah Ashkenazi of Cracow (1593), a writer on moral subjects; Edel Mendels of Cracow who, in the 17th century, wrote a history book for women, and historian and printer, Bella Hurwitz who lived in Prague in the early 1700's.

Lita of Regensburg, an author whose origins remain a mystery, wrote a translation of the book of Samuel in Yiddish verse, called the *Schmuel Buch*. The first record of it appeared in 1544 when it was printed by Chaim (Hayyim) Schwartz. The inscription in the Hamburg, Germany manuscript read:

> This book I wrote with my hand, Liva (Lita) of Re-gensburg is my name. My dear *generin's* (patroness') name is Breidlen, may she use and read it in joy. This I desire. [17]

Because of the vagueness of the inscription, male historians felt that the book was merely copied, or that it was by a man. They reasoned that no woman was capable of actually composing such an exceptional work. However, Johann Christoph Wolf, a noted bib-liographer of Jewish books,[18] believed that the actual author was a woman, Lita, and other sources attribute the work to her as well.

Another women scholar was Eva (Hava) Bacharach, also known as Hava of Prague. She lived from 1580 to 1651. Eva came from a scholarly family and produced learned children, all dedicated to Judaism. Her father was Rabbi Samson and her mother's name was Vogele Cohen. Her son was elected Rabbi of Moravia, and her grandson, Jair Bacharach, wrote and published 238 responsa, which he named in honor of Eva, his erudite grandmother from Prague. The collection was called *Havat Jair,* or Jair's Eva.[19]

Eva, however, did not depend on her illustrious family for her personal fame. She was an expert in rabbinical and biblical writings and her opinions were sought on obscure passages. Later in her life she journeyed to Palestine in the hope of fulfilling a long held wish to see the Holy Land. She died on her way there, before reaching her goal.

The Middle Ages was a time of extreme hardship for much of European and Asian civilization. For some Jewish women, however, it was also a time of growth, as they became more educated and committed to Jewish life and learning. From England to Byzantium, from Poland to Kurdistan and beyond, Jewish women were accomplishing, building, and working to create the next generation of learned and dedicated Jews—and this in spite of all odds and adversities. Jewish women suffered the same tribulations as Jewish men in the medieval world: special Jew badges and hats, special taxes, persecution, instability, and periodic expulsions. In addition, they experienced the special prejudices that Jewish men often felt toward them and their "accepted" role. Still, they managed to overcome many of their difficulties.

Rebecca Tiktiner

Jewish women overcame not only the social and physical difficulties of their time. They also overcame the silence which sometimes surrounded their proudest accomplishments. Rebecca Tiktiner is the perfect example of this. Rediscovering Rebecca was an exciting adventure that came to represent our search for all the forgotten women of Jewish history.

Except for a few brief references to her name and work, Rebecca was unknown to us.[20] Bibliographies and card catalogues failed to turn up any more facts about her. Encyclopedias either ignored her or provided scanty information. Who was Rebecca and what had happened to her work?

Rebecca Tiktiner was the daughter of Rabbi Meir Tiktiner. Although no exact date is found for the birth of this daughter, we do know that she probably lived in Prague or Poland about 1520, and died around 1550. Her book, *Meneket Rivka* (Rebecca's Nurse), was first published in 1609.

In the 1500's, at a time when Protestants and Catholics were fighting for mastery of Europe, the Jews of Prague lived in a ghetto. Less· than one hundred years after the expulsion of the Jews from Spain, the bulk of the Jewish community was now concentrated to the east of the Rhine River. Talmudic scholarship had been well established for many centuries. When Rebecca Tiktiner began writing, the *Schulchan Aruch*, the "set table" codifying Jewish law for the layman, was being written and amended for the Ashkenazi community.[21]

We knew she had written a book in old Judeo-

German called *Meneket Rivka* (Rebecca's Nurse). The title is a reference to the Biblical story of Rebecca who brings her nurse (personal governess) with her when she leaves home to join Isaac, her new husband (*Genesis* 24:59 and 35:8). The book contained moral teachings, selections from the Talmud and Mishna, and poetry. Rebecca was also known as the translator of a famous ethical treatise entitled *Duties of the Heart*, an extremely popular work which had been written in Hebrew by Bahya ibn Pakuda in the eleventh century. But where were these examples of her scholarship?

After exhausting the regular libraries and researching rare book collections, we went to YIVO, the Institute for Jewish Research.[22] The YIVO Library did not have a copy of *Meneket Rivka* but a staff librarian believed there was still one in existence at the Jewish Theological Seminary. He added that "it is an extremely rare book and was so even in the 18th century."[23] We began to realize that we were looking for something special.

Searching the Jewish Theological Seminary files, our next clue was an article written by Dr. Menahem Schmelzer, the Librarian at the Seminary. In a column of the Library Newsletter in Spring of 1974, he had written an article about the very book we were looking for: *Meneket Rivka*. He quoted S. Y. Agnon, Nobel Laureate:

> In our provinces, I never saw the book. . . .*Meneket Rivka*, which was not even seen by the greatest bibliographers. I had found an incomplete copy of *Meneket Rivka* among the remnants of burned books after the fire in my house, and I gave it to my brother-in-law Alexander Marx, of blessed memory, and he gave it to the Library of the Jewish Theological Seminary of

America. Whether the book had survived the fire in my house only to be consumed in the fire of the Library of the Jewish Theological Seminary, I do not know.

Dr. Schmelzer continued by stating that the slim volume placed by Alexander Marx, then the Seminary's Chief Librarian, on the shelves of the Rare Book Room had indeed escaped the fire in the Seminary in 1966 as it had from Agnon's home in 1924.[24]

Finally having tracked it down to its last location, we were ushered into the Seminary Library's Rare Book Room and a copy of *Meneket Rivka* was placed in our hands. It was the second edition of this book, printed in Cracow in 1618. (The first edition, printed in 1609 in Prague, had not been found.) The binding of the book is dark parchment—discolored with years—and the outlines of a faded Latin manuscript can still be seen on the inside of the cover. Each page, darkened and stiff, stands as a witness to the centuries this book has endured.

In the Introduction, the printer has written:

> This book is called Meneket Rivka (Genesis 35:8) in order to remember the name of the authoress and in honor of all women to prove that a woman can also compose a work of ethics and offer good interpretations, as well as many a man.[25]

The printer goes on to describe Rebecca as a learned woman and a preacher, who died in Prague in the middle of the 16th century. In addition to the printer's words, we also discovered that 101 years after publication of *Meneket Rivka,* a book had been written about Rebecca Tiktiner. It is a 36-page study in Latin by George Zeltner (1672-1738) devoted completely to a discussion of Rebecca and her work. Zeltner was a German Lutheran theologian, a Christian Hebraist and a "missionary to the Jews". He describes this distinguished writer as:

> The Polish Rebecca, a rather rare example of learned women in the Jewish nation.[26]

The search for Rebecca Tiktiner was rewarded. Although we are not able to reproduce all of her writings here, Rebecca surely should not be buried in our archives. Having overcome the silence of history, she can still speak to us today.

The following is the printer's introduction written on the first page of Rebecca Tiktiner's book *Meneket Rivka*, in the Cracow edition of 1618. The printer, a man, displays his own sense of surprise at finding a woman so learned and wise. "Who ever heard of such a wonder!", he says. He nevertheless gives her full credit for her work, praising her ability "to read biblical verse and homiletical commentary" and to give explanations "that men would agree with."

Haver in Hebrew means friend. In the sense that it is used in the following paragraph, it means much more than that. The printer's allusion to a woman also being a *"haver"* implies her ability to enter into the learned society of men. This is indeed rare praise.

Photograph of *Meneket Rivka* by Rebecca Tiktiner, Cracow, 1618.

Listen, all you dear, blessed, pious women. You may read and look upon this translated book and let your soul trust in the Omnipotent. In this way this new work will be created. When you have gotten to know the respected woman, Rebbitzen-Preacher Mrs. Rivka, may her memory be blessed, the daughter of the brilliant scholar, Rabbi Meir Ticktiner, may his memory be blessed, your mind will think and concentrate and, through her, your fear of God will be renewed and your thoughts will not be diverted. Who ever heard of such a wonder! For everlasting time it has happened that a woman, out of her own mind, became a *Haver* and was able to read Biblical verses and homiletical commentary on Scripture aloud. Therefore I let this be printed, in order that you dear women who will read this will buy one and will say the following: Mrs. Rivka taught us righteousness and, in honor of all women, stated that a woman can also be a *Haver*, teaching good explanations that men would agree with. In spite of their being spread over seven chapters, they are short, without using unnecessary words. By this merit may you be privileged to witness the coming of the Messiah. Divine Presence will return to Israel and in this way God's will shall be fulfilled.

Here, the Holy Community in Krakow.[27]

Translated from the Yiddish
by William Ungar.

This is Rebecca Titktiner's own introduction to her work. It is basically a prayer to God, and describes, in moving metaphor, her decision to write this book. From her own satisfaction and fulfillment in Jewish learning, she conceived the desire to "bring to all my

Ernestine Rose, suffragist, 19th century (See chapter XIV, pp. 212-243).

near ones" . . . "That they will drink for the length of their days."

Rebecca speaks of herself as having fulfilled God's commandments and followed in the Torah. She generally displays a deep love of God's law and of study, which she likens to "a well of fresh water."

I had seen. In my heart I meditated. With my voice I called out. Here, I have now come. And today I walked. And a well of fresh water I found. And I discovered the big stone from the well. And from it I drank. And I was still thirsty. And I said in my heart. I will go and I will bring. To all my near ones. And my bones will rejoice. That they will drink for the length of their days. To fulfill what is said: drink blessed water and you will be blessed by the Blessed. And so with those who are sheltered in Your shade. And so it was promised to us by Your prophets. It will not be removed from the mouths of the seed of your seed. And I also, Your handmaid. The daughter of Your righteous ones. To fulfill Your words. And I shall also come after You. And I fulfilled Your commandments. To follow in Your Torah. Because all of my good, all, is from You. And my resting place is after (in) You. And I will look to Your ways. For Your words are a candle to my feet. In order that You be just in all Your judgments. For You are close to all who call out to You. And to all who desire to see You. They will merit resting in the pleasure of Your eyes. [28]

Translated from the Yiddish
by William Ungar.

The following poem, written by Rebecca Tiktiner, is a special *techinah* (prayer) to be recited on Simchat Torah. In structure and content it is similar to the synagogue prayers still in use today. It is a hymn of hope and faith, praising God, the Creator of all things. Here, as in so many of the prayers composed by women, all generic terms are avoided and God is referred to as "Creator" or the "Living and Eternal." God is not called "king," but one who "lives . . . on Your heavenly throne."

> Our God is one—You are my God,
> Who created my soul and body—Hallelujah!
>
> You created Heaven and Earth,
> Therefore is your praise eternal—Hallelujah!
>
> You were and will be eternally
> You created us all—Hallelujah!
>
> All things are in Your power;
> Therefore we praise You day and night—Hallelujah!
>
> True and pure is Your Command
> Therefore we thank You, O True God, Hallelujah!
>
> Living and Eternal, You are our Consolation
> As You did promise us—Hallelujah!
>
> You live eternally on Your heavenly throne,
> For the prayers, You keep their reward, Hallelujah!
>
> Take as Your help the heavenly Host;
> Everything will prove true—Hallelujah![29]

Q. D. B. V.

DE

REBECCA

POLONA

Eruditarum in Gente Judaica Fœminarum

Rariori Exemplo

P R A E S I D E

GVSTAVO GEORGIO

ZELTNER

D. P. P. & P.

A. R. S. MDCCXIX. a. d. III. Kal. April.

disputabit

IOH. CONRADVS LVFFT

Fischbaco-Noric.

ALTDORFII,

Litteris I od. Gvil. Kohlesii, Vniversit. Typogr.

1719

De Rebecca Polona; by Gustavo Zeltner, 1719. *Courtesy of Jewish Theological Seminary*

Anxious Letters

As the following letters will show, not all women of this period were as educated and secure as Rebecca Tiktiner and some of the other women scholars and writers of those centuries. This first moving letter was written sometime during the thirteenth century by Donna Sarah, an Italian Jewess. The letter was sent to her husband, Rabbi Solomon the scribe, who had left their home town in Italy and journeyed to Egypt in order to obtain relief from paying certain taxes. We will never know whether Rabbi Solomon ever received the letter or if he did return home. The document was found among the Hebrew letters of the Cairo Geniza. Even though it was written so long ago, Donna Sarah's longing for her husband, her indignation at his absence, and her need for support and help are familiar feelings now, as they must have been then.

Yet, Donna Sarah's plea has a deeper meaning than that. The deserted woman (*agunah*) according to Jewish law, holds a unique and lonely place in the Jewish community. Should Rabbi Solomon have failed to return, Donna Sarah would have been left without the possibility of remarrying for the rest of her life. Lacking a witness necessary to prove his death, she could not have claimed status as a widow. And since the Jewish woman herself is not able to initiate a divorce, nor is the court able to grant her one without the husband's ultimate consent,[30] Donna Sarah would have been doomed to a lonely life.

Even though the problem of the *agunah* still exists for many observant Jews, the desperate urgency of this dilemma in Donna Sarah's time cannot fully be appreciated today, when Jews have access to civil law and Jewish courts are not legally binding. Donna Sarah, as a member of the Jewish community of Italy, was legally bound by rabbinic law and had no recourse to appeal to any other authority, even if she had wished to. These facts bring to her words ("I swear to the Lord, if you do this, you must not speak with us any more; and if you do this, which will make the world despise us. . . .") a poignancy that would not otherwise be apparent.

DONNA SARAH TO HER HUSBAND SOLOMON

May ample peace and welfare be with my master and ruler, the light of my eyes, the crown of my head, my master and husband, the learned Rabbi Solomon, the Scribe, may he live long. May ample peace be bestowed upon you by the Master of peace and from Donna Sarah your wife, your daughters Reina and Rachel, from R. Moses, your son-in-law, and Rebecca.

We are all longing to see your sweet face, as one longs after the face of God, and we are wondering that you have not answered the numerous letters we have sent you. We have written you often begging you to return, but—no answer at all. If you can manage with the help of the esteemed physician. Rabbi Solomon, may he live long, to obtain release from taxes it will be greatly to your profit, and this kindness will exceed all benefits which he has conferred on you. May the Lord grant him a rich reward in this world and the world to come, and may he educate his son for Torah, marriage and good works.

And now let us return to the previous subject. We are all assembled, your wife, your daughters and your son-in-law Moses, to implore you from the bottom of our hearts not to go further, either by sea or by land, because we have heard that you have the intention of leaving for Turkey. I swear to the Lord that, if you do this, you must not speak with us any more; and if you do this, which will make the world despise us and cause a quarrel between your son-in-law and your daughter, who is in certain circumstances, you will inflict pain upon your daughter and perhaps she will suffer a miscarriage. And you will also endanger the happiness of your daughter Rachel, who has grown up and has become a beautiful and modest maiden.

People will talk scandal and say: "Here is a respectable old scribe, who left his wife and daughters and has been missing for many years. Perhaps he is mad. For he went to a distant country and you know what the verse says: 'The eyes of a fool are in the ends of the earth.' " Beg the physician, Rabbi Solomon, therefore to provide you a confirmation about the release from the taxes; otherwise come home (in the name of) the Blessed one! . . . Do nothing else. And Peace![31]

Lady Maliha lived in Byzantium, generally known as the Eastern Roman Empire. Her letter to her brothers shows the closeness of family ties in this period, and hints at some of the events and practices of the times.

There is no place name on the letter, nor any address, but since it was found in the Cairo Geniza, it was probably addressed to her brothers in Egypt. It is not specifically known where Lady Maliha was living, but because the letter reminds her brothers that "many Jews are being fetched from Byzantium", it might be reasonable to assume that she was living in or near Constantinople, the Byzantine capital itself. In this city, the Jewish quarter had been sacked and burned by Latin Crusaders in 1204 after the fourth Crusade. The area was in a general state of turmoil.[32] Lady Maliha may well have wanted to leave this situation and return to the comparative stability of Egypt.

Another interesting point mentioned in the letter is Maliha's use of the Torah as an omen. ("I consulted a Torah scroll and obtained a disappointing answer which boded no good . . . ") The concept of using a Torah scroll as a Jewish "crystal ball" is strange to modern thinking and was most certainly frowned on by rabbis even in the eleventh and twelfth centuries. However, looking for omens was an old superstition that dates back to biblical times. King Saul consulted the High Priest for an omen before deciding whether to go to battle against the Philistines.[33]

Maliha decided that the omen was not auspicious enough for her to take a trip at that time. This apparently did not preclude her brothers' coming to take her. The risk was in her travelling alone.

Why does Maliha appeal to her brothers and not her husband for her protection? Indeed, why is she alone in "Byzantium" with her daughter while her family is elsewhere? Is her "Master, the fourth" that she refers to in the letter their father or her husband, or someone else? These questions must remain unanswered.

Maliha's letter, written originally in Hebrew and full of references to Bible stories, shows her as a learned woman. She gives us a brief glimpse into a little known world where one crisis followed another, where travelling and even communication were fraught with danger, and long separations were common. In such an atmosphere, family ties and responsibilities bolstered by the structure of Jewish law, could mean the difference between life and death for women like Lady Maliha. Understanding this makes

her loving appeal to her brothers much clearer and
more logical.

LADY MALIHA'S LETTER

May this letter be delivered in gladness to my excellent brothers, Abu Said and Solomon, from your sister
Maliha. May peace from Heaven like the drops of
water from above (and abundant) like the fishes in the
depths (of the sea) be bestowed upon you and
strength, vigour, favour, mercy and pity and a long
life like his who became father of the people [Ab-
raham], or his who was bound as a victim on a high
mountain [Isaac], or of Jacob the plain man, or of him
who dreamed [Joseph] or of him who sprinkled the
blood on the altar seven times [Aaron]. May all
blessings come and be gathered and accumulated
upon the heads of my brothers, Solomon and Abu
Said, gentle and most beloved brothers from your sister Maliha. And heartiest greetings from my little
daughter Zoe.

We are in good health and trust in the Rock of your
welfare that you, too, are well and safe, prosperous
and free, in good heart without trouble and sorrows.
But I, while wishing you good, am not myself in good
humour, for when I think of you, my heart sinks, my
knees quiver, my limbs tremble, my strength dwindles,
because I have been separated from you for many
years and am desirous of seeing your faces. I should
like to run to you like a lion, nay, to fly! Oh for the
wings of a dove, that I could fly and join my brothers,
and also our Master, the fourth. I am, however, not
able to come, as the hour is not favorable. I was ready
to go with this man [the bearer of the letter], but I
consulted a Torah scroll [using the passage that
turned up for an omen] and obtained a disappointing

answer which boded no good for myself. Thus I could not join them.

And for Heaven's sake, do you not see that many Jews are being fetched from Byzantium, by their relatives? Why does not one of you make up his mind to come over here in order to bring me back? You will understand that I am reluctant to engage strange people. If I should go alone, may God not deprive me of luck, but if anything evil should befall me during the voyage, it might be fatal to me and I should die. For I have been devoted to you since your infancy. . . .[34]

Rebbetzin Mizrachi

The Middle East, like the Western world, also had its share of noteworthy Jewish women. Among those most deserving of recognition is the Rebbetzin Mizrachi, who was a learned woman of the sixteenth century. History has failed to preserve her first name, but her correspondence has miraculously been preserved.[35] From these letters we know that "Mrs." Mizrachi lived in Kurdistan, then a part of the Ottoman Empire, and was the wife of Rabbi Jacob Mizrachi.

The Kurdish people, although never politically independent, had an independent spirit. Kurdish women fared better than other Moslem women. Although severely limited by Moslem custom, these women were nevertheless held in relatively high esteem in society and even occasionally achieved prominence in tribal leadership.[36] Jewish women naturally benefited from this freer social atmosphere.

Scholarship was valued among the Kurdish Jews and during the time of Turkish rule (from approximately 1500), the Jews were relatively better off and able to develop Jewish learning and skills. Kurdish Jewish poets sprang up in this era and one of the most famous was a woman named Osnath, who wrote in the seventeenth century. She was the daughter of the well-known poet, R. Samuel ben Nathanel HaLevi Barazani.[37]

The Jewish community in Kurdistan traced its origins back to the original ten tribes who were exiled by the Assyrian king, Shalmanesir. They spoke Aramaic and were devout followers of Jewish Law.[38] There was a fairly large population of Jews, especially around the

Kurdish city of Amadiya, and Jewish scholars and leaders there exerted a great deal of influence on the surrounding Jewish communities.

It was in Amadiya that Jacob Mizrachi lived with his wife and children, studied, and administered a yeshiva. His wife had been given a thorough education by her father, himself a famous scholar. When she was offered in marriage, her father stipulated that she must never be troubled with housework. Accordingly, she worked as a teacher in her husband's yeshiva, assuming most of the burden of running the school and teaching the students while her husband pursued his own studies. When Jacob Mizrachi died, he left his widow with a young son and daughter, an entire school to administer, and very little funds.

Although learned women were not unheard of in the 1500's, they were certainly not commonplace. Even more unusual was the fact that Rebbetzin Mizrachi remained head of a school for so many years despite her financial difficulties. She refused to give up the yeshiva, but maintained it until her son, Samuel, was old enough to assist in the work.

In Moslem lands it was not customary for women to travel, or even walk about the streets alone (a fact that she alludes to in her letters). Yet Mrs. Mizrachi managed to continue teaching and running the school. Her debts brought her further difficulties with the rulers of Amadiya, who sent collection agents into her home to confiscate her personal property in lieu of payment. Even this did not deter her, nor persuade her to abandon her efforts to maintain the yeshiva. It merely encouraged her to write an appeal for help.

The excerpt included here is from one of these appeals to the community of Amadiya. The original is written in beautiful Hebrew, rich in Biblical and Talmudic allusions. The first part is a long poem, describing her plight, and begging for assistance. She then reverts to prose for her more practical requests. The mood of her writing changes from supplication to strident demands and back to supplication.

It is interesting to note that throughout the lengthy letter she never refers to the school as hers, or to herself as its head. She alludes to herself as acting either for the honor of her deceased husband, or in the name of her minor son. Probably well aware of the uniqueness of her position, she never mentions her daughter as a possible successor.

Mrs. Mizrachi may have felt that her appeal only had a chance if it was sent in the name of learned men like her well-known father and husband. At one point in her poem she alludes to the students who will: "In the shadow of (her) father and (her) husband, sit and study Torah."[39]

Whatever the reason for her humility—whether it was truly how she felt, or a shrewd assessment of how the elders of the community felt—it did not help much. Several years later, a similar letter, written by her then-grown son, was sent to the same community referring to the neglect of his family and the yeshiva.

In spite of the unsympathetic reactions of her own contemporaries to her problems, the words of this gallant woman can still evoke our concern and admiration. With her courage and determination, she succeeded in keeping the school at a time when many others would have failed to do so.

She ends her letter with a final plea, practically throwing herself at the mercy of the community, and signing simply "your servant." With this humble gesture she has forever denied us the privilege of knowing the name of this talented and scholarly woman.

Photograph of Rebbetzin Mizrachi letter, in Hebrew,
Courtesy of Hebrew Union College, Cincinnati.

REBBETZIN MIZRACHI'S PLEA FOR HELP

To whom can I turn?
To the generous people that can cure my ills.
You righteous ones, please spare me,
And remember my deeds and the Torah of my God.
Not for my pleasure or my personal benefit am I crying here.
Not for the need of my household, my clothes, or my food.
But only to preserve the Midrashot, [biblical explanations]
That my valour will not be shattered. . . .

. . . If the students of God will be scattered,
What will become of my world,
Of my days and nights?
Therefore, listen, pious and righteous people. . . .

Mrs. Mizrachi then continues in prose to explain her problem in detail.

. . . And here is where I am going to tell you about my own problem. They caught me and hit me. . . . They sent a judgment with people that took over my house and they sold everything: my clothes and my daughter's clothes. They even took the books that were before me! And in addition they told me that I owed them one hundred grush. And I have no place to run or find shelter. Only from your mercy and the mercy of God. For the grave of my father and the rabbi [her husband], that their Torah may not be abolished, and their names will not disappear from the congregation. Because I am the one who is left to teach and preach the Torah: who demands Sabbath ablutions and laws of purity. And this is my problem: because I fell into debt because of the interest that I mentioned before and I have nothing to sell. And I don't have a grown son or a messenger that can solicit for us in the community. Because it is not the custom of a woman to solicit in the community. Her honor is to be a daughter of a king, sitting on a throne, wearing gold and rubies.

I, in my day, was the key to my household. The daughter of a queen did not go out. I was raised on the knees of the greatest scholars, the pride and joy of my father. And no work did he teach me except the ways of heaven. And I studied day and night. He didn't have any sons and he even had my husband swear that he wouldn't make me do any work. At the beginning my husband was very busy with his own studies and didn't have time to teach the students. And I was teaching them in his place. I was his helpmate. And now, because of our many sins, he went to his rest and left me and the children to our sorrows . . .

Mrs. Mizrachi concludes her appeal in poetry:

. . . And it will be known in Israel that I am tender,
And carry the burden of these orphans (her children)
Woe is me from them, and from my husband.
You, the congregation, perhaps you can lift your prominent hands,
And you will receive this letter with kindness and mercy,
And you will again be eating at my table. . . .
With great humility,
Your servant who kisses your hand. . . . [40]

Translated from the Hebrew
by Isaac Taitz

VIII

Scribes and Printers

"She perceiveth that her merchandise is good;
Her lamp goeth not out by night."

PROVERBS 31:18

Imagine the scribe leaning over a manuscript and carefully copying treasured words and letters—precious ideas transmitted from one manuscript to another with nothing but a simple pen and ink, and perhaps the sunlight from a window. It was difficult and tedious work. Yet in this way hundreds of books were placed in circulation in Jewish communities, and most are surprisingly accurate. It was rare to find a footnote such as this one by an anonymous woman:

> I beseech the reader not to judge me harshly when he finds that mistakes have crept into this work; for when I was engaged in copying it, God blessed me with a son, and thus I could not attend to my business properly.[1]

Books and the reproduction of books have always been important to the Jewish people. Before the advent of printing we depended on scribes to make copies of the Bible and the increasing commentaries on the Bible. These careful workers were engaged in a sacred and honored profession. The completion of one book could be a matter of years and the few women who worked as scribes might very well have begun writing a manuscript, then have conceived and borne a child before it was completed.

It was not common for women to be taught how to write at all in medieval Europe or the near East, but, as always, there were notable exceptions. Miriam Ben-ayahu was perhaps one of the most notable. In San'ya, Yemen, where her family lived, women were generally excluded from all religious learning. Yet Miriam, a scribe of renown, copied the Torah — the Five Books of Moses, and with it a note in her own hand which reads:

> Do not condemn me for any errors that you may find
> for I am a nursing woman.
> Miriam, the daughter of Benayahu, the Scribe.[2]

Miriam's family was famous during the fourteenth century and afterwards for producing over four hundred books for synagogues and private individuals. These books are still known and remembered for their beauty and accuracy.

In Europe, other women scribes were known for their accomplishments. One of the earliest on record is Paula Dei Mansi of Italy, the learned daughter of Nathan ben Yehiel. Paula translated a collection of Bible commentaries (1280 and 1288) and added her own. Her translations were reported to be in the Seminary Library of Breslau, Germany as late as the 19th century.[3]

Frommet Arwyller is another name that has been preserved for us by a chance inscription. She lived in the 1400's and presented a copy of the rabbinic code, *Kizzur Mordecai*, as a gift to her husband. This book, which is in the Biblioteque Nationale in Paris, includes the following short statement:

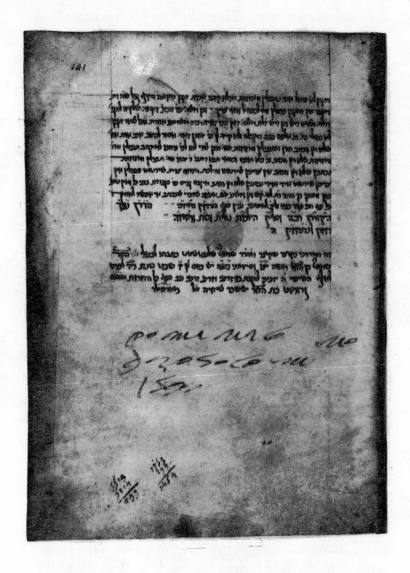

Inscription by Scribe Frommet of Arwyller, 1454, on Kizzur Mordecai.

This copy has been executed by Frommet, daughter of Arwyller, for her husband, Samuel ben Moses, 1454.[4]

Considering the skill and time involved in this undertaking, the woman who gave such a gift to her husband truly gave of herself.

With the development of printing in the fifteenth century, the reproduction of multiple copies of books became more feasible. The typesetting and printing itself were hardly less difficult than the work of the scribe. But once it was done, hundreds of books could be produced instead of just one.

Some of the earliest presses were founded for the printing of Hebrew books. In 1476, Estellina Conat, one of the first women printers, operated a printing shop in Mantua, Italy with her husband, Abraham. At this time, a Hebrew word for printing was not yet invented. Instead, Estellina uses the word 'write' *(kotev)* in her inscription for *Investigations of the World*. Thus she says "I . . . wrote this book."

> I, Estellina, (wife of my master, my husband, the honored Rabbi Abraham Conat, may he be blessed with children, and may his days be prolonged, Amen,) wrote this book, *'Investigations of the World'* with the aid of the Youth Jacob Levi of Provence, of Tarascon, may he live. [5]

An accepted Hebrew word was first developed for the printing process in 1477 (one year after the above inscription was written) by Abraham Dyer of Ferarra. He called it (in Hebrew) *difus*, adapted from the Greek.[6] But a year before that, Abraham Conat, Estellina's husband, referred to the process as writing, also, and proudly says of his wife: "She wrote the book with many pens, without the aid of a miracle."[7]

As printing grew, literacy increased among women as well as men, and some Jewish women gained prominence in the printing field. M. Steinschneider, the famous bibliographer, has catalogued the names of all the typographers and printers of Jewish books until 1732, among which can be found many women, such as Bat Sheba of Verona (1594), Gutel Kohen of Prague (1627), and Rebecca and Rachel Judels of Wilmersdorf (1677).[8] Most of them belonged to families of typesetters, but some learned the craft by other means. Often they were skilled translators as well.

There was Roizl Fishels of Cracow who worked in the late 1500's, when Cracow and Prague were the great printing centers of the Jewish book world. She translated psalms into Yiddish poetry and published many volumes, using as her model the *Schmuel Buch* written in verse by Lita of Regensburg. Much later, in the late 1600's, there were Bella Hurwitz Chassen of Prague who wrote a history of the House of David,[9] and Elis bat Mordecai Michals of Slutzk.[10] Among Elis bat Mordecai's many translations from Hebrew into Judeo-German was a special collection of prayers for the sick and dying called *Maavor Yabbok*, which she completed in 1704. Joseph Caro's code, one of the most extensive discussions of Jewish law, based on Jacob ben Asher's code called *Turim*, was first printed in 1727 by Fiola Hirsch of Bavaria together with her husband.[11]

All these names stand as witnesses to the abilities and the varied activities of the Jewish woman. Not only did she compose and create, but she was involved in every way in the process of educating her fellow

Jews and disseminating information in her world. Following are some of the writings of these women printers. Many are rare treasures, carefully preserved by libraries and museums. Although most of the "writings" of these printers and translators are just a few lines on a fly leaf—an acknowledgement of work done, or a short prayer or poem—they give us a glimpse into the otherwise unknown world of Jewish working girls and women.

Surely one of the treasures of the history of Jewish women must be a brief passage, written at the bottom of one page of a prayer book. The book, in Hebrew with a Yiddish translation, was printed in Dessau in 1696. The writer of the passage is named Ella.[12] In a few lines she states simply that she set the type for this translation. She is only nine years old and in view of her youth, she asks to be forgiven for any printer's errors.[13]

Reyna Nasi was the daughter of the famed philanthropist and businesswoman Dona Gracia Nasi (see Chapter X). She lived in Constantinople, Turkey and established a printing press for the publication of Hebrew and other Jewish books. Her first printing press was located at Belvedere, Constantinople and ran from 1592 to 1594. Her second enterprise began in 1597 and operated for two years at Kuru Tschechme, Turkey. The printed inscriptions inside these books give a clue to the esteem in which she was held in the community.

שיר הכבוד   סדר החרולקין מכה

הקב"ה ודרוס מיד ודר סביר מכן מה וְאוֹתָהּ קַח חֶלְקְךָ בִּכְשָׁמִסְרֹאשׁ: יַעֲרַב
ער ביסטזב ט־מא אחכט נישון מא נָא שִׂיחִי עָלָיו כִּי נַפְשִׁי תַעֲרוֹג אֵלֶיךָ:
סאחרקד ציון: וברבבאי מא חו סוף
אכ דיך וואכטאו לבר וועכן לו אידאיטט ריין קחמ רמ איטט איין אכ וולו ריד אקביל זיין
מא־ברכלה נכם לו דריר מודים היפם נאירין דיח אן החס נישאו לורמן קטור ת מנולו רען
סאן־האנמת (יערכל) טוטואל אין רמ מן חוקביס דיך איר־רד מיולדיד וטבן אין ליב סרידטט
לודיד איט ורד תבלה:

ורע מן אוין רער שול ניט וזא זאגט מן דאש יהי:

יְהִי יְיָ אֱלֹהֵינוּ עִמָּנוּ כַּאֲשֶׁר הָיָה וְלִשְׁלוֹם מֵעַתָּה וְעַד עוֹלָם ·
עָסְאֲבוֹתֵינוּ אַל יַעַזְבֵנוּ וְאַל הַשְׁקִיפָה מִמְּעוֹן קָדְשְׁךָ מִן
יִטְּשֵׁנוּ · לְהַטּוֹת לְבָבֵנוּ אֵלָיו הַשָּׁמַיִם וּבָרֵךְ אֶת עַמְּךָ אֶת
לָלֶכֶת בְּכָל דְּרָכָיו וְלִשְׁמוֹר יִשְׂרָאֵל וְאֵת הָאֲדָמָה אֲשֶׁר
מִצְוֹתָיו וְחֻקָּיו וּמִשְׁפָּטָיו כַּאֲשֶׁר נִשְׁבַּעְתָּ לַאֲבוֹתֵינוּ לָתֶת לָנוּ אֶרֶץ
צִוָּה אֶת אֲבוֹתֵינוּ · וְהָיוּ נָא זָבַת חָלָב וּדְבָשׁ · אֵל הַכָּבוֹד
דְּבָרַי אֵלֶּה אֲשֶׁר הִתְחַנַּנְתִּי לִפְנֵי אַחֵן לָךְ שִׁיר וַהֲלֵל · וְאֶעֱבוֹד לָךְ
יְיָ קְרוֹבִים אֶל יְיָ אֱלֹהֵינוּ יוֹמָם יוֹם וָלֵיל · בָּרוּךְ יָחִיד וּמֵיוחָד הָיָה
וָלַיְלָה לַעֲשׂוֹת מִשְׁפַּט עַבְדּוֹ הֹוֶה וְיִהְיֶה · יְיָ אֱלֹהִים אֱהֶ־יִשְׂרָאֵל
וּמִשְׁפַּט עַמּוֹ יִשְׂרָאֵל דְּבַר יוֹם מֶלֶךְ מַלְכֵי הַמְּלָכִים הַקָּדוֹשׁ
בְּיוֹמוֹ · לְמַעַן דַּעַת כָּל עַמֵּי הָאָרֶץ בָּרוּךְ הוּא · הוּא אֱלֹהִים חַיִּים
כִּי יְיָ הוּא הָאֱלֹהִים אֵין עוֹד · יְיָ מֶלֶךְ חַי וְקַיָּם לָעַד וּלְעוֹלְמֵי עַד ·
נְתַן בְּצִדְקָתָהּ לְמַעַן שֹׁרְרָי הַיָּשָׁר בָּרוּךְ שֶׁהַכָּבוֹד מַלְכוּתוֹ לְשָׁלוֹם
לְפָנֶיךָ דַּרְכֶּךָ · וַאֲנִי בְּחַסְדִּי אֶהֱלֵךְ וָזָר · לִישׁוּעָתְךָ קִוִּיתִי יְיָ · כִּי
פְדֵנִי וְהַגְאֵנִי כִּי יָחִיד וְעָנִי אָנִי · רַגְלִי כָל הָעַצְמִים יֵלְכוּ אִישׁ בְּשֵׁם
עֲמָדָה בְמִישׁוֹר בְּמַקְהֵלִים אֲבָרֵךְ אֱלֹהָיו · וַאֲנִי אֵלֵךְ בְּשֵׁם יְיָ אֱלֹהִים
יְיָ שׁוֹמְרִי צִלִּי עַל יַד יְמִינִי · חַיִּים וּמֶלֶךְ עוֹלָם · עָרֵי מַעַם
עָרֵי מַעַם יְיָ עוֹשֶׂה שָׁמַיִם וָאָרֶץ · יְיָ עוֹשֶׂה שָׁמַיִם וָאָרֶץ · יְיָ יִמְלוֹךְ
יְיָ יִשְׁמוֹר צֵאתִי וּבוֹאִי לְחַיִּים לְעוֹלָם וָעֶד:

ﷺ עַל יְדֵי הַפּוֹעֵל בִּמְלֶאכֶת הַקּוֹדֶשׁ נְאֻם יִשְׂרָאֵל ﷺ
בֵּן כְּהֹרֵר מֹשֶׁה שְׁלִיט:

ריח שיטט מי מתלית הכב־אין נישלמ איט איר־ר הזמו׳ עֲלֵה בֹּת כהר"ר מֹשֶׁה אוי
האמ־ר: איר־י ירי וין אין ולבר פג־ין ׳ לוטן ועכם קזרד בין אין אין כ־ת חדה חזין:
ורכן וו־לו חד־ר מין סטלולן נילהוו · מא־נידאכ־ק ׳ רם צב הטע מ־מרט ׳ נולש אין קן ־ר :

Prayer book with Yiddish verse by printer's daughter, Ella
of Dessau, age 9 years, 1696.

Printed in the palace of the Honored woman Reyna Nasi, widow of the Duke Don Joseph Nasi, at Belvedere, which is near Constantinople, under the rule of Sultan Murad.[14]

or:

Printed in the house and with the type of the Crowned Lady, crown of descent and excellency, Reyna (may she be blessed of women in the tent!) widow of the Duke, Prince and Noble in Israel, Don Joseph Nasi of Blessed Memory . . . near Constantinople, the great city which is under the rule of the great and mighty King Sultan Mohammed (may his might increase!).[15]

Gela is another young "daughter of Israel" who, in 1713, included these moving lines at the beginning of a translation of prayers for which she set the type.

Of this beautiful prayerbook from beginning to end,
I set all the letters in type with my own hands.
I, Gela, the daughter of Moses the printer, and whose mother was Freide, the daughter of R. Israel Katz, may his memory be for a blessing.
She bore me among ten children:
I am a maiden still somewhat under twelve years.
Be not surprised that I must work;
The tender and delicate daughter of Israel has been in exile for a long time.
One year passes and another comes
And we have not yet heard of any redemption.
We cry and beg of God each year
That our prayers may come before Him Blessed Be He,

For I must be silent.
I and my father's house may not speak much.
As will happen to all Israel,
So may it also happen to us,
for the Biblical verse says
All people will rejoice
Who lamented over the destruction of Jerusalem
And those who endured great sufferings in exile
Will have great joy at the redemption.
(1713)[16]

IX

Liberated Women: Renaissance Style

"Give her of the fruit of her hands;
And let her works praise her in the gates."
PROVERBS 31:36

Much has been written about Renaissance Man and very little about Renaissance Woman, leaving us to believe that she was a shadowy figure hovering in the background, confined to her household chores. This was not always the case. Jewish women of the Renaissance period (the late 15th and 16th centuries) did not remain uneducated while those around them enjoyed wider horizons.

Italy, where Renaissance thought flourished as nowhere else, was known as a haven for Jews for many centuries. Jewish settlement began there in the earliest days of the Roman Empire, even before the destruction of the Second Temple. The level of Jewish learning among these early inhabitants benefited considerably from their proximity to the Palestinian academies which were active in the first centuries of the common era.[1] When those centers of learning disappeared, there was already a strong foundation of Jewish scholarship in Italy. By the tenth and eleventh centuries, scholars and houses of study were known there.

Jews who fled from the Inquisition found refuge in many of the Italian cities, where they discovered that culture and the arts were as advanced as they had been in Spain in the height of the Golden Age. Yet, Italy was also the originator of the compulsory ghetto for Jews in the mid-1500's.[2] This policy, which had as its goal the limiting of any intercourse between Jews and Christians, was the result of the Reformation.

When Martin Luther became an active advocate of a new Christianity which directly challenged the Catholic Church, the Pope had to defend himself. The Jews were an added danger to his universal rule and a threat to the unquestioning loyalty of the population. In addition to setting up laws to restrict the Jews to ghettos, the Pope also banned them from many professions. Ultimately the wide range of Jewish activities lessened until the only professions allowed to Jews were money lending and dealing in second hand goods.[3]

The Italians enforced these restrictive, anti-Jewish laws with more or less severity, depending on economic conditions. The promise of the Renaissance enlightenment was not quickly forgotten by the general population, and the Pope could not easily limit the centuries-old tradition of interaction between Italian Christians and Jews. Nor could he prevent the Jews from studies and development of the intellect, the arts, or the practice of medicine—fields in which they had long participated in Italian society. There are many examples of Jewish physicians who served as doctors for prominent Christians even after it had technically been forbidden. There were Jewish entertainers, musicians, playwrights, and poets as well, and the Pope's ban did not always succeed in eliminating the roots and flowers of this cultural tradition.

Women too, joined in these pursuits and often became prominent. There is record of a woman physician named Perna who was licensed in 1460

Torah ark curtain, executed by Leah Ottolenghi, embroidered 17th century, *Courtesy of Jewish Museum, N.Y.*

at Fano, Italy.[4] Others followed her. Women entertainers were also common among the Jews. One of the best known of these is Madonna Bellina, who lived in the mid-sixteenth century. It is said of her that she "played and composed to admiration and sang like a thousand nightingales."[5] Another woman singer was Madame Europa. She was a participant in Monteverdi's earliest opera, *L'Arianna* in which she performed with a "delicate and sweet" voice which brought tears to the eyes of her audience.[6]

Although the learning of Talmud was not universal for women, it was still found frequently, especially among the upper classes. There was a Talmud Torah for girls which flourished in Rome as early as 1475.[7] Many women were known to have been teachers during the later Renaissance period in Italy, and even after the establishment of the ghetto.[8] A fascinating by-product of the thorough education of women in Jewish ritual and Law, was their employment by the community as *shochtot* (ritual meat slaughterers).[9]

Most well known for their Talmudic scholarship was the family of de Modena. Pomona de Modena of Ferrara was reputed to be the equal of any male Talmudic scholar. Her son, Abraham ben Jehiel Modena, immortalized his mother's piety in over one thousand liturgical poems composed between 1536 and 1552. Of Pomona de Modena's own writings there is no trace.[10]

Another woman in that family, called Bathsheba (or Fioretta) was a disciplined and dedicated scholar. She devised a systematic scheme of progressive weekly study for herself, concentrating a great deal on Maimonides' writings. She was the ancestor of a line of distinguished savants and scholars. These appear to be the only testament that Bathsheba bequeathed to the world. Like so many other women, only the accomplishments of her children and grandchildren remain as witnesses to her talents.

Devora Ascarelli

Along with all other arts and scholarly pursuits, poetry thrived in Renaissance Italy. Jewish women, enjoying a high level of literacy, participated in the poetic experience as both patronesses and poets. Much of their work has been lost, but one of the few whose poems are still available today is Devora Ascarelli.[11]

Devora was married to Joseph Ascarelli, a successful merchant and the president of the Catalan Synagogue. She translated many Hebrew hymns into Italian and was the translator of two well-known works of her time: *Meon Ha-Shoalim* and *Mikdash Me'at,* both written by Moses da Rieti.[12] This gifted woman was not only famous for her translations, but also for the creative talent she displayed in her own poetry. She may have been one of the first Jewish women to have her work printed in Italian. Devora's poetry shows a sensitivity and a dedication to Judaism that could be found among many of her contemporaries in Italy. Her work was first published in 1601-2,[13] and then republished in 1925 by a descendant Pellegrino Ascarelli. This last publication was, perhaps, an attempt to remind the then growing Italian Fascists of the contribution Italian Jews had made to the culture of their country.[14]

The Bible and the Apocryphal books were favorite subjects of Renaissance writers. One story that was especially popular among them, and which was retold in poetry and dramatic form in many languages, was the story of Susannah and the Elders. Once included in the Book of Daniel, it subsequently became a popular story of the Apocrypha.[15]

Devora Ascarelli also chose the theme of Susannah as the subject of one of her poems. It is the story of a beautiful and pure young woman, married to Joachim of Babylon, who is falsely accused of adultery by two elders of the community. These two men passionately desire her favors and plan a way to gain them by threatening to tell the people that she has been unfaithful to her husband. Faced with the choice, Susannah says: "It is better for me to fall into your hands and not do it, than to sin in the sight of the Lord."[16]

The elders falsely declare her an adulteress. Just before she is to be put to death, God comes to her aid by sending Daniel, who questions the two men separately. Finding an inconsistency in their testimonies (each swears he saw her under a different tree), Daniel declares Susannah innocent and the elders guilty of bearing false witness—a crime also punishable by death in any trial involving the death penalty for the accused.

In her first stanza, Devora gives her own description of the beautiful and righteous Susannah. The second verse is written in praise of this woman with the "chaste heart" and her excellent example of "thoughts and words" which bring the soul closer to God.

THE PORTRAIT OF SUSANNAH

Although a beautiful shock of golden hair swings across her forehead
And love finds nourishment in her eyes
The chaste Susannah never strays from the right path
And harbors not one thought without the Lord.

Hence those who, casting caution aside, ogle her
And see beauty in her, and grace, and worth,
Finally notice that in a chaste heart
There is no place for deception, flattery, or suspicion.

Whatever in me is of heaven
Is born because from your blossoms
I collect the gentle honeydew
And find delight and satisfaction
In feasting eagerly on your Ambrosia.
From you comes the sweet liquid
From you issues the true Love
And your thoughts and your words
Awaken the soul to the Creator of the Sun.[17]
                    translated from Italian
                            by Dr. Vladimir Rus

IL RITRATTO DI SUSANNA

Se ben in fronte un bel crin d'or l'ondeggia,
E ne begl'occhi suoi si nutre Amore
Susanna casta punto non vaneggia,
Nè pensier tien che sia contra il Signore.
Onde l'incauta copia, che vagheggia,
In lei beltade, in lei gratia, e valore;
S'accorge al fin che dentro un casto petto,
Non fan frodi, lusinghe, nè suspetto.

                    * * *

Quanto è in me di Celeste
Nasce che da' tuoi fiori
Colgo suavi, e rugiadosi umori,
Mentre lieta, e contenta
Sono a cibarmi di tua Ambrosia intenta;
Surge da te dunque il dolce liquore,

Surge da te dunque il vero Amore,
Son i concetti tuoi, le tue parole,
Che destan l'alme al Creator del Sole.

Devorà Ascarelli.

Sara Coppia Sullam

Sara Coppia Sullam is another remarkable product
of Renaissance Italy. She was born in the Venetian
Ghetto in 1590. Despite the many limitations of ghetto
life, she had a fine humanistic education and was able
to read Latin, Greek and Spanish as well as Hebrew
and Italian by the time she was fifteen. In addition to
being a poetess, she was noted as a singer and per-
former on the lute and harpsichord. After she married Joseph Sullam, a wealthy and well known Jew of
Italy, Sara established a literary salon in their home
which was popular with both Jews and non-Jews. She
often entertained her many distinguished guests with
readings of her own poetry, but since it was never
published in her lifetime, very little of it remains today.[18]

Because of her prominence in the cultural life of
the Venetian community, repeated efforts were made
to convert Sara to Christianity. She remained true to
her faith, but apparently suffered from rumors and
accusations involving her religious philosophy. These
false reports moved her, in 1621, to write a pamphlet
entitled *Manifesto of Sara Coppia Sullam, Jewess, in which
she refutes the opinion denying immortality of the soul,
falsely attributed to her by Sr. Bonifaccio.* She dedicated
this short essay, written in Italian, to her father who
had died fifteen years before, when she was a young
girl of sixteen.

Addressed to "Signor Coppio, my most beloved creator," Sara wrote:

> This little but necessary work could not properly be dedicated to anybody else than to him who has passed the threshold of this transient life, because it confirms the thesis which I prove in this work, namely, that I undoubtedly believe in the immortality of the soul.

She continued her dedication in the tone of extreme modesty and humility which marked learned women throughout the centuries:

> I should like to contribute to the increase of thy heavenly pleasures by the modest fame I was able to acquire, which, I trust, will be not less dear to thee because it was produced by a woman most desirous but unable to do as much for the perpetuation of thy name as a son would have done. . . . Accept, therefore, this humble token of the unlimited devotion of thy daughter, whom thou lovedst so much, and who, if it will be allowed to me to enjoy life and health, as a certain amount of creative ability has already been bestowed upon me, will live for the honor of thy name no less than for her own.[19]

Sara Coppia Sullam died in 1641. For some, the cloud of suspicion that rested on her may still have lingered, but she remained a loyal and dedicated Jew until the end of her life.

In this sonnet, Sara again alludes to the malicious and false charges of which she was accused. She appeals

to God who knows "my inmost hope and thought,"
to protect her from the "venom" of the "lying
tongue's deceit."

> O Lord, You know my inmost hope and thought,
> You know when e'er before Thy judgment throne
> I shed salt tears, and uttered many a moan.
> It was not for vanities I sought.
> O turn on me Thy look with mercy fraught,
> And see how envious malice makes me groan!
>
> The Pall upon my heart by error thrown,
> Remove: illume me with Thy radiant thought.
> At truth let not the wicked scorner mock,
> O'Thou, that breathed in me a spark divine.
> The lying tongue's deceit with silence blight.
> Protect me from its venom, Thou My Rock,
> And show the spiteful slanderer by this sign
> That Thou dost shield me with Thy endless might.[20]

Cover of manuscript of the Hebrew prayer, *Adon Olam,* showing woman seated at writing table. (1714).

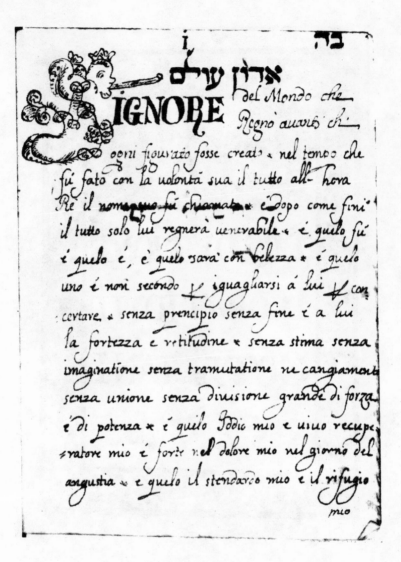

Italian transliteration of Hebrew prayer *Adon Olam*, Illie
bat Menachem, of the Meshullam family. (1714).

מעשה ידי הבחורה יראת ײ
ומשכלת מרת אילי מבת בת
איש חיל רב פעלים כמ׳ מנחם
הלוי משולמס יצ׳ו ‎‏‎—‏‎—‏ ‎˙˙

ויהי השלמתו ברביעי בשבת יום
ראש השנה לשנות טו לחדש
שלום ברכה טובה בשנת
למן תלמוד לראה
את ײ :

Last page of manuscript of *Adon Olam* indicating the writer to be an educated Italian Jewish woman, Illie, the daugher of Menachem the Levite, Meshullamim, 1714.

X

Women of Influence

"She is not afraid of the snow for her household;
For all her household are clothed with scarlet
She maketh for herself coverlets;
Her clothing is fine linen and purple."

PROVERBS 31:21-22

Power, money and fame: these were a man's goals and were part of a man's vocabulary. Women—especially women who lived before the twentieth century—could hardly achieve any of the three in their own name. Or could they?

In the 1500's, long before women's liberation became an issue, two women liberated themselves in their own way. They each achieved more power, fame, and money than most men could even dream of. They were Benvenida Abrabanel and Beatrice de Luna (also known as Dona Gracia Nasi). In the same century, at a time and place when women were supposed to have been mainly concerned with the home, another woman—Esther Kiera—was playing power politics and negotiating favors with one of the strongest empires in the world.

The Byzantine Empire, the longstanding bulwark of Christian power in Eastern Europe and Asia Minor, had disappeared by the sixteenth century.[1] Turkey had captured the Byzantine capital city of Constantinople in the spring of 1453 and had established there a more enlightened regime which welcomed Jews. The Jews had already been expelled from Spain in 1492 and soon afterwards (1497), from Portugal. Millions of them—the Marranos—secretly adhered to

Judaism while outwardly converting to Catholicism so that they might remain in their homes. As new Catholics, they avoided expulsion, but now faced the dangers of the Inquisition, which was the Church's method of rigorously controlling the behavior and practices of Catholics. Thousands of other Jews, spurning conversion, left Spain and Portugal where they had enjoyed a Golden Age beyond compare, and scattered to the four corners of the world. Holland, Belgium, France, Italy, North Africa, Turkey—all received a portion of the Jewish people wending their way out of the Iberian Peninsula to build a new life.[2]

Benvenida Abrabanel

One of the families who chose to leave Spain in 1492 was the renowned Abrabanels.[3] Isaac Abrabanel, the most famous member of the family, was a good friend of King Ferdinand and Queen Isabella, the rulers of Spain. He pleaded with them to reverse the expulsion decree which demanded that all practicing Jews leave the country. However, Ferdinand granted him alone the right to remain in Spain. Therefore, the Abrabanel family elected to go into exile along with thousands of other Jews, and finally settled in Naples.

Isaac Abrabanel had three sons. The youngest was named Samuel. Isaac's brother, Joseph, had a daughter named Benvenida. These two cousins married (it was Samuel's second marriage) and remained in Naples until 1541 when that city-state came under the rule of Spain and, following the Spanish precedent of 1492, decided to expel its Jews. From there, Samuel and Benvenida moved to Ferrara, where they lived peacefully and prospered.

In the home of Benvenida, who had an excellent education and had enjoyed the pleasures of wealth all her life, scholars gathered to discuss ideas and hear opinions.[4] While yet in Naples, she had been called upon to teach Leonora, daughter of the Spanish viceroy. Through this association the two women developed an intimate and lifelong friendship. When Leonora became Duchess of Tuscany, Benvenida enjoyed many advantages from this relationship.

The Abrabanels' business prospered, and when Samuel died in 1547, she continued running his affairs. It was said that Benvenida, a strong and noble woman, conducted her business on a grand scale and was able to obtain important commercial privileges in Tuscany through her friend Leonora, the Duchess.[5]

Riches were not Benvenida's only claim to honor. She was a sincere and pious Jewess who gave generously to charity. With her own money, she ransomed more than one thousand Jewish captives. She was well known in Palestine for her acts of charity and philanthropy, and her learning was praised by all those who knew her.

When Benvenida died in 1560, she was described as one of the "most noble and high-spirited matrons who (has) existed in Israel since the time of the dispersion . . . a pattern of chastity, of piety, of prudence and of worth."[6]

Dona Gracia Nasi

Unlike Benvenida Abrabanel, Beatrice de Luna belonged to a family that had chosen to become Marranos so that they could remain in their home in Portugal. They had a successful business and a rich life. Beatrice was born in 1510, thirteen years after the expulsion of all practicing Portuguese Jews. Those remaining in Portugal worked hard to hide any Jewish allegiance from the world. In this atmosphere of tension and secrecy, Beatrice's brother had managed to become the royal physician and her family continued to prosper.[7]

When she married, at the age of 18, Beatrice's fortune did not diminish. Her husband was Francisco Mendes, a wealthy banker who acted as a broker for the purchase and sale of commodities overseas, and transmitted payments from one country to another. The couple had a daughter whom they named Brianda (later known as Reyna).[8]

Beatrice was widowed when Reyna was still a young child. Life at that time was becoming more and more perilous for the Marranos. The Inquisition was everywhere, tracking down secret Jews and putting them to the rack for Judaizing or being unfaithful to the Church. At 26 years of age, Beatrice had her little daughter to protect, as well as half of her husband's vast fortune which she had inherited at his death.

Facing these difficult decisions alone, she left Portugal with her child, her sister, and her brother's son Joao. Eventually she arrived in Antwerp, where her brother-in-law, Diogo, ran a branch of her late husband's extensive business. The two brothers had been partners and Beatrice shared the inheritance with Diogo.

It did not take long for this enterprising and determined woman to form an association with Diogo and actively participate in the running of the business. They did well but nevertheless considered leaving Antwerp,[9] a city allied with Spain, where harsh laws stifled Jewish expression.

Despite the fact that Beatricè and her family were now free from the Inquisition, they did not openly embrace Judaism. Perhaps that was another of this woman's wise decisions. Although outwardly Catholics, Beatrice and her family did not feel comfortable in Antwerp's atmosphere of persecution. Before they could leave, however, Beatrice's brother-in law and partner died. She was left to administer his estate and to manage, alone, the vast network of financial enterprises that had previously been a joint responsibility.

Dona Beatrice's daughter, Reyna, was now approaching young womanhood, and Don Francisco de Aragon, a Catholic nobleman, requested her hand in marriage. Fearing serious consequences if she refused this offer for her daughter, Dona Beatrice made another difficult decision. Rather than have Reyna marry a Catholic, she would flee the country.

One morning the Mendes' mansion, where Beatrice and Reyna lived, was found abandoned. The family had slipped out of Antwerp without telling anyone of their plans. Dona Beatrice took with her only her money and personal jewelry.

Shortly after her disappearance from Antwerp, Beatrice de Luna, together with her daughter, arrived in Venice. With her came her sister and her household, as well as her nephew, Joao, who was by this time active in her business. The year was 1544.

By then the ghetto was well established in the Italian city, but Beatrice and her family did not join the Jews there.[10] They lived outside the ghetto. Little is known of her affairs at that period, except that she gradually sent property to her agents in Constantinople where she had influential friends. She remained in Venice for four years, and endured a confinement in prison as a result of a family dispute in which her sister denounced her as a Jew.[11]

When she was released, some arrangement had apparently been made. The family went to Ferrara, Italy, under special safe conduct passes and with a letter of welcome from the Duke of Ferrara. It was here that she finally felt free enough to proclaim her true religion, and she lived openly as a Jew for the first time, calling herself Dona Gracia Nasi. Gracia was the name she was called as a child (the equivalent of her Hebrew name, Hannah) and the name by which she became most famous.[12] Nasi, meaning leader in Hebrew, may be an allusion to the fact that she was a descendant of the rulers of Israel.

As a Jew, Dona Gracia had no trouble adopting the traditional values of her people. She used her riches to rescue many Portuguese Jews. Even as a Marrano in her early days in Antwerp, Dona Gracia had been active in the rescue of others who wanted to escape, maintaining her own style of 'underground railroad' through her network of trade and business. Her agents and representatives in various cities acted as "stations" to help Jews who were fleeing from the Inquisition. The admission of her Judaism allowed her to do even more.

Dona Gracia also became a patroness of letters. Even in her short stay in Ferrara, she had won enough honor and fame to have the new Ferrara Bible, then being translated from Hebrew to Spanish, dedicated to her. The dedication reads:

Prologue to the Very Magnificent Lady. We are
about to print the Bible in our Spanish tongue (translated from the Hebrew word for word—so rare a work
never before known until our day.) Therefore we desired to direct it to your Honor, as being a person
whose merits have always earned the most sublime
place among our people.[13]

When she left Ferrara for Turkey in 1552, Dona
Gracia travelled with her family and an enormous re-
tinue of servants and possessions in four roomy
coaches. In Constantinople, she lived royally and
dominated Jewish life with her philanthropies. She
generously supported hospitals, synagogues, schools
and individual scholars within the entire Ottoman
Empire. Her own merchant ships carried on a large
overseas business, trading in wool, pepper and grain.
She was one of the largest importers of textiles and
cloth.[14]

Before her death, Dona Gracia saw her daughter
Reyna, now a grown woman, marry her cousin Joao
Miguez. Joao became Joseph Nasi when Beatrice
changed her name to Gracia Nasi, and he represented
his mother-in-law's interests abroad. He was given the
title of Duke of Naxos by Sultan Selim II of Turkey.[15]

By the time of Dona Gracia's death at 55, she had
achieved fame and riches beyond imagination. She has
been described by many people in many different
ways. One man spoke of her as "the heart of her
People."[16] Another called her "the crown of glory of
goodly women".[17] But Cecil Roth, the great Jewish
historian who wrote a book about this outstanding
woman, gave her the highest praise.

"No other woman in Jewish history," says Roth,
"has been surrounded with such devotion and affec-

tion. No other woman in Jewish history it seems, has deserved it more."[18]

No one knows if these two great figures in history, Gracia Nasi and Benvenida Abrabanel, ever met. Although the paths of these two women did cross during Dona Gracia's brief sojourn in Ferrara, Italy, there is no record of any communication between them. Nevertheless, they shared a way of life and a set of ideals that contributed much to their people.

Anna the Hebrew

In contrast to the greatness of Benvenida Abrabanel and Dona Gracia Nasi, Anna, a Jewish woman cosmetics dealer, was relatively unknown. However, like others of her profession, she was in a position to exert a great deal of indirect influence. Signing herself "Anna the Hebrew," she wrote and addressed a letter to Catherine Sforza in 1508.[19]

Catherine was a high born woman, related by birth to the ruling family of Forli as well as the Sforza's of Milan. She was not afraid to use her influence and in 1490, had advised anti-Jewish officials of the economic advantages of welcoming Jewish bankers into her city of Forli.

In a growing economy, it had become increasingly necessary for businessmen to be able to obtain large amounts of money on interest. Since the Catholic Church forbade this profession (banking, or moneylending) to their followers, Jews who engaged in it became increasingly valuable to the community. It was Catherine's idea to invite a wealthy Jew of Bologna to Forli. He was to provide credit for the local citizens and, in turn, his capital was guaranteed by the town officials.[20] It may have been Anna's knowledge of this incident that prompted her to write to this royal lady, hoping at least for a sympathetic response, or at best, for a profitable business relationship selling cosmetics.

After three husbands and eight children, Catherine Sforza, a forty-five year old noblewoman, was still concerned about her appearance. Surrounded by political enemies, Catherine did not know whom she could trust with her personal concerns. She may well have been moved by Anna's thoughtful postscript which showed an awareness of this problem and an understanding of Catherine's fear of being poisoned.

The following letter, written by Anna the Hebrew, is unique because it is one of the few of its kind that was preserved. Anna proudly proclaimed her Jewishness while offering a sincere business relationship that would be beneficial both to herself and Catherine Sforza. If your Highness will apply these things, says Anna, "I am quite sure that you will order from us continually."

Had the relationship flourished, Anna, like so many others who appealed to the vanity of Italian royal women and thereby gained their trust, might well have been able to ask for favors for herself or her people. Other Jewish cosmeticians had had success in this way. In Florence, the Jews were saved from expulsion because of the Jewish cosmeticians there who had served Bianca Capello, an Italian noblewoman, so faithfully and so well.[21] Unfortunately, Catherine died the following year and the possible effects of Anna's quiet diplomacy will forever remain unknown.

To the Most Illustrious Madonna, Caterina de Rear-
lis, Sfortiz Vicecomitissa, Countess de Imola, my most
honored patroness. Wherever she may be.

Permit me most illustrious`Madonna, to commend my-
self to you and to send greetings. Messer Antonio
Melozo, Esquire, has been here on behalf of your
Highness to inquire of me if I will not give him as
many kinds of facial cream as I have.

To begin with, I gave him a black salve which removed roughness of the face, and makes the flesh
supple and smooth . . .
(Anna goes on to carefully describe how the salve and
other creams, lotions and powders are to be used, and
itemizes the prices for each one.)

. . . Now if your illustrious Highness will apply these
things, I am quite sure that you will order from us
continually. Rome, the 15th of March, 1508.
Your Highness' servant.
Anna the Hebrew

P.S. The black salve is bitter. If it should happen to go
into the mouth, you may be assured that it is nothing
dangerous; the bitterness comes from the aloes in it.[22]

(This is a most relevant postscript. In an age where
political assassinations often occurred, poison was frequently used to dispose of one's enemies.)

Esther Kiera

Benvenida Abrabanel was living grandly in Ferrara, Italy, and Gracia Nasi was a young Marrano woman of 20, when a Jewish baby girl named Esther was born in 1530.

Not very much is known of Esther's origins or of her childhood, except that she was probably of Spanish descent. She married a merchant named Elias Handali and together the couple sold trinkets and jewelry to the Sultan's harem in Constantinople, Turkey.[23]

Through this business, Esther became known at the Court of the Sultan, and especially to the female members of the royal family. She was called Esther Kiera (Kiera being the Turkish equivalent of her Hebrew name, Esther), and was first rewarded by the Sultan Suleiman I in 1548 for services to his mother.

After her husband died, Esther became the chief lady's maid to the harem. She is known to have assisted with childbirth, obtained cosmetics, and carried messages, as part of her duties.

The job that Esther Kiera Handali held was a job often held by Jewish women in the Turkish Court. Since Muslim women could not be in the company of men—indeed, could not move around in society at all—it was imperative that a suitable female "go-between" be found to handle their affairs. She had to be able to move about freely in both the world of the harem and the world of the streets, as well as have enough intelligence to handle all the personal and business matters of the women at the Royal Court. Esther Kiera met all these requirements.[24]

She became a special friend of the Sultana Baffa (also known as Safieh). Baffa was the favorite wife of

Murad III, a weak emperor who ruled the Ottoman Empire from 1574-1595. Esther acquired privileges as a friend of this royal lady, each granted in a separate *firman* or decree from Sultan Murad.

In 1584, Esther had another chance to serve the Sultana. In that year, Catherine de Medici, Queen Mother of France, wrote to Sultana Baffa seeking the support of the Turkish fleet against Spain.[25] Esther was employed either to make sure of the accuracy of the Turkish translations accompanying the Italian texts, or as a spy to communicate copies of the correspondence to Venice. From this we can gather that she was something of a linguist and was in a position of the highest trust.

Esther must have pleased Sultana Baffa as well as the Venetians (who were, at this time, allied with Turkey) with her services, because in 1587 Esther was rewarded with a letter of recommendation and approval to start a lottery in the Venetian Republic.[26] This was the first time a foreigner, and especially a Turk, was allowed this privilege in Venice, which had only recently become allied with the Ottoman Empire after years of warfare. In connection with this new business venture, not less than seven firmans were issued granting Esther Kiera specific privileges in the Venetian Republic. All this was made possible for her with the cooperation of Baffa and her other friends at the Sultan's harem. It was written that Esther Kiera:

> . . . . stood high in the favor of the Imperial Harem; she was considered by foreign diplomatic observers to be one of the most influential persons at court.[27]

As a Jew, Esther Kiera had a reputation for helping Jewish merchants who suffered at the hands of Muslim plunderers during the frequent periods of unrest in the Empire. When the shops and homes of well-to-do Jews were burned and looted, Esther came to their aid. She also sponsored the printing of Hebrew books and gave money to Jewish scholars. Her concern for the Jewish community continued almost until her death.

Meanwhile, Esther's career took her from the apartments of the various Sultans' women, to the highest military and administrative offices of the Ottoman Empire. She lived first under the reign of Suleiman I, then Selim II, but achieved the height of her powers under the reign of Murad III. Already a mature woman when Murad III ascended the throne of the Ottoman Empire, Esther shrewdly took every advantage that her friendship with the Emperor's wife offered her. Her reputation for intrigue and taking bribes, especially where it involved the appointment of high officials, left her with many enemies. Over the years, much animosity was built up against her and it eventually proved to be her downfall.[28]

Turkey was filled with unrest during the late 1500's. Continuing warfare with Spain, Venice, Persia, the Balkans, and even within the Turkish provinces, created an unstable political situation. Various disputing factions had long existed within the Moslem empire. One of these factions was the *Spahis,* the feudal horsemen and warriors of the Turkish provinces,[29] who became angered by one of Esther's military appointments. After Murad III died and his son Mohammed ascended the throne, the *Spahis* plotted to kill Esther. In 1600, they led a mob into the palace, surrounded it, and overcame the guard.

The mob dragged Esther from the protection of the Palace, cut off her limbs and nailed them to the doorways of all those who had gained favors through her influence. At least two of her sons were killed with her, but one is known to have survived. Her vast fortune was then confiscated by the Turkish government despite Sultana Baffa's attempts to prevent this.[30]

It was not until many years after her death that the family of Esther Kiera was restored to royal favor. In 1618, Osman II reissued to her grandchildren the privileges once granted to Esther.

Esther Kiera used and misused power in her life but she is one of the few who obtained so much of it without the benefit of inheritance. Beginning as a peddler, she ended her life as one of the most influential people in the Ottoman Empire. There is some evidence that she converted and became a Muslim during her last years, but there is no question of the fact that she lived most of her life as a Jew.[31] Although not a typical heroine, she has the added distinction (along with Dona Gracia Nasi) of being one of the very few Jewish women who is known by her own name, not by the surname of a husband or father. Esther Kiera's name and life were so well known that they formed the basis of a novel written long after her death.[32] In the English-speaking world her exploits and intrigues have been neglected, but here, along with many other women, she has been rediscovered.

Esperanza Malchi

Esperanza Malchi must have been a brave woman to take on the job of chief lady's maid to the Sultan's harem, after her predecessor, Esther Kiera, came to such a violent and unhappy end in that same position. But this important post was traditionally held by a Jewish woman and it contained opportunities of power and influence far beyond the actual work.

Although the Jews had been expelled from England in 1290,[33] this did not prevent Esperanza Malchi from writing to Queen Elizabeth of England in 1599 on behalf of her mistress, the Sultana of Turkey, and stating plainly that she was "a Hebrew by law and nation."[34]

In the following letter, Esperanza writes as the go-between for the Sultana. Yet she clearly inserts her own views and feelings. They show a concern both for her mistress and for the Queen, a concern that included a sincere desire for their health and well-being as well as their immediate pleasures. Securing small items for the diversion of the royal women was part of her job and she took it seriously. It is not surprising that women like Esperanza eventually endeared themselves to the women of the royal courts and were in a position of demanding and receiving important concessions. Esperanza Malchi wrote the following letter in Italian:

> To the most Serene Queen of England, France and Ireland:
> As the Sun with his rays shines upon the Earth, so the virtue and greatness of your Majesty extend over the whole Universe, so much so that those who are of different nations and laws desire to serve your Majesty.

This I say as to myself, who being a Hebrew, by law and nation, have from the first hour that it pleased the Lord God to put into the heart of this most Serene Queen Mother to make use of my services, ever been desirous that an occasion might arise on which I might show that disposition which I cherish . . .

. . . the most serene Queen wishing to prove to your Majesty the love she bears you, sends a robe and a girdle, and two kerchiefs wrought in gold, and three wrought in silk . . . a necklace of pearls and rubies . . . and I have delivered . . . a wreath of diamonds from the jewels of her Highness, which she says she hopes your Majesty will be pleased to wear for the love of her and give information of the receipt.

And your Majesty . . . I venture to (make) the following request; namely that, since there are to be met with in your Kingdom distilled waters of every description for the face, and odiferous oils for the hands, your Majesty would favor me by transmitting some by my hand for this Queen, by my hand as being articles for ladies, she does not wish them through other hands. Likewise, if there are to be had in your kingdom cloths of silk or wool, articles of fancy suited for so high a Queen as my Mistress, your Majesty may be pleased to send them, as she will be more gratified by such objects than any valuables your Majesty could send her.

I have nothing further to add, but . . . that your Majesty may be ever prosperous and happy. Amen.

Your Majesty's most humble,
Esperanza Malchi

XI

Voices From the Ghetto

"She looketh well to the ways of her household,
And eateth not the bread of idleness."

PROVERBS 31:27

The Prague Letters

Voices from the past do not always speak clearly. Most are forever lost, or are recreated sketchily by historians. Only rarely does a piece of time become frozen for posterity, so that hundreds of years after it all happened, we can enter, for a few moments, into the minds and hearts of the people who once lived.

The time was 1619, the month of November. The place: Prague, capital of Bohemia. In 1619, Prague housed one of the largest Jewish ghettos in Europe. It was a center of Jewish printing and Jewish learning. It boasted synagogues and community centers and a Jewish population that could trace its origins back to the tenth century.[1]

Outside the ghetto, a war had begun that would continue on and off for thirty years and drastically affect the lives of hundreds of thousands of people: Jew and gentile, man and woman. The Thirty Years War started with a rebellion in Prague against the Hapsburgs, rulers of the Austrian Empire.[2] It gradually drew in all the tiny city-states and duchys of Germany and, at one time or another, involved almost every country in Europe.

A Jewish man and woman, Loeb and Sarel Gutman,

ran a mail service out of the Prague ghetto to Vienna in 1619. It was set up mostly to facilitate their own communication with each other, for Loeb was often in Vienna on business. On November 22, just before the Sabbath began, their messenger was on his way with a sack of mail.

It had only been two weeks since a new king was crowned in Prague—the Protestant, Frederick I. He was viewed by the Catholic Hapsburg rulers as a dangerous threat to the Empire, and Austrian soldiers were on the alert. As the messenger was traversing the 160 miles between Prague and Vienna, he was apprehended, and all the letters confiscated lest they contain any valuable information concerning the enemies of the Austrian Empire.[3]

Found to be politically useless, the sack and all its contents were thrown aside and never delivered. The messenger disappeared from history, but a slice of life was frozen forever.

When the letters were finally discovered by historians in the Austrian archives, and published in the early part of the twentieth century, three hundred years had passed. Twentieth century people could now read the personal letters and glimpse the intimate relationships, the daily lives and problems of others who had long passed on.

Many of the letters were written by women to husbands, or to other family members. The writers of the letters seem to be both intelligent and aware. Although they were concerned for the fate of their loved ones in a war in which they could have no say, and no real benefit, they nevertheless continued a lively interest in life. Fashions and clothing, requests for money, and interest in family affairs, continued despite a perilous existence filled with riots, epidemics and many other insecurities. Travellers caught on the highways and robbed of all their possessions; ransoms paid for prisoners; destruction of property; these are some of the problems alluded to in their letters. Franz Kobler, who has edited a *Treasury of Jewish Letters*,[4] including some from the Prague ghetto that were translated into English from the Yiddish, points out that the letters of the women, unlike those of the men, concern themselves with the politics of the day. "There was obviously no room," says Kobler, "for such profane news in the letters of the serious-minded men . . . "[5]

Talk of political developments and mention of secular events as well as names of friends and relatives with whom these women were involved can all be found throughout the letters. The reader cannot help but wonder what happened to these very real women and their touching human concerns.

Did Loeb Gutman return home safely? Did Mirel Auerbach ever receive her fashionable new coat? Did Hannah's mother escape another riot in the neighborhood, or did she fall victim to the next one? Reading letters from the Prague ghetto is like tuning into a television soap opera for one day. The viewer enters immediately into the concerns of the characters, but is never able to tune in again and find out how it all worked out.

Sarel Gutman, who signs her letters as the "daughter of Moses," was the woman who, together with her husband, ran the mail service that brought letters back and forth between Prague and Vienna. This letter, written to her husband, reflects the turmoil that existed during the early part of the Thirty Years War. Sarel was obviously worried about her husband's health and his whereabouts. She found time, however, to include in her letter the news about the coronation of King Frederick I and his wife Elizabeth of England (although she made a mistake in the date, and wrote it as the 28th of Heshvan instead of the 27th).[6] She is the only one, of all the letterwriters from the Prague ghetto that day, who included this item of news in her writings.

There is apparently some question as to whether Sarel wrote the following letter by herself or had it written for her. Certainly it was not uncommon for women to be illiterate in those times, although her obvious intelligence and capability in running the messenger service would suggest otherwise. It was Sarel's job, when the letters arrived, to distribute them to the recipients and to collect money according to a rate schedule which she and her husband had decided. In a second letter to her husband she states:

"Now about the main point, as I cannot write you about all things in detail. As you have sent me a separate slip saying to whom the letters belong and how much the people are to pay me, I, too, send you the enclosed slip (with a list of those) who paid when they received the letters, and (of those) who paid when they delivered the letters (for Vienna)."

Kobler, editor of the letters in English, points out that the letter excerpted above and the letter following, have a handwriting identical to the letter written by Sarel's son-in-law Meir Epstein.[7] Certainly it is unlikely that *she* wrote the letter for *him*, but several other possibilities present themselves. Although capable of writing, Sarel may have felt her writing skill was inadequate for such a long letter. Or, disturbed by the events of the war and worried about her husband, she may have been too distraught to write, and requested the help of her son-in-law. Whatever the situation, the words are most certainly hers, even down to her subtle complaint about her husband, to whom she says: "You have never become entirely settled, and thus, you think: out of sight, out of mind. . . ." These words and all the others that Sarel has written to her husband have the ring of authenticity familiar to any woman in any age whose husband is away and who must face difficulties alone.

Many good, blessed and pleasant years, may they surely come to you and to your head and hairs! To the hands of my lovely, dear, beloved husband, the pious and prudent, worthy Rabbi [a title which noted respect] Loeb, may his Rock and Redeemer keep him. First know of our good health; you, too, shall be so always and in every hour. Further, my lovely, dear beloved husband, you shall know that I was very eager to write you much but I was afraid that I should have to pay too great a fee to the messenger, so much I have to write to you. I have been ever grieved because I have not heard a word from you for seven weeks, where you are in the world, especially in such a situation as that which we have now. May the Lord, be He praised, turn everything to good soon. I was, indeed, at my wits' end, and did not know what I should think about all that. Honestly, I do not know how I live in my great distress, the Lord be He praised, knows how I feel. I do not eat, I do not drink, I do not sleep, my life is no life for me. For in good days, if I did not have two letters a week, I thought that I should not be able to live longer. . . . And now I do not at all know for such a long time where you are in the world. But

what shall I do now? I have worried about so many
things, I must rely upon God, may He be praised. But
there is nothing for which I care so much as your long
life to a hundred years, this is my prayer in the morning and late, may He grant it . . . I must say to everything: even this will be for good. Now my heart has
been calmed a little, because a messenger came from
Linz today, who met Jokel at the fair; he had asked
Jokel about you, and he said that you are in Linz. You
can believe me, I have heard an angel, if I may say so.
First I was troubled again that you have not written. I
wonder that you let a bird fly (namely, the messenger)
in such a time without writing, as this is not your
manner. But at any time if I had been given 100
ducats it would not have pleased me so much, although for me every penny is now like a thousand,
you can believe me indeed. Nevertheless cursed be all
money, and the only good is if I hear of your dear
health to long years. I thank God, may He be praised,
for this (so much), as I cannot write you. I had much
to write you about horrible things, but I cannot write,
about the affliction we had to endure here when riots
almost occurred in our streets. It was like at the destruction of the Temple. What shall I tell you about
this? I think you are clever enough to imagine what
could happen in such a time. Now we have been saved
from this peril, we have certainly profited by the
merits of our ancestors. And I particularly have suffered terribly. I have not saved a penny for my own
needs, if, God forbid, my life were to be endangered.
Nowadays nobody is ready to lend anything to other
people, from one hand into the other. When I needed
something for a living, I was obliged to offer double
pledges and to pay high interest. What shall I do? I
wriggled about like a worm before I was prepared to
borrow money on pawn in such a time. The saying

goes: Need breaks iron, if you will or not. You must eat, domestics must eat, you may be as careful as you like, you must have money anyhow . . . What shall one do? The rich and the poor are nowadays all equal, one gains just as much as the other. Believe me, therefore; my head tells me not to wish you now here, I think you are yourself prudent enough for this, it is not necessary to teach you much. If I only hear where you are in the world, if I only hear about you and I have a letter from you every week and know that you have a good job. For here one cannot do anything nowadays, until the Lord, be He praised, will change it soon for the better.

Besides, you should know that they have crowned the King here with great honours, and her too; him on Monday, the 28th of Heshvan, and her on Thursday, the New Moon of Kislev. Write, too, what is going on, so that one may know what is happening. . . .

Therefore, my dear beloved husband, . . . write me a letter whenever you can, and delight me once again with news about your health, long may it last Amen.

Further you may know that just as we were writing, people arrived from Vienna and did not bring me a letter either. This has frightened me even more, and they told me that you have sent a letter through a messenger and are looking forward to my answer. But I have not seen any letter at all. Therefore do not upset me any longer and write me certainly about all things and thoroughly. I have no rest in my heart. They told me that you were having quite a nice time there. I, too, should like to enjoy it. But I do not blame you. You have never become entirely settled, and thus you think; out of sight out of mind. . . .

And thus, good night from your loving wife, who remembers you always, and who has no rest in her heart until she hears of your good health, to long years.

Sarel, daughter of Moses, may his memory be blessed.[8]

The following letter, written in a very flowery Yiddish, is by Henele to her sister Bona and her brother-in-law Simon Wolf Auerbach. It is a good example of the type of language commonly used in this period. Although the religious phrases found repeatedly throughout this and all the other ghetto letters were formalized and almost automatic, they nevertheless reflected a general religious piety that went unquestioned. Every event—from the recuperation of a seriously ill relative to the receipt of a letter—was cause to praise God. Phrases such as: "may His name be praised," "may the Lord protect you," or, referring to an individual: "may he live long" can be found in every letter.

To judge by this letter, it would seem that Bona had been seriously ill and had recovered. Henele gives a hint of the type of relationship expected between a husband and wife in that period when she says: "I have also been told how your dear husband stayed with you and did not move from you; he has behaved not like a husband but like a father."

Henele's letter is one of the very few which have any mention of political events happening outside the ghetto. She refers to Maximillian, the Duke of Bavaria having captured Nordlingen (a town in Bavaria). As soon as Frederick I—a Protestant—was crowned king of Bohemia, the Catholic Maximillian sent his troops against him.[9] Henele has apparently heard rumors to the effect that Nordlingen was captured by the Catholics but seeks confirmation from her relatives in Vienna.

Not only does Henele's letter show a tenderness and concern for her sister and her sister's family, but also a fine style of writing. Indeed, she refers to her father as her teacher, which may offer a further clue to the fact that Henele was literate and educated.

Much peace and health, ever and always: as much as you desire and can speak with your mouth, to my most beloved sister, the virtuous and pious, the king's daughter all glorious within, the wife of the Rabbi, lady Bona, may she live, and to your lovely and beloved husband, the dear, sensible and God-fearing man, his learned excellency, Rabbi Wolf, may his Rock and Redeemer keep him, and to your dear little children, each of them, according to their names.

First of all you shall know that I am well; I wish to hear the same of you as well, my most beloved sister and most beloved brother-in-law (whom I love) like my own brother. You shall know that I was very pleased when I heard that you, (may you live) for long years, are well and that the Lord, may His name be praised, let you reap the reward of your righteousness and piety and has saved and helped you that no harm, God forbid, has been done to you. . . .

I don't want you to read anything that will disgust you, and will, therefore, not complain, because the Lord, may His name be praised, has done us such miracles and restored you, thanks to God. Everybody says how you and your lovely dear husband have done so many kind and good works. I have also been told how your dear husband stayed with you and did not move from you; he has behaved not like a husband but like a father. . . .

My lovely dear sister and brother, I have been told that the Duke of Bavaria has captured Nordlingen, I should like to know whether this is true. I had no let-

ters from our sister Gutle, may she live, I should like
to hear and see much good for good, therefore write
me often, please, so that each may at least know of the
other's health, particularly in these days when sinful
man has so much trouble again. . . I don't waste words;
nobody knows in whose hands the letters may fall.
You shall know that Samuel son of R. Abraham Wal-
lerstein arrived here naked and stripped of everything
except a shirt and an old suit. He told us that they
took everything from him in Nikolsburg. His father
gave him a nice suit. He will go away again whatever
the danger. . . . I don't want to waste words until I
shall receive, with God's help, good letters from you.
And thus may the Lord protect you from all trouble,
this is the desire and prayer of her who loves and
honours you, your sister Henele, daughter of my
father and teacher, the excellent and learned Abraham Levi Heller, his memory be blessed in the
world to come, who day and night thinks of you for
good, and would like to see you. . . . In great haste
Friday, on the eve of the holy Sabbath, 15th Kislev. . . . [10]

Resel Landau, an inhabitant of Prague, wrote the following letter to her daughter who lived in Vienna. She
mentions a young girl (referred to as a maid) who
travelled from Vienna to Prague and escaped great
danger, by offering her possessions as ransom for
herself. Apparently a young woman travelling alone
was not as unusual in the European communities as it
was in the near East, but it evoked particular comment in this letter because of the woman's subsequent
adventures.
It would seem that Resel Landau's daughter Hannah is less aware of world events than her mother,
who has to point out that: " . . . even if I could get it

(the veil her daughter had requested) for nothing, I could not send it away . . . " However, in those times when communication was difficult and slow, perhaps Resel Landau's daughter should not be blamed too much for her lack of awareness.

May peace and healthy days be your lot always; to my much beloved daughter, may you live long, you who are pious and virtuous, lady Hannah, may she live, and to all who are dear to you. First of all you may know of our health, may I hear the same from you always. Further, my darling, know that I received your letter from the messenger today, Friday, the 15th of Kislev. I was very pleased with such a rare letter, particularly in these days. The Lord, may He be praised, shall further protect Israel, Amen. My darling, on Monday, before the messenger arrived, the daughter of Bela and Matel came and brought me no letter. I nearly died (of fear), but they swore to me that you and all your dear ones are well. Thus I felt a little more satisfied. The whole community cannot wonder enough that they have sent the maid hither now. She had a narrow escape. They would have brought her into the camp, if she had not had her belongings with her; with them she was able, with God's help, to ransom herself. . . . She has certainly benefitted from the merits of our ancestors. . . . She was the first not allowed to enter (the city) and is in Lieben now, for there is a rumour that a great epidemic, God forbid, is raging, and that the maid was sent hither for this reason. Therefore I am again very anxious to have a letter from you. My darling, when you write that so many strangers are with you, this is no wonder. Here too there are as many strangers as people of this country. What shall we do? What the Lord does is rightly done, may He be praised. Shall I write you how we

are? May the Lord, may He be praised, spread blessing everywhere. We hardly escaped when a riot
occurred once; it passed thanks to God, well, we have
profited by the merits of our ancestors. May the Lord,
may He be praised, further protect Israel. My darling,
you write for a veil; even if I could get it for nothing,
I could not send it away; if we should lack nothing
else than veils, it would be all right. Therefore, my
darling, be patient a little while; as soon as I can I
shall send it to you. . . .

. . . And thus, many blessed years from the Lord, may
He be praised, and from your apprehensive mother
Resel Landau. Remember me to Isaac and the dear
children, may they live long, and all our dear heads
and everybody who is dear to you and sends kind regards to me. [11]

This last letter is included as an example of the
many different types of women that must have lived
in the Prague ghetto. Freidel, the daughter of Israel
Hamerschlag, wrote the following to her relative,
Mirel, then residing in Vienna. No mention is made
here of war or politics or family affairs. The only concern is a coat which Mirel has ordered to have made
up for her.

The detailed description of the coat itself, shows
that it is clearly an elegant, fashionable, and expensive
item. It makes an interesting comparison for those
who may picture the woman of the ghetto as the "typical" Jewish housewife with long dress, apron and ker-
chief. Quite clearly, neither Mirel nor Freidel would
fit this stereotype.

Many good times and hours to my dear relative and
good friend. My dear relative and good friend, I let
you know that I discharged your commission well and

ordered the coat to be made for you in the best and finest fashion possible in the world. Lining inside, namely, double damask; . . . laces . . linen-cloth, velvet for laces . . . silk, (and payment for) wages for the tailor.

Therefore, do not omit to send me more money in order that I can give it to Abner son of Henoch Schik, of blessed memory, that he may buy a beautiful smooth otter fur in Poland; I think if you send me forty gulden more, that I shall have enough for all. I buy everything as economically as if it were my own. I have written you many times, but I suppose that the letters did not arrive. I could obtain otter fur here, but they are dyed. Write me through whom I shall send it to you. I want to have it made as fine as possible and send it to you. And thus, blessings of the Lord, may he be praised, from your good friend Freidel daughter of the excellent and learned Israel Hammerschlag. Remember me to your father and to all who ask after me for good.[12]

Emma Goldman

Hannah Solomon

and 20th Century Jewish Women
(See p. 214 and p. 254)

Rosa Sonneschein

Anzia Yezierska

Rebecca Kohut

Twentieth Century Jewish Women
(See chapter XV).

Bertha Pappenheim

Glückel of Hameln

In 1646, while the Thirty Years War was winding to a close, a baby girl was born to pious Jewish parents in Hamburg, Germany. She was called *Glückel,* meaning "luck" in the Judeo-German dialect. Her life spanned 70 years and almost a century of events that have all been documented by historians as well as by *Glückel* herself.

When the Thirty Years War finally ended, the German cities, in the same state of political disorganization as before, were gasping for breath. The German population had suffered from the plague as well as from the war and its aftermath.[13] Riots, killings, religious persecutions, and disease had resulted in a general breakdown of the economic system, trade and travel. Basically, the long drawn out battle had solved very little. The middle European countries were still divided among feuding factions of Catholics, Lutherans, and Calvinists. The Jews were still very much the outsiders, secluded in ghettos and forced to pay high taxes to the individual noblemen in whatever city they attempted to live.

Trade and small business were the mainstay of the Jewish community in the German and middle-European towns. Glückel's husband was a trader in seed pearls who made his living buying and selling at the local fairs and speculating in the pearl market for a profit. As was the custom in that time, he shared the responsibilities of his business with his wife. Together they faced the dangers of a changing and often hostile world.

By the time Glückel had reached 40 years, she had borne thirteen children, and seen the results of two events in Jewish life that shook the foundations of the whole European Jewish community.

The first of these, the Chmelnitzki massacres, beginning in 1648, occurred when Glückel was very young. Chmelnitzki was an officer in the Polish army who revolted and fled to the Ukraine. Here, he organized the Cossacks and returned to Poland for an orgy of killing and looting which lasted ten years and destroyed Poles and Jews indiscriminately. The Jewish community in Poland suffered such a severe blow from the Chmelnitzki revolt that the effects of it could not be contained.[14] The gloom and hopelessness were transmitted, along with a stream of refugees, into Germany and Western Europe. This series of events paved the way for a popular revival of Messianism throughout the Jewish world.

When Sabbatai Zvi, a Turkish born Sephardic Jew, announced in 1648 that he was the Messiah of the Jews, he was in a synagogue in Smyrna, Turkey,[15] Chmelnitzki was riding across Poland, and Glückel was a little girl in Hamburg, still too young to learn to read. Both the Chmelnitzki massacres and the Messianic movement triggered by Sabbatai Zvi would powerfully affect Glückel's life as they indeed shaped the whole course of Jewish history in her time.

By the time the Polish massacres had subsided, the fame of Sabbatai Zvi, the self-proclaimed Messiah of the Jews, had spread over Europe and the Middle East. Everywhere his avid and committed followers rejoiced at the nearness of the redemption, packed their household goods, sold their businesses, and waited for his call for a return to the Holy Land. Their hope was never to be fulfilled. Sabbatai Zvi, received with joy and loud acclaim, ultimately failed his people. Faced with the Turkish ultimatum of conversion or death, Sabbatai, the man who had created a vision of Jewish redemption, chose to convert to Islam. His plans for the Jewish people's return to the Holy Land faded away, and his adoring worshippers, now disillusioned, returned to their everyday lives. Glückel writes in her memoirs about the packages of household goods and dried foods packed by her husband's parents in anticipation of their departure to Palestine led by the Messiah, Sabbatai Zvi. The sealed packages stood in her home for many years, until finally a letter came from her in-laws advising them to open the bundles of food and eat it before it spoiled. Even after that, the boxes remained as a symbol of the hoped for redemption that never came in their days.

In 1691, Glückel was 45 years old and a widow. To wile away her lonely evenings she began to write down the story of her life so that her children and grandchildren might read it and find out about their origins. After Glückel's death, these memoirs were found (in 1724) and copied over by her grandson, Moses Hameln, chief Rabbi of Baiersdorf. The life of a Jewish woman was, by her own efforts, thus preserved for the future.

Glückel's diary offers a vivid picture of Jewish life in seventeenth century Germany as well as insight into the feelings of a Jewish woman. If the Prague ghetto letters suggest one episode of a soap opera, then Glückel's life is a whole series, played till the end. Writing simply and forthrightly about the events in her life, Glückel shows herself to be a strong and independent woman. Through joy and misfortune she persists, doing what she feels she must do and putting her complete faith in God. She travels to fairs to buy and sell, makes business and family decisions, helps her children, and all this with no hint of self-doubt or feelings of inadequacy. She never whines or complains, but stands firmly in the face of all the troubles and hardships that life brings, ready to work hard for herself and her family.

Glückel relates all her business dealings matter-of-factly and never suspects that they might be unusual or exemplary. After her husband's death she runs the business singlehandedly explaining:

> At that time I was still quite energetic in business, so that every month I sold goods . . . Besides this, I went twice a year to the Brunswick Fair and at every fair sold goods for several thousands . . . I did good business, received wares from Holland, bought much goods in Hamburg and sold them in my own shop. I did not spare myself but travelled summer and winter and all day rushed about the town. Besides this, I had a fine business in "seed" pearls. I bought from all the Jews, picked and sorted the pearls and sold them to the places where I knew they were wanted. I had large credits. When the Borse was open and I wanted . . . cash, I could get it. [16]

One cannot help but wonder how anyone could see Glückel as other than an industrious, brave, and loyal woman, truly religious and wise in her simplicity. Yet Solomon Schechter, in reviewing her work in his essay *Memoirs of a 17th Century Jewess*, says of Glückel:

> She was a simple-minded woman, a mere 'mother in Israel', as foolish as all mothers, hence doomed to many disappointments . . .[17]

Following are several selections from the diary of this outstanding woman—the first such book written by a Jewish woman—so that the reader can judge her by her own words.

Glückel's memoirs are divided into seven small books. She begins the first book by admonishing her children to have faith and trust in God. This is her philosophy of life. Her firm belief in God, in spite of everything, permeates the entire book.

> My children, be devout and good. Serve the Lord God with all your heart as well if things go well with you as when, God forbid, all is not well. As we have to bless God for good, so also must we for evil (Talmud). If He punishes you, do not be too grieved. Remember everything comes from the Lord. Should, God forbid, children and dear friends die, do not grieve too much, for you did not create them. Almighty God, who created them, when He desires, takes them again to Him. What can the helpless mortal do? He himself must go the same way.... So, my dear children, no matter what you may lose, be patient for nothing belongs; it is only lent. [18]

In Book II, Glückel begins by describing her childhood. She loved and respected her parents very much and has nothing but good to say of them and of her household. She remembers that "whoever came into the house hungry, went out satisfied."[19] Glückel went to *heder*[20] (the Jewish school) as a child where she received a religious education. She tells us that her father "had his daughters taught religious and worldly things."[21] This was apparently unusual enough to merit comment as education for girls was by no means universal. It was only in Germany that girls went to *heder*. In Eastern Europe it was not generally the custom for girls to be educated formally, although they were often taught at home by their parents. Some picked up their reading and writing skills by listening and watching their brothers studying.

In Hamburg, where Glückel grew up, the Portuguese Jews had the right of residence in the town, but the Ashkenazi Jews did not. This meant that each individual Jewish family had to buy a special pass to live in the city. Every month the pass was renewed by payment of a special tax. In telling about her life, Glückel remembers those passes and some of the other conditions that the Jews endured.

> Still, it was a very hard life especially for the poor and needy, who risked going without a pass; if they were caught they were imprisoned. This meant ransoming them and called for much expense and trouble before they were released. . . .When they (the men, returning from work in the evening) passed through the gates (of the ghetto) their lives were in continual peril from attacks by sailors, soldiers and all sorts of hooligans. Each woman thanked God when her husband returned safely home. [22]

Glückel described her wedding in detail. Although she was a young child when she was betrothed, and an adolescent at marriage, she never gave any hint of worry or fear. She told of the events relating to her marriage matter-of-factly and with good humour. It never occurred to her to question her parents' judgment nor the suitability of the match. And events proved that she had no need to. She was devoted to her husband and his family, and he returned her love, until his death.

> Before I was 12 years old I was betrothed and the betrothal lasted two years. My wedding was celebrated in Hameln. My parents, accompanied by a party of twenty people, drove there with me. . . .

In the evening we had a great feast. My parents-in-law were good, honest people, and my father-in-law, Reb Joseph, of blessed memory, had few to equal him. At the feast he toasted my mother with a large glass of wine. . . .
After my wedding my parents returned home and left me, a child not yet fourteen, in a strange town, among strangers. I was not unhappy but even had much joy because my parents-in-law were respectable, devout people and looked after me better than I deserved.[23]

Glückel was a married woman and a mother many times over when Sabbatai Zvi, the self-proclaimed messiah of the Jews, gained popularity in Europe. Glückel described the impact of this messianic movement on her community, and the results of Sabbatai Zvi's downfall, in her own very female metaphor. She compared the Jews of Europe to a woman who is in labor. After the final stages of labor are completed, the child is not born. It was all for nothing.

It was just about this time that Glückel herself, bore another child—a daughter, Mattie—who, in her third year became ill and died. Perhaps associating the two events in her mind helped to create such a vivid comparison.

During this time I was brought to bed with my daughter Mattie; she was a beautiful child. And also about this time, people began to talk of Sabbatai Zvi, but woe unto us, for we have sinned, for we did not live to see that which we had heard and hoped to see. When I remember the penance done by young and old—it is indescribable, though it is well enough known in the whole world. O Lord of the Universe, at that time we hoped that you, O Merciful God, would have mercy on your people Israel and redeem us from

our exile. We were like a woman in travail, a woman
on the labour-stool who, after great labour and sore
pains, expects to rejoice in the birth of a child, but
finds it is nothing but wind. This, my great God and
King, happened to us. All your servants and children
did much penance, recited many prayers, gave away
much in charity, throughout the world. For two or
three years your people Israel sat on the labour-
stool—but nothing came save wind. We did not merit
to see the longed for child, but because of our sins, we
were left neither here nor there—but in the middle.
The joy, when letters arrived, (telling about Sabbatai
Zvi) is not to be described. Most of the letters were received by the Portuguese (Jews). They took them to
their synagogue and read them aloud there. The
Germans, young and old, went into the Portuguese
synagogue to hear them. The young Portuguese on
these occasions all wore their best clothes and each
tied a broad green silk ribbon round his waist—this
was Sabbatai Zvi's colour. So all . . . went with
joy . . . to hear the letters read. Many people sold
home, hearth, and everything they possessed, awaiting
redemption."[24]

In recent years, much has been written about the
widow and her unique kind of loneliness. This is not a
new phenomenon, nor a newly recognized one. Glückel
describes her own feelings at the death of her husband poignantly and realistically, with full awareness
of her needs and her vulnerability. She writes: ". . . for
the mood of a widow who so suddenly loses such a
kingdom is such that she easily imagines that everyone
wrongs her. May God forgive me this."[25]
Speaking about her experiences during the period
of mourning for her beloved husband, Glückel strikes

a universal chord that will be familiar to anyone, in any age, who has suffered the death of a loved one.

What shall I write, my dear children, of our great loss? To lose such a husband! I who had been held so precious by him, was left with eight orphaned children (the others had already married) of whom my daughter Esther was a bride. May God have mercy and be father to my orphans, for He is the only father of the fatherless. But though I silence my weeping and lamentations, I shall have to mourn my friend all the days of my life. . . .

The whole community mourned and lamented him; the unexpected blow had fallen so suddenly. Surrounded by my children, I sat the seven days of mourning,[26] a pitiful sight, I and my twelve children thus seated. . . . All our friends and acquaintances, men and women, came every day of the week of mourning, to console us. My children, brothers, sisters and friends comforted me as well as they could. But each one went home with a loved one, while I remained in my house in sorrow with my orphans. . . .

My dear mother, sisters and brothers comforted me, but their comfort only increased my sorrow and poured more oil on the fire, so that the flames grew ever higher. These comfortings lasted two or three weeks; after that no one knew me. . . . [27]

Lillian D. Wald, 20th century social worker (See chapter XV, pp. 249-256).

XII

One Step Ahead: Hasidic Women

"The heart of her husband doth safely trust
in her,
And he hath no lack of gain.
She doeth him good and not evil
All the days of her life."

PROVERBS, 31: 11-12

Flower children, defenders of the poor, and fighters against conventional life are not peculiar to the twentieth century. They are found throughout history. In the 1700-1800's, they were represented by a group of Jews who called themselves *Hasidim*—pious ones. This sect began with a young Polish Jew named Israel (later called *Israel Baal Shem Tov*). It cultivated the belief that learning and study were not the most important things in Jewish life. Love of God, piety, emotion, and sincerity were all equally important, and God loved the simple, illiterate Jew as much as the Talmudic scholar.

During the 1700's, Polish and Eastern European Jewry had not yet recovered completely from the chaos of the Chmelnitzki uprisings in 1648, when thousands of Jews were murdered by the Cossacks. Disillusionment had also set in after Sabbatai Zvi, the false messiah, whose messianic hopes had fired Jews throughout Europe, abandoned his followers and converted to Islam in 1666. To those debacles was added the final blow of Frankism, the new messianic movement of the 1700's whose leader, Jacob Frank, and all his followers ultimately converted to Catholicism.

Hasidism offered a new outlook on life and a chance for the poor and uneducated to actively participate in their religion. Because so much stress had been put on Talmudic learning, it was time for a reaction. Hasidism was that reaction. Israel ben Eliezer, its founder, was himself not educated in Talmud. He was a nature lover and was known to wander through the countryside alone. He lived in poverty and obscurity until his fortieth year, when he emerged as a pious and saintly man, a miracle worker and a believer in *Kabbalah*, the doctrine of Jewish mysticism and metaphysics. He became known as Israel *Baal Shem Tov* (Master of a Good Name) and his following grew.

Hasidism began as a rebel group within Judaism which drew its support from the simple people—the uneducated and poor. As the uneducated came to be considered as esteemed as the learned, women also began to look at themselves in a new way.

For centuries, Jewish learning had been stressed as the most holy and the most worthy of all occupations for the Jew. At the same time, all Jews were aware that the *mitzvah* to study Torah and Talmud was not obligatory on women. For the most part, and despite the many learned women cited in these pages, women were not educated in Bible and Talmud on an equal level with men and this fact in itself made them less worthy in the eyes of the Jewish community. Hasidism changed the religious self-image of the average Jew by introducing the idea that one's emotional response to God is equally, if not more important than Talmudic study. Many women felt emancipated by this movement and were quick to respond to the new openness around them.[1]

As Hasidism evolved over the centuries from a revolutionary group to a more conservative faction, the outstanding women who helped to build it up were forgotten. Fortunately some of their names and a few stories about them still remain.

The first of these noteworthy Hasidic women was Edel (variously spelled Adel, Oudil, or Udel), the only daughter of the Baal Shem himself.[2] She was known to be outgoing and charming, everyone's favorite and close to her father, whom she often accompanied on his travels. Hasidim honored Edel as if she were a *rebbe* herself and believed that the *Shechina* (the presence of God) rested on her face. Far overshadowing her brother, Reb Tzvi-Hirsch, who was retiring and sad, Edel was joyous, and involved with the early Hasidim who flocked to her father. Encouraged to participate, she was near him in all his prayers, celebrations and gatherings. When he was sick, it was she who was at his bedside to nurse him. This special bond between the Baal Shem Tov and his daughter was explained by him through her name, the acronym for the Hebrew expression *Esh daat lamo,* (EDL) translated as "a fiery Law unto them."[3]

A legend from the collection of *Hassidic Stories* by Meyer Levin,[4] relates how Edel met her husband. It is a tale rich in modern-day psychological symbolism.

When Edel was grown she asked her father when she would marry and whether she would have any children. The Baal Shem Tov told her: "Your husband is hidden among the scholars who come here. You must wait until a sign points him out to you."

Edel waited till *Simchat Torah,* the celebration of the Law. The Baal Shem's students were all dancing wildly around the Torah. During the dancing, the shoe of one of the students flew off his foot. Seeing this, he sang out a popular song:

A maiden will put the shoe on my foot
A mother will rock the babe in her cradle.

Edel's father, seeing this, called to his daughter. She, in
turn, became so confused that she could not find the
student's shoe. Instead, she sat down, removed both her
own slippers, and offered them to the student. It was
this same student, Yehiel Ashkenazi, who became her
husband. Together they had three children.

In addition to the religious activities she shared
with her father, Edel cared for Yehiel and their
three children. She supported the family by managing their grocery store, while her husband involved
himself in study and prayer as was the custom.

Edel's children grew to be famous in their own right.
Her first son, Moses Chaim Ephraim, became a respected scholar and writer. The younger, Baruch, was
a successor to his grandfather, the Baal Shem Tov. A
story from a collection of tales, *In Praise of the Baal Shem
Tov,* tells how Edel conceived his child and demonstrates
belief in her father's magic.

Edel's only daughter, Feige, inherited many of her
mother's attributes. She was said to be a woman of
unusual ability and understanding. Her son, the
beloved Hasidic spiritual leader and storyteller,
Nachman of Bratislav, holds a high place in Hasidic
history and literature. R. Nachman had great respect
for his grandmother, Edel, and said of her: "All the
tzaddikim believed her to be endowed with Divine
Inspiration, and a woman of great perception."[6] Feige,
too, was famous for her "Divine Inspiration", and is
herself credited with encouraging her son's Hasidic
leanings.[7]

At a time when Jewish life was rocked by the battles
of the Hasidim against the *Mitnagdim* (literally, "op-

posers"), urging one's son to join this rebel group was no casual decision. In 1772 and again 'in 1796, the *Mitnagdim* had actually ruled to excommunicate all Hasidim.[8] Yet Feige was not the only one who had the courage of her convictions.

Another such woman was Malkah, the wife of Shalom Rokeach of Belz. She urged her husband to become a Hasid, and in accordance with her wishes, he went to study with Rabbi Shlomo of Lutzk. He was eventually named the rabbinical head of Belz and established a Hasidic court there. Through all this, his wife Malkah did not remain in the background. She was a leader in her own right at the court of Belz, and prominent men were counted among her spiritual-devotees.[9]

Their daughter Eidele, followed in the footsteps of her parents. She married Rabbi Isaac Rubin of Sokolov and because of his reluctance to take on the role of *rebbe* (spiritual leader), she had an opportunity to use her talents. Eidele delivered discourses on the Sabbath, distributed food to the poor, and played a leading role in the community.[10]

In the mid-1700's, as Hasidism was growing among the masses of southern Poland, another woman, called Soreh, bore a son whom she named Yehudah Leib ben Bezalel. Shortly after his birth, Yehudah Leib's father died. The widowed Soreh brought her son up by herself and taught him to follow in the paths of Hasidism. When Yehudah Leib was in his teens, he joined the circle of the *Baal Shem Tov*. As an honor to his mother, he was called Leib Soreh, and is still known today by that name.[11]

There were other noted Hasidim who took on their mother's names or were known as the son or daughter of their female parent. Within the Hasidic movement particularly, this use of the mother's name became the accepted formula for prayers and requests.[12] **When a woman came to the** *rebbe* **with a special problem, it would be put in the form of a prayer such as:**

> With the Grace of God, Jacob, the son of Sarah, for his son Samuel, that he may recover from his illness.

or

> With the Grace of God, Isaac, son of Hannah, for his daughter Rachel, may she secure a good match.

Hasidism, more than any other group in Judaism, had a personality cult. Each individual village or town had its own *rebbe* who was also known as the *tzaddik* (righteous one). Men and women came to the *rebbe* to seek advice, to hear stories of wisdom, to observe examples of pious living, and to seek intervention with God on their behalf. The *tzaddik* turned no one away, and every problem was promised a favorable solution.

Women came personally to these leaders with problems of marriage or business, requests to heal the sick, and help the poor. They composed their own little *kvittelech* (prayer petitions) and gave them to the *rebbe* together with small sums of money called *pidyon* (redemption) money.[13]

The *Baal Shem* himself believed that the prayers of women were especially meaningful to God. Following this belief, the *tzaddik* encouraged the women to come to him. He made them feel that they were important members of the community. Often, their support of Hasidism was instrumental in guiding individuals or whole families, into the movement. Even those women who were not learned and not specifically concerned with Hasidism freed their husbands and sons for study and devotion to the *rebbe's* court by their efforts in business and their hard work in supporting their families.

The *rebbe* had to be charismatic as well as pious. To be sure, there were many *tzaddikim* who were also wise, but the requirement of learning was not considered crucial. The original appeal of Hasidism was that no one was excluded from closeness to God or participation in any area of Jewish life because of poverty or lack of learning. Joy in Torah was more important than a thorough and precise knowledge of the Law. This situation opened up a new opportunity to many women to be not merely a part of the *rebbe's* court, but to be the *rebbe*. As long as a group of people believed that a particular person, whether it be through wisdom, righteousness or piety, could help them or intervene with God on their behalf, this constituted a following. In such an open atmosphere, more than a few women found their places as leaders.

Women's names abound in the Hasidic literature. Freida, the daughter of Shneur Zalman of Liadi (the founder of the Habad sect of Hasidism) was an honored woman who wrote a number of manuscripts based on her father's wise sayings. Perele, daughter of Israel of Kozienice, was an ascetic woman with her own disciples. She wore *tzitzit* (ritual fringes)[14] and regularly fasted on Mondays and Thursdays. Her large following supported her with money, most of which she distributed to the poor. Sarah, daughter of Joshua Heschel Teumim Frankel, acted as *rebbe* after the death of her husband. She was known far and wide for her wise parables and was consulted by famous rabbis. Malkele the Triskerin (the Queen from Trisk) sponsored public meals, distributed food, and received petitions from Hasidim twice a day.[15]

These few names only hint at the active role women may have taken in the Hasidic courts. Others such as

Hannah Havah, daughter of Rabbi Mordecai Twersky; Rachel, daughter of Rabbi Abraham Joshua Heschel of Opatow;[16] Sarah, mother of Aryeh Leib Sarah;[17] and Merish, daughter of Rabbi Elimelech of Lezajsk[18] were also known throughout the Hasidic world. These women were examples of piety and wisdom, mothers and daughters of famous Hasidic figures, and spiritual leaders with followings of their own.

Still more *rabbaniot* (women rabbis) and *tzadkaniot* (righteous women) have been forgotten due to destroyed or lost community records and books. Discovering details about their lives may now be impossible. But no amount of lost documents, burned community records, or faulty memories could completely blot out the most famous Hasidic woman *rebbe* of all—Hannah Rachel Werbermacher.

Hannah Rachel was born in 1805 in Ludomir, Poland. She was a lonely and melancholy girl who was always hungry for knowledge. This pursuit of knowledge and education led her to the study of *Midrash* and *Aggadah*. Although she was betrothed at an early age, the engagement was broken off and Hannah did not marry until she was forty years old. Possibly for this reason, she was known as the Maid of Ludomir.

One day, on one of her frequent visits to her mother's grave, Hannah Rachel had a mystical experience which was to affect her life. She emerged from it by proclaiming: "I have just returned from the Heavenly Court."[19] From that time, the Maid of Ludomir wore *tzitzit* and prayed with *tallit* and *tfillin*. She preached sermons on the Sabbath from her apartment adjacent to the synagogue built for her by the community. Her synagogue, called *die Grune Schule* (the green synagogue), was filled with rabbis and scholars who came to hear her speak.

In his book, *Shosha,*[20] I. B. Singer uses the life of Hannah Rachel Werbermacher as the subject of the hero's play, *The Ludmir Maiden.* Singer, versed in Hasidic lore, referred to Hannah Rachel as "a girl who wanted to live like a man. She studied Torah, wore ritual fringes, a prayer shawl...put on phylacteries, became a rabbi and held court for Hasidim." (However, she reputedly covered her face with a veil when she preached Torah.)

After finally being persuaded to marry by Rabbi Mordecai of Czernobiel, Hannah's influence waned, and she emigrated to Palestine. There she concentrated on Kabbalistic studies and mystical plans to help speed the coming of the Messiah.[21] Hannah Rachel, the Maid of Ludomir, died in Jerusalem in 1892. She had no children, and by the time of her death, the world was changing. The industrial revolution and the resulting concern with materialism left little room for women of Hannah's spirituality and religious devotion.

The Jewish ghettos were opened by the late 1800's, and the *Haskalah* (secular enlightenment) had begun to make serious inroads into the Jewish community. The massive immigration of Jews to America had begun, (1881) and the First Zionist Congress, which took place in 1897, was being organized by Theodore Herzl. Hasidism had evolved from a revolutionary movement, one hundred and fifty years before, to the conservative bastion of Jewish life and traditionalism.

While the twentieth century controversy rages as to the "traditional" role of Jewish women and their place in synagogue ritual, it would be appropriate to recall Hannah Rachel Werbermacher, the Maid of Ludomir, and the many other women who helped make Hasidism a vital part of the Jewish landscape of Eastern Europe.

XIII

The Three Portals

"Grace is deceitful, and beauty is vain;
But a woman who fearest the Lord, she shall be praised."
PROVERBS 31:30

Sarah Bat Tovim and Others

The three *mitzvot* (commandments) that Jewish
women are specifically required to perform are: the
lighting of the candles on the Sabbath and holidays,
the separation of a small part of the dough when bak-
ing *challah* (bread), and the laws of ritual purity. In
the period when Eastern European and Italian Jewry
flourished, women observed these *mitzvot* with great
care. But that was not all they did. There were always
women who branched out from their households into
other areas of Jewish life. These women lead us
through the portals of three important areas of
activity—religion and prayer; political and community
affairs; and the arts—activities that helped sustain
Jewish life from the 1600's into modern times.

The migration of the Jews throughout Europe resulted in pockets of learning and culture, first in one
area, then in another. By the turn of the 16th century, the cultural center of Jewish life was well established in Poland, parts of Russia, and the Slavic countries. As this community developed and matured, the
Jewish language developed with it.

Yiddish had developed hundreds of years before as a dialect of the Middle High German that the Jews spoke in parts of Germany.[1] They wrote it in their own Hebrew alphabet and added to it familiar Hebrew words. As these Jews moved from place to place, they took their language with them and it became more widespread. Words from other languages which the Jews spoke were added. Originally referred to as Judeo-German in the German-speaking areas, it eventually became Yiddish, the universal language of the Ashkenazi Jews throughout Central and Eastern Europe.

The learned studied Hebrew, which still remained the language of the Bible. For those who did not or could not learn Hebrew, however, there was Yiddish. Hebrew was the holy tongue; Yiddish was the language of the people.

As it was not generally the custom for women to be taught Hebrew, they embraced the folk literature of stories, poems and prayers. Written in Yiddish, mainly for women, and sometimes by women, these works preserved and developed the Yiddish language as a literary form, and created the styles that are still familiar today.[2] Not deemed as important as Hebrew studies, this literature was often passed over by Jewish scholars and historians. Yet it represented a meaningful folk culture not only to women, but to all the ordinary people for whom Yiddish was the only language in which they could read the weekly Torah selections and the explanations of Biblical stories. Among the most popular and famous of the books aimed primarily at a female audience of readers was *Brantspiegel (Fiery Mirror)* by Moses Henoch Altschuler, (Basel, 1602) which discussed the moral conduct of modest women, and later *Lev Tov (The Good Heart)* by Isaac ben Eleakim (Prague, 1620). But the most famous of all was certainly the *Tze'ena U-re'ena (Go Forth and See)* by Jacob ben Isaac Ashkenazi of Yanov, which appeared in 1618. So great was the popularity of this book, that it became known as the "Women's Torah." It retold Biblical stories in Yiddish, drawing also on Jewish literature and legends, the Talmud, and the Midrash.

A great advance in opening religion to a fuller participation by women, and by less educated men, was the composition and translation of personal prayers, called *techinot*, from Hebrew into Yiddish. Among the many women who created the *techinah* style, the most popular and famous was Sarah Bat Tovim. Very little is known of her life, but she was probably a *firzogerin*, or foresayer in the women's section of the synagogue. Although it would have been unusual for her not to have married, nothing is known of her marital status. We do know that her great grandfather, Mordecai, was the chief rabbi of Brest-Litovsk, a town in Western Russia, and that she herself lived in the first decades of the eighteenth century somewhere in the Ukraine. Her parents were Mordecai and Leah. Bat Tovim is a pen-name meaning daughter of goodness or daughter of distinguished men.[3]

The Ukraine was still reeling from the Chmelnitzki uprisings and was trying to recover from the economic instability of the Polish government, when Sarah Bat Tovim grew to womanhood in the early 1700's. She may have been unaware that fellow Jews were reaching colonies in the New World across the ocean, or that England had finally agreed to re-admit Jews in 1655-1657, three hundred and sixty five years after their expulsion from that land. Eastern Europe was a vibrant center of Jewish life, and despite its problems, was autonomous and self-contained.

Born into a rich Jewish family with learned parents who educated her, Sarah went regularly to synagogue and became a foresayer (in Yiddish, a *firzogerin*), leading and explaining the prayers in the women's section of the synagogue, and translating the prayers from Hebrew into Yiddish. This responsibility required greater learning than that received by the average woman.

There were many women *firzogerins* in the Jewish world. Often, they expanded their activities to include writing original *techinot* which applied to specific feminine situations. They created prayers for the health of children and the safety of husbands, additional prayers to say after lighting the candles or on holidays, and special prayers after childbirth and for widows. These prayers were usually addressed not to the God of our Fathers, Abraham, Isaac and Jacob, but to the God of our Mothers, Sarah, Rebecca, Leah and Rachel, with whom the women identified. Sarah Bat Tovim and other women writers appealed to the God of their Ancestors—an all-inclusive term with no gender connotations. For them, as for their Biblical ancestor Hannah, who was the first to make a personal appeal to God (Sam. I 1: 9-16), prayer was intimate and meaningful. God was close and listened to their pleas. Just in case God did not, surely Sarah and Rebecca, Leah and Rachel, mothers and wives like themselves, would understand and intervene.

From this deeply personal belief and sincere desire to come close to God, a whole literature developed and was nurtured by women in the Yiddish-speaking world. It centered around their lives and their interests: home, family, and the three positive commandments that women had to perform. These commandments were the lighting of the candles on Friday night to usher in the Sabbath, the observance of family laws of purity and regular ritual immersions at the *mikveh* after menstruation, and the separation of the dough. This last was in memory of the portion given to the priests during the time of the Holy Temple in Jerusalem. After the destruction of the Second Temple in 70 C.E., when a woman baked the loaves of *Challah* on Friday before Sabbath, she was commanded to separate a small piece of dough, say a blessing, and toss it into the oven to be burned.

Sarah Bat Tovim was intimately aware of each of these commandments. She wrote a prayer pamphlet for women which included the special prayers for each *mitzvah*. The pamphlet also included prayers and comments for *Rosh Hodesh* (the new month), and prayers for the High Holidays *(Rosh HaShana* and *Yom Kippur)*. *(Rosh Hodesh* was the ancient celebration of the appearance of the New Moon which had been preserved by women as a special half-holiday long after the men gave up its observance.)[4] Sarah called this little book *Shlosha Shearim* (or *Three Portals*) and in her own words explains:

> The first portal (or gate) is based on the three *mitzvot* we women must perform: to take *Challah* and burn a piece. Women's purity—*Niddah*, Lighting of the candles. In the second portal, a prayer for *Rosh Hodesh*. In the third portal, a prayer for the solemn days.[5]

This small publication was extremely popular among women. It was reprinted several times even after Sarah's death and is still available today.

Sarah Bat Tovim, born into a prosperous home at a time when most Eastern European Jews were far from rich, suffered a reversal of fortune later in life. It may have been the result of the political and economic turmoil of that period, or of new anti-Jewish laws which were constantly being enacted. It may have been the result of her being widowed at a time when her husband was in debt. No records remain to give us a clue to her misfortunes. Sarah attributed her trouble to her own sins. She refers to herself in her writings as "homeless" and believes her situation is a punishment for talking in the synagogue when she was young.

The date and circumstances of Sarah's death are unknown. She must have died sometime in the mid or late 1700's, perhaps time enough to witness the beginnings of *Hasidism*, a Jewish religious movement that was being founded in the mid-eighteenth century. She left behind no will or records, but did bequeath a series of beautiful prayers that were still being reprinted as late as 1838 in places as far away from Sarah's home as Jerusalem.

After her death, Sarah's name was used by other writers of *techinot*, both men and women, who tried to imitate her style and profit from the fame and respect that Sarah had achieved in her lifetime. This situation led many to believe that she herself was only a legend. But Sarah Bat Tovim was real and she holds first place in the Jewish world as innovator of the personal *techinah* in Yiddish literature.[6]

Some of the many prayers that Sarah Bat Tovim wrote, were included in a collection entitled *Sheker HaChen (Grace is Deceitful)* (Proverbs 31:30). At the beginning of this volume, Sarah's introduction explains how these *techinot* came to be written and when they should be recited. It would seem from her explanation that not all the prayers are original.

Sarah points to one prayer in particular which was written by her. The "new *techinah*" as she refers to it,

came from her at a time of sorrow and she suggests
that it was divinely inspired. The actual prayer was
not quoted in our sources, and the original volume of
Sarah Bat Tovim's *Sheker HaChen* may be as rare as
Rebecca Tiktiner's book, *Meneket Rivka*.[7]

Sarah's reference that her *techinah* "may be a
memorial after my death" is taken to imply that she
had no children to carry on after she died.

> Dear women and girls. Read this *techinah*, and your
> heart will rejoice. The prayers were taken out of books
> (words missing in the text). . . .In the merit of this you
> will be privileged to come to the Land of Israel. I have
> set before you a beautiful new *techinah* that should be
> said Mondays and Thursdays and on fast days and the
> Days of Awe. "Grace is deceitful and beauty is vain"
> *(sheker ha-chen ve-hevel ha-yofi)*. Beauty is nothing, only
> virtuous deeds are good. "Every wise woman builds
> her house." The chief thing is that the woman should
> conduct her household in such a way that those in it
> can study Torah and that she may lead her children in
> the right way to the service of God. I, a poor woman,
> was scattered and undone. I could not sleep. My heart
> murmured in me, and so I reminded myself, whence I
> came, and whither I shall go, and how I shall be tak-
> en. And a great fear came upon me. And so I begged
> the living God, Blessed Be He, weeping bitterly, that
> this *techinah* may come forth from me.

> I, Sarah Bat Tovim, the distinguished and well-known
> woman, who has no strange thought but who made
> this *techinah* for the sake of dear God, Blessed Be He,
> that it may be a memorial after my death. I Sarah Bat
> Tovim, the daughter of the scholar, the rabbi, distin-
> guished in Torah and renowned our teacher Rabbi
> Mordecai, the son of the Rabbi, the great light, our

teacher Rabbi Isaac, may his memory be for a blessing, of the holy community of Satanov, may God be over her. Amen.[8]

Sarah Bat Tovim's work, *Shlosha Shearim*, contains comments, advice, and many short prayers to be recited on special occasions, such as the lighting of candles. Sarah refers to the three commandments performed by women, with the use of one Hebrew acronym, *Chanah*, which is made up of the first letter of each of the three: Ch for *Challah*, N for *Niddah*, and H for *Hadlachat Nerot* (candle lighting).

Women of the seventeenth and eighteenth centuries took the fulfillment of these *mitzvot* very seriously, (as did those before them) and the prayers reflect their attitude. The Jewish housewife who lit her candles on Friday evening may well have felt herself to be carrying on the work of the High Priest in the Holy Temple.

With the ever-living God's help, I am writing these new prayers with much love, great fear and trembling. God should have great compassion for me and for all Israel. I should not be homeless for long, in His Righteousness and of our Matriarchs, Sarah, Rebecca, Rachel and Leah. My beloved mother Leah should plead on my behalf. The fact that I am homeless should be a sacrifice for my sins. God Almighty, blessed be He, should forgive me for talking in the Synagogue during services in my youth. *Chanah* represents the Three *Mitzvot: Challah, Niddah*, and Lighting the Candles.

If you fulfill these three *mitzvot*, you will never be in need. In olden days, the Kohen sacrificed the first fruits, the Levi gave a tenth for charity, and the poor

man gave a smaller amount. After lighting the candles, I utter the following prayers:
'My mitzvah of candle lighting should be accepted as
the equivalent of the High Priest lighting the candles
in the Temple.'
My special prayer for Yom Kippur candle lighting:
"Almighty God, I beg you to be a compassionate God.
Accept my prayers with lighting. May it be Your Will
that we be inscribed for good and be worthy for the
time that Israel and the Temple will be restored.'⁹

Translated from Yiddish
by Joseph Adler

Sarah Bat Tovim ends her pamphlet, *Shlosha
Shearim,* with one last bit of advice. Although there is a
certain naiveté in her belief that she was punished for
her "great sin" with homelessness and wandering, this
cause and effect idea was widespread among men and
women in the time that she lived. Her sensitive and
astute comparison of the fasting person to the poor
person whose heart is bitter because of involuntary
fasting, is a comparison that would still be apt today.
Sarah's sincerity, her concern for her people, and her
humility, come through despite the span of years that
separates her from today's world.

I, Sarah, beg you young women not to sin by talking
in the Synagogue as I did for it was a great sin. I
was punished for this by homelessness and wandering,
and therefore warn you, you will not be punished.
Confess your sins before God, Blessed be He. I entreat you also to have mercy on widows, and orphans,
on strangers and captives, on aged people and sick
people.

When you fast, your heart is bitter, and so believe that the poor man's heart is bitter too, because he cannot refresh himself. . . . .Stand in the dear synagogue with fear and dread. I wrote these good new *techinot* to atone for my sins. Through our remembering our sins, may God Blessed Be He grant us life, Amen. Selah. The woman, Sarah Bat Tovim, daughter of Rabbi Mordecai, may his memory be for a blessing. [10]

Sarah Bat Tovim was not the only writer who wrote prayers for women in Yiddish. Another was Serel, wife of Rabbi Mordecai Katz Rapoport, president of the rabbinic court of Olesnica, and daughter of Rabbi Jacob HaLevi Segal of Dubnow. The following beautiful *techinot* were published in Vilna in 1852 (perhaps after Serel's death) and reflect the accepted style of appealing to Sarah, Rebecca, Leah and Rachel as intermediaries to God. The first prayer was to be recited on Rosh Hodesh Elul, (the month of repentance preceding the New Year), the second at the sounding of the shofar on the High Holidays.

With lovingkindness and great mercy, I entreat you to do with me; accept my petition. . . . .I pray that You may accept my tears as you did those of the angels who wept when Abraham, our father, bound his dear son; but the tears of the angels fell on Abraham's knife, and he could not slay Isaac, [Genesis 22]. So may my tears before You prevent me, my husband, my children and good friends from being taken from this world. . . . 'All gates are closed, but the gate of tears is not closed.[11] Merciful Father, accept my tears . . . wash away our sins with the tears and look on us, with mercy, rather than strict justice. Amen.

May the four Matriarchs' merit, the three Patriarchs' merit, and the merit of Moses and Aaron be present for us at judgment. . . . .We beg our mother Sarah pray for us at the hour of judgment, that we may go free . . . . .Have mercy, our mother, on us your children and pray for our children, that they are not separated from us. You know the bitterness of a child taken from its mother, as you grieved when Isaac was taken from you. Pray now, at the blowing of the shofar of the ram, so God may remember Isaac's merit who let himself be bound as a sacrifice. Ask for mercy on our behalf.

I beg mother Rebecca to pray for her children and that our father and mother be not separated from us. You know how strongly you long for a father and mother, as you wept greatly when you were taken from your father and mother to your husband Isaac.

Therefore pray for our father and mother, that they may have a good year of life, and I and my children, and good livelihood. We entreat mother Rachel to inscribe and seal us for a good year, without grief . . .We know you cannot endure the sorrow of your children. . .as when your dear son Joseph was taken to Egypt and afflicted, he fell on your grave and wept: Mother, have mercy on your child. How can you look on my sorrow, when you loved me so much.

So you could not see your child's affliction and you answered: My dear child, I hear your bitter weeping and will always have mercy, and pray for you and listen to your sorrow.

So have mercy on our sorrow. . . . .and pray for us, that a good year may be inscribed for us, Amen.[12]

Mamael, like so many other writers of *techinot*, was the daughter of a reknowned rabbi, Rabbi Tzvi Hirsch, and the wife of Rabbi Isaac of Belz. She wrote a *techinah* pleading for the well being of her children and for protection in her old age. In her prayer she refers to the "pious Hannah" whose prayer is part of the Haftorah reading for the first day of the New Year. Hannah is often considered to be the first woman to appeal to God with personal problems (I Samuel Ch. 1-2), and along with the four Matriarchs, she was much admired. Prayers like this one reflect the feeling of an intimate relationship with God, a feeling not uncommon among women of this period.

A techinah omnipotence, charity and prayer . . . made by the woman Mamael. . . . .let me benefit from the merit of our pious Hannah, who went to the temple to pray before Eli the priest. She moved only her lips, and he said to her: Depart hence, you drunken woman. She answered: No, my Lord, I am a woman with a grieved spirit. And as you answered her, I beg You to answer me too. Dear God, do not punish me with anger, but with Jacob's mercy. . . . .How should I beg not to have any sorrow with my children when I know the troubles Jacob endured before he raised his children.

I know I ask too much, but You desire that men pray to You, so I beg your compassion and pray that you do not cast me off in my old age.[13]

This old, handwritten *techinah*, written by an anonymous *firzogerin*, probably dates back to the beginning of the seventeenth century. The writer uses the term God of our Ancestors, instead of the more common God of our Fathers. This, and other names for God such as Your Holiness, Creator, and Your Will are used repeatedly in the women's prayers. God is rarely alluded to as He, nor are God's people referred to in generic terms. The women who wrote and read these *techinot* were very sure that they were children of God and that the Almighty was not only the God of their Fathers, but the God of their Mothers as well.

This prayer, like many others of the period, may have been a paraphrasing, in Yiddish, of part of the Hebrew prayer book used in the synagogue.

> May it be Your will, God of our Ancestors, our Creator, Creator of the whole world from the beginning of the world with the word of Your Holiness, with Your Will and the will of those who fear You and the will of Your household Israel. You were alone, and no one else will be in eternity. One only and no one alongside You to rule this world and the other world. Here I, Your maidservant, come; daughter of Your holiness, with great humility, that You may give me honorable sustenance.....me and my husband and children, and all who trust in You.[14]

Frumet Wolf

Following in the footsteps of Sarah Bat Tovim, but from very different parts of Europe, were two women whose lives personified the Jewish woman's devotion and concern for her community.

During the time that these women lived, the American and French Revolutions had made waves that were slowly rocking the boats of Europe as far east as Russia. Napoleon's Army had advanced through Austria by 1800, and up until the time of his final defeat in 1815, had made a strong impression throughout Europe. Jews were beginning to turn to the outside world with more interest and more hope. With the encouragement of men like Moses Mendelssohn Jewish life broadened. This noted German-Jewish scholar tried to combine both the Jewish and the gentile worlds by urging secular education for Jews.[15] The ghettos of Germany and Austria were opening up and English Jewry was thriving and mingling in the social circles of high society. In Eastern Europe a bitter battle between *Hasidism*, the fast-growing and popular sect which emphasized the importance of an emotional response to God, and the *Mitnagdim*, the scholarly Jews who believed in the primacy of Talmudic study, was threatening to destroy Jewish unity.

Frumet (Fani) Wolf was born in the late 1700's into the Beilin family of Eisenstadt, Hungary. She was well-known for her acts of charity and helpfulness and was said to have inspired in others a desire to be independent and productive.

Frumet Wolf was a young wife when she composed a pamphlet, allegedly of a controversial nature, and published it anonymously.[16] Exactly what the pamphlet was about is open to conjecture. It may have taken issue with Jewish community leaders on secular political concerns, or matters of interest to the Jewish population. Whatever the subject, the pamphlet was said to be "full of acid invectives against the communal heads of Eisenstadt."[17] The result of this bit of boldness was that a rabbinical ban was issued against the anonymous writer and the pamphlet's distributors.

Not content to let the issue die and allow herself to escape the rabbinical ban, Frumet Wolf stepped forward to admit her authorship of the controversial material. She subsequently spent many years trying to have the ban against her retracted. With the help of her husband, who acted as her mediator, Frumet's efforts ended in success. Years after, she was still fighting against the inclusion of a note referring to this ban, in the diary of the community. Frumet's determination and success is our loss. Nothing remains in the records except her will which she wrote in 1829. Neither her pamphlet nor the reasons for the ban against her could be traced any further.

Frumet Wolf's writing reveals a religious commitment, strength of character, and a basic practical nature, not unlike the writing of Glückel of Hameln who lived one hundred years before her. While exhorting her children to live in a manner she believed good and right, Frumet fully realized the irony of trying to rule over them after her death. She openly states: "What if your obedience is buried with me?" then very practically goes on to list the stipulations which she has inserted into her will to insure that they will not ignore her wishes.

Frumet died in 1849, but this will was written some twenty years before. In 1829, shortly after her husband died, Frau Wolf saw fit to make provisions to dispose of her considerable fortune in a way which she thought suitable. The inclusion of instructions and rules of conduct was fairly common in what were called "ethical wills" but this is a rare example of a will of this type written by a woman.

THE LAST WILL OF FRAU FRUMET WOLF

.... Here then, my dear children, I have revealed my last will. If some of you expected that better care should have been taken of you, while others perhaps, wish that I had omitted to make a will at all, I certainly find this quite natural. But believe me, just as it is difficult and even almost impossible to comply fully, in a testament, with the wishes of all concerned, so it is unjust and unreasonable to part from one's dear ones without having made a last will, and thus leave the distribution of the inheritance to existing customs and laws which do not and cannot make individual distinctions.

As I know your righteousness and your filial love and obedience toward me, I may expect that you will respect my last provisions with due reverence and fulfill them unaltered. But what if I have gone too far in my good opinion of you? What if your obedience is buried with me? If, because I am no longer alive and therefore of no further use to you, you should forget your lost mother as well as her last will covering the inheritance....(a series of provisions aimed at safeguarding the fulfillment of the last will follow here.)

To be sure, I know well that my suspicion is unfounded, and that it will deeply hurt you, my dear children, that I could doubt your obedience and your conscientiousness even for a moment. But do not bear a grudge against a careful mother who could not content herself until she had secured the ultimate execution of her will.

I wanted, on the occasion of my farewell, to leave you, my dear children, instructions and rules for conduct. As all of you, however, are grown up, I cannot advise you as is usual with minors. I shall therefore limit myself to some general though important instructions.

Above all I admonish you to cherish virtue and fear God; otherwise you can neither achieve full happiness on earth nor find peace and reward in the world to come. Content yourself with your fate and fortune and accommodate your needs to your income, behave peacefully to everybody and among yourselves. Do not allow yourselves to become involved in harmful family conflicts. Live, moreover, in concord and assist one each other with advice and deeds.
You must hold together ever more closely and firmly. You need such closeness, and you will need it more than ever, once the sad event occurs—so much sadder for you than for me—your mother's being torn from you, and thus, as it were, the center disappearing from the circle.

Farewell, and accept the blessing of your always faithful mother,

Fani Wolf[18]

Judith Montefiore

While Frumet struggled to protect her honor and integrity in Eisenstadt, a contemporary of hers was gracefully developing a role of fame and leadership in England. She was Lady Judith Montefiore, a woman who entertained and mingled with high society and royalty in London and throughout Europe. At about the time when Fani Wolf finished writing her will, Judith Montefiore had returned from her first visit to Palestine with her husband, Moses. She commented in her diary on the fact that "only six European females are said to have visited Palestine in the course of a century."[19]

Judith Montefiore had no children. She was devoted to her husband, with whom she spent much time and money helping the Jewish people throughout Europe and in Palestine. After their first visit to the Holy Land in 1827, Moses Montefiore conceived of a plan to help the Jews of that area set up farms, engage in agriculture, and thus become self-sufficient. Judith supported him in every endeavor towards that end and also sponsored causes of her own. Her good name and charitable reputation prompted the leaders of both the Ashkenazi and Sephardic communities in Palestine to direct a letter to her appealing for help. It was addressed to:

> The honoured and pious Judith Lady Montefiore who pursueth righteousness and mercy, who is an ornament to her sex and a bright example to the women of Israel.

The letter asked for her help in building a hospital and reminded her of past kindnesses:

Were we not already convinced by the many tokens
of your benevolence of the active interest you take in
the affairs of mourning Jerusalem—had we not received many proofs of your sympathy with the
afflicted Land of Holiness, we should not venture to
address you...But you have on so many occasions
joined your noble and august consort in his benevolence ... you have been so frequently his companion
in his journeys for the defense of Israel ... that we
are encouraged to appeal to you as well as to Sir
Moses, to make known and publish our distresses
among your numerous circle of friends among the
women of Judah and Israel in Europe. [20]

Judith's strong commitment to Jewish life was in-
stilled during her childhood. Born in the late 1700's
(possibly 1784)[21] into a rich family, she grew up in a
fine neighborhood surrounded by educated and cultured people. Judith's parents, Levi and Lydia Cohen,
were Ashkenazim who had come to England from
Holland in the mid-1700's. They gave their daughter
a good education with private tutors. Judith learned
English literature, music, singing, French, Italian,
German and Hebrew. Her home was an observant
one and members of the family regularly attended
Sabbath services in the Great Synagogue, the main
synagogue of London.[22]

Judith herself was very conscientious about not
speaking in the synagogue—perhaps a bit of advice
she had learned from reading Sarah Bat Tovim.[23] In
her mature years, she often commented disapprov-
ingly in her diaries about the fact that women spoke
during the services and were not attentive. On one occasion in Florence, Italy, she wrote:

Several German females were present and they wished to be very conversant; but I, as usual, at a place of devotion was as determined to be taciturn. [24]

Her parents' concern for their children's loyalty to Judaism was expressed in the Will of Judith's mother, Lydia Cohen, written shortly before her death in 1819. To her daughters she says:

I beg and pray for you not to forget that you are Jews and keep your religion and always have in your memory your father who is in Heaven and take example from him. [25]

Although conversion was not uncommon among Jews of that period (the Disraeli children, including the future Prime Minister, were baptized in 1817), both Judith and her sister Hannah remained steadfastly loyal to their faith. Hannah married Nathan Mayer Rothschild, of the noted banking family, and Judith married Moses Montefiore. At the time of their marriage, Moses was a respected Sephardic Jewish businessman. He later became one of the best-loved Jews in England—both among his own people and among the English. He was the first Jew to be knighted by the Queen of England. Judith enjoyed a similar reputation, not merely as the wife of Moses, but truly earned by her own acts of graciousness, charity and educated concern.

In 1862, shortly after celebrating her fiftieth wedding anniversary, Judith died. As a memorial to this great woman, her husband founded the Judith Lady Montefiore College at Ramsgate, England. Before his own death, twenty three years later, he wrote in his journal:

... May I become deserving, more and more deserving of the blessed happiness of being again her companion in Heaven. [26]

Both Judith Montefiore and Frumet Wolf lived in very different circumstances, and their energies and interests reflected this difference. Based on the little we know of Frumet's life, she was not content to watch the world and comment on it from the safety of her home any more than was her contemporary, Judith . Frumet spoke up for what she believed, even when it was not in her best interests to do so. Hers was a more modest impression than the one that Judith Montefiore left us. Nevertheless one cannot fail to see a commonality in the goals of both women—a desire to improve the world in which they lived.

Rachel Morpurgo

The expression of Jewish life and thought took many forms, of which the arts, especially writing and poetry, were never neglected. Sarah Bat Tovim and others like her concerned themselves with religion and prayer. Judith Montefiore and Frumet Wolf were more political and community minded. Rachel Morpurgo was a poet. However differently they expressed themselves, these women were all nourished and inspired by their faith in God and their belief in Jewish values.

Like so many other Jewish poets, Rachel Morpurgo's main topics concerned the sorrows of Israel, hopes for the redemption of her people, and faith in the future of a rebuilt Zion. Unlike Sarah Bat Tovim who wrote in Yiddish, Rachel wrote in the Hebrew language. Although Yiddish was the dialect in daily use in many areas of Europe at that time, it had never spread to the Jews then living in Italy and other Mediterranean lands.

Rachel Morpurgo was born Rachel Luzzatto in Trieste. Even though Trieste had been part of Austria since 1382 and would remain so until 1919, the cultural ties of the people were with Italy, and the language spoken there was Italian.[27] The small community of Jews that lived there always fared well in comparison to those in other Austrian or Italian cities. The ghetto of Trieste had already started to disappear early in the 1700's, well before the larger, more established ones in Germany and the Austrian Empire. Final emancipation of the German Jews was not accomplished till 1869.

By the time Rachel was born in 1790, the Jews (estimated at 150 to 200 at most) were living outside the ghetto and many had gained prominence. Her family, the Luzzattos, was famous and respected for their scholarship and Rachel was included in this distinction. She studied Torah in her home with her uncles Hezekiah and David, was familiar with Hebrew and Aramaic, and learned to expound Talmud and other medieval rabbinic texts. It is said of Rachel that at the age of 12, she could read in Hebrew Bahya ibn Pakudah's *Hovot Ha-L'vavot (Duties of the Heart)*[28] and that at 14 years, she could read Talmud.[29] When Rachel reached 18, she began writing poetry and continued this occupation until her death. She also studied Italian literature, mathematics, Rashi's commentaries and the *Zohar*. Rachel's poetry was admired by other contemporary Jewish scholars and was published on several occasions during her life and after her death. She often signed her work with the initials of the three words: Rachel Morpugo Hak'tanah (the small one). In Hebrew these initials spell out *Rimah*, the worm,[30] and attest to her extreme modesty, a trait commonly cultivated among Jewish women.

The circumstances surrounding Rachel's marriage show her to be a woman of determination as well as modesty. In spite of the disapproval of her parents, Rachel chose Jacob Morpurgo to be her husband and refused to marry anyone else. She finally married at the age of 29, when her family gave in to her wishes. Their disapproval of Morpurgo may have stemmed from the fact that while Rachel was from a prominent and wealthy Italian Jewish family with such notable members as Haim Moses Luzzatto, the renowned philosopher and cabbalist (1707-1747), and Samuel David Luzzatto, writer and scholar (1800-1865), he was not. Jacob Morpurgo was a simple merchant of Austrian Jewish descent, although his family also included many important scholars and leaders.

Accounts of their married life differ. One of Rachel's biographers says they were blissfully happy.[31] Rachel, a mother of four, attended to all her household duties and still found time to write and publish her poetry, meet and correspond with Jewish scholars, and lecture to young men who sought her wisdom.

Other students of her life put a very different slant on the same facts. They contend that she lived in near poverty and could only find time for her writing at night.[32] She is said to have written her poems after her household chores were completed, or on New Moons, when it was customary for women to observe a half-holiday[33] and thus not feel obliged to do their sewing.

Rachel Morpurgo died in 1871 at the age of 81. In her later years she became acquainted with Judith Montefiore and journeyed with the Montefiores to Palestine, thus joining the ranks of those few women who had visited the impoverished Holy Land during that century.

Professor Vittorio Castiglioni, noted scholar, native of Trieste, and chief Rabbi of the Jewish community of Rome, was an admirer of Rachel Morpurgo. In 1890, one hundred years after her birth, he published a volume of her collected letters and poems entitled *Rachel's Harp*. In the forward to the book he commented on the situation of women in Judaism, vehemently denying the current Christian assumption that to the Jews "woman was as abhorrent and disdainful in their eyes as a servant and that she counted as chattel."[34] Castiglioni asserts that even if we suppose that woman's place is not as important as man's, we can find no law or rule in our books that justifies the attitude that Judaism disdains her. He alleges that just the opposite is true. Not only are there no obstacles in the way of women, nothing forcing them to stay within the home, but that women could also sit in the government or prophesy, Castiglioni says of Rachel Morpurgo:

> She is dear to us in three ways. From the point of view of our faith, because she is an Israelite, from the point of our city, because she was a native of Trieste, and from the point of literature, because she is an exalted poetess. She is a ready writer, who by her pleasant writings added beauty and glory to our holy language. [35]

Castiglioni may have exaggerated when he said

that there were no obstacles for Jewish women who wanted to leave the traditional role. However, Rachel herself, and her remarkable contemporaries, are women who by their creativity proved that such obstacles could be overcome. They all "added beauty and glory" to our heritage by opening the many portals of Jewish life.

In the following work, Rachel took as her inspiration the Austrian revolution of 1848 which was a struggle by the people against the Austrian dynasty. Many Jews participated in this early struggle for democracy.[36] Even though the subject of the poem is a political one, the metaphor is still religious. Like so many women, both before and after her time, Rachel condemns war and violence as being useless and pointless. Only God, she suggests, "will sound the great trumpet to summon the Deliverer." In Rachel Morpurgo's poetry, as in most Hebrew poetry of that period, the trend was towards expressions of love and faith in God. It was not that different from what we know as synagogue liturgy; it was, in fact, sometimes used for that purpose. The poem was originally written as a sonnet but is here translated into free verse.

He who bringeth low the proud, has brought low all the kings of the earth. . . .He has sent disaster and ruin into the fortified cities, and sated with blood their cringing defenders.

All, both young and old, gird on the sword, greedier for prey than the beasts of the forest; they all cry for liberty, the wise and the boors; the fury of the battle rages like the billows of the stormy sea.

Not thus the servants of God, the valiant of His host.
They do battle day and night with their evil inclina-
tions. Patiently they bear the yoke of their Rock, and
increase cometh to their strength. My Friend is like a
hart, like a sportive gazelle. He will sound the great
trumpet to summon the Deliverer. [37]

(Sonnet of 1848)

This poem, written in 1853 when Rachel Morpurgo
was 63 years old, describes in beautiful metaphor, her
vision of the coming of the Messiah and the restoration of Zion. Rachel skillfully includes in her poem
reference to Rav Hananel, the man to whom it is
dedicated.

THEN WE'LL BE PRIVILEGED

We'll be privileged to go out
Chanting and dancing
To sing with a voice so pleasing,
To the Good Shepherd.

The mountains and hills
Will break forth in song.
The tree leaves will clap
Their hands.

To give thanks unto the Lord
In the Temple Ariel
Then the entire nation will see!

Into Zion comes a saviour
The salvation of Israel.
And in their lead, Hananel. [38]

translated from Hebrew by Elisa Blankstein

In 1855, Rachel Morpurgo penned this poignant song of hope for the restoration of her people. The popular belief in the Messiah is reflected in her words: "Hasten and lift the nation's Chosen One."

1855

My God, my redeeming rock—
Look and see and hear my voice.
I'll weep, I'll cry, I'll beg.
Oh! Have pity and compassion for a troubled nation.

Help erect my tent.
For no one questions, no one helps.
Sons will return to their borders
Crowned with the world's joy.

I beseech Thee, carry the weight of their
Transgressions.
Hasten and lift up the nation's chosen one.
O Cry no more. For God is gracious.

Though He tarry, I will hope for Him.
He'll build the walls of His House
And Rachel will rejoice
In a new song. [39]

translated from the Hebrew
by Elisa Blankstein

Perhaps the best way to appreciate the depth of emotion of Rachel Morpurgo's work is by reading a literal translation of one of her poems. This poem was translated in the early twentieth century by Nina Davis Salaman, one of the foremost translators of Hebrew poetry. Although it does not reproduce the original poetic structure, it does reveal the strong mystical and religious feelings which distinguished Rachel's work from that of other poets of that period.

Emek Akor (The Dark Valley)

O dark valley, covered with night and mist, how long will you keep me bound with chains. Better to die and abide under the shadow of the Almighty, than sit desolate in seething waters.

I discern them from afar, the hills of eternity, their ever enduring summits clothed with garlands of bloom. O that I might rise on wings like the eagle, fly upward with my eyes, and raise my countenance and gaze into the heart of the sun.

O Heaven, how beautiful are thy paths, they lead to where liberty reigns, forever. How gentle the zephyrs wafted over Thy heights. Who has words to tell? [40]

Rachel was a prolific writer and wrote poetry from the age of eighteen until her death in 1871. One of her last poems includes the following moving verse:

Alas my wit is weak,
My wound in despair.
See my days draw to the close
I acknowledge my sins.
I return home to God
I serve my Creator
With willing heart,
I thank Him for all He has done for me. [41]

XIV

Opening Doors:
Women Ahead of
Their Time

"Late born and woman-souled, I dare not hope."

EMMA LAZARUS

Just before the turn of the century, a German-Jewish woman, in discussing the fact that it was not traditional for women to study Jewish Law, said:

> The Jews had no knowledge of that class of lonely,
> desolate women, old maids, who are met with so fre-
> quently in modern society. They were not aware that
> there could be women without husbands, without chil-
> dren . . . women sound in body and mind, who are try-
> ing to forget their loneliness in outside occupation, as
> they have no homes. Happy are those among them
> who find earnest study to fill their mind and who
> are able, by propagation of knowledge, to make them-
> selves useful.[1]

This characterization of the unmarried Jewish woman might make the modern reader squirm. How-ever it is appropriate to remember that Jewish Law considered marriage the only acceptable state for men *and* women, and pitied the unmarried man as much as the single woman. It was the *choice* between family *or* study that made the woman's situation distinct from her male counterpart. Men never had to make this choice. Most civilizations allowed the man to freely use his creativity even after his marriage. In fact, it was marriage that was supposed to have freed him for a productive role, whereas woman's creativity was to be channelled into her home and family.

This situation was acceptable as long as home life and community life were inextricably intertwined in the Jewish community. It did not really limit the Jewish woman as much as is commonly believed. Until the French Revolution ushered in the modern age, industry, work, and study were home activities. The woman who was "at home," probably worked as well.[2] Printing, trading, tailoring, writing, translating, manufacturing, all were done at home. Community activities such as selling, helping the poor, and studying in the local *Bet HaMidrash* (house of study), did not take one more than a few blocks away from home. In the days of the ghetto, those who ventured outside their circumscribed area were always anxious to return to the safety of home.

When the world began to change (after French civil and political emancipation in 1791),[3] the home orientation of Jewish life changed with it. The Industrial Revolution brought people out of home industry and into factories. Country after country granted citizenship to each man and woman living within its borders regardless of race or religion. In return, the government demanded primary allegiance to the State, including military service and direct individual payment of taxes.[4]

The Jew was no longer limited to or by his own community. Greater commercial and educational opportunities were opening up for Jews as well as non-Jews, and as the men emerged from the home and the small community into this secular world of opportunity, they left their wives behind. Concerned with a home which was less and less the center of life, the Jewish woman saw her opportunity for creativity diminishing and her world becoming smaller as her husband's grew broader. Increasingly, the Jewish wife was looked upon as an "enabler" rather than as a doer.

Being "enablers" meant that women themselves were less creative. It was no longer a reasonable possibility to divide their energies between home and the commercial and communal activities which continued to move ever farther away from their spheres. In such a situation, women who were not married or who had no children were in a freer position to use their own talents most efficiently and to the best interests of the community at large. We can already see a hint of this situation in the 1700's and early 1800's. Sarah Bat Tovim was apparently childless, as was Judith Montefiore. Frau Frumet Wolf[5] was widowed early and Hannah Rachel Werbermacher[6] married late in life.

There continued to be women who managed multiple roles at home and in cultural and community affairs. The poet Rachel Morpurgo[7] (1790-1871), Hannah G. Solomon[8] (1858-1952), founder of the National Council of Jewish Women, Rosa Sonneschein[9] (1847-1932), journalist and publisher of the *American Jewess,* (the only Jewish publication by and for American Jewish women predating LILITH in the 1970's), and Nina Davis Salaman (1877-1925), the English poet and translator, were all wives and mothers. Salaman had six children, and was a scholar who published a life of Rachel Morpurgo. Her poem, *Lost Songs,* which follows, seems more contemporary in the 1980's than of her own time. Her words personify the dilemma of many women who refuse to make the choice between marriage and creativity; who struggle with both during their lives:

LOST SONGS

How long the singing voices in my heart
Have all been silent! Day by day the sound
Of noisy nothings whirling through their round
Of restless nullity has dulled the smart
Which silencing of life's whole truer part
Must cost the soul; and hours and days abound
When not one space for hearkening may be found
And not one stillness for the tears to start.
Only at night, amid the quiet rain,
Or scent of flowers, or in the full moon's sight,
Sometimes a thought comes back, and then the pain
Of some lost poem floating on the night
Brings to the heart its inmost song again,
The weakening whispers of its old delight.[10]

In Nina Salaman's poetry it is possible to see the conflict between domestic responsibility and self-realization which had become so marked for women. Nowhere was the conflict more apparent than in the industrially developed nations of Western Europe, and in America, the new land of opportunity.

America had received its first Jewish settlers as early as 1654, and their first congregations developed soon after. In 1729-30 the first synagogue structure was built in New York, followed quickly by others in Charleston, S.C., Newport, and Philadelphia. By pre-Revolutionary days women's names began to appear in the records. Abigail Levy Franks, the wife of David Franks, spearheaded the fundraising campaign for the building of that first synagogue in New York.[11] Abigail Minis (1701-94), and Esther Etting Hayes (d. 1799) were patriots who actively worked for the Revolution as well as for the Jewish community.[12] Abigail Minis, matriarch of the Jews of Georgia, was expelled from Savannah during the Revolutionary War for her anti-

British sympathies. Esther Etting Hayes braved the dangers of hostile British soldiers when she passed through enemy lines with supplies for the Colonial Army hidden in her petticoat. [13]

A scant 2% of the population of New York City, and even less elsewhere in the colonies, early American Jews had no restrictive structure to hinder their movement in society. Generally accepted in the American gentile world, with no communal institutions to arrange traditional marriages, and a narrow choice of Jewish partners, intermarriage and assimilation inevitably occurred. Many Jewish women were distressed by this trend and some families sent children abroad to England to be educated and to seek mates. [14] Others had no choice but to accept the fact that offspring either did not marry or left Judaism to disappear into the new post-Revolutionary American culture.

In the period from 1800 to 1875, some of the most creative and productive Jewish women were unmarried. Educated, enlightened, free from family responsibility, and with many doors into secular society open to them for the first time in hundreds of years, these women nevertheless chose to work in Jewish education and charity, and use Jewish themes in their writings. Choosing Judaism did not preclude an active involvement in the non-Jewish world, and numbers of women moved with ease between Jewish and non-Jewish society, respected in their chosen fields. This was true not only in America, where Jewish community structures and mores were never strong; it was also the case in countries like England, France and Germany where barriers of intolerance were breaking down for the first time, taking with them both the good and the bad of the old Jewish communal structure.

The women cited on the pages which follow achieved beyond the boundaries of established family and communal life. They chose roles which, while not entirely new, had to be adapted to a totally new environment; a more fluid intellectual and religious climate where men and women were now free to choose not only marriage partners, but religious affiliation. Each of these women took important beginning steps in directions that were innovative for their time. The Hebrew Sunday School, initiated by Rebecca Gratz, was a first for the new Jewish communities of America. Modeled on the church Sunday School, it provided the only cultural or religious education given American Jewish children, and created a precedent for an evolving American system of Jewish education. Women had composed prayers for other *women* before Penina Moise began writing, but Moise wrote prayers and hymns for the entire congregation. When feminism and equal rights were just emerging in England, Grace Aguilar influenced women by her scholarly example and educated them in Jewish history and law. Emma Lazarus, a Jewish American poet and scholar, recognized by the broader literary community, was important for dramatically presenting the plight of impoverished East European immigrants to the attention of an unconcerned public.

Although volunteerism has recently fallen into disfavor, the significant accomplishments of women in creating social service organizations of the 19th and 20th century that focused on real needs in the Jewish community cannot be diminished. Gratz, Moise, Aguilar and Lazarus all formulated and performed important services in their time. Rebekah Kohut acted to meet critical health, cultural and recreational needs,

which government was later to fund. Women like
those who took the first steps through newly opened
doors helped build the foundations for the modern
Jewish communities of today.

Rebecca Gratz

Born in 1789, Rebecca Gratz represents a Jewish
woman who, whether through preference or default,
chose a life outside the traditional home. She was
born into a prosperous and patriotic Jewish family of
Philadelphia merchants and landowners. Educated according to the upper class standards of an expanding
America, she grew up to find her possibilities for
marriage severely limited because of the scarcity of
Jewish men of her class. Rather than marry a Christian, (a choice that was made by two of her brothers),
Rebecca chose to remain single.

From a twentieth century viewpoint, this charming
and attractive young woman may appear to be very
conventional and accepting of her life and its limitations. However, she did not live in rebellious times,
and although she may never have critically examined
her role as a woman in a man's world, she did expand
it to its fullest.

The period when Rebecca lived was known as the
Era of Good Feeling—a period of relative political
calm. For the Jewish people, it was marked by a rein-
forcement of the position which the Jews had
achieved in America. The Jewish community was
neither large nor as organized as it would become after
1848 with the influx of German Jews. The new

American Jews worked to maintain the privileges of
citizenship that they had won. They helped to develop
thriving communities and protected their new country
by financing and fighting in the Revolutionary War[15]
and the War of 1812. Many individual Jews were
isolated in small towns, with no possibility of obtaining
a Jewish education for themselves or for their offspring. As a result of their small numbers as well as
their acceptance by the gentile community, intermarriage became a common occurrence. [16]

The new nation was full of possibilities and hopes
for each citizen. Still, there were very few anchors
which a Jew could hold onto in order to remain a Jew,
since strong Jewish community services (hospitals,
schools, social agencies) had not yet been developed.

It is in this world that Rebecca gracefully moved,
and found a way to enjoy fresh opportunities without
losing sight of the anchors of Jewish life. She
socialized with the young women of her class and
went to dances and teas as they did, yet she made a
commitment to do much more. Rebecca chose activities according to the acceptable mode of her day
and to each cause she gave her complete devotion.
She was active in the Female Association for Relief of
Women and Children in Reduced Circumstances, and
helped to organize the Philadelphia Orphan Society
and a Jewish Foster Home.[17]

Her most important contribution to Jewish life was
the establishment of the Hebrew Sunday School Society. She founded the Society in 1838 and served as its
first superintendent and president for more than 25
years. With this Society, she opened up the possibilities of Jewish education to many families for the
first time.

Rebecca also gained fame from being used as a
"model" for the Jewish heroine in Sir Walter Scott's

famous novel, *Ivanhoe*. Rebecca was well aware of this and discussed her namesake, as well as the book itself, in her letters. Scott had first heard of her through a mutual friend, Washington Irving, who was one of her many prominent associates. The lovely Miss Gratz was included in the circles of Philadelphia society, and was considered a philanthropist and an educator.

Rebecca Gratz also enjoyed a close relationship with her entire family. One among twelve brothers and sisters (two brothers died in infancy), she corresponded regularly with them and their spouses. This familial devotion showed itself after her sister Rachel's untimely death, when Rebecca helped her brother-in-law to raise his nine motherless children.

Although she was not a poetess or a philosopher, Rebecca was a prolific letter writer. Her many letters give us a glimpse into the feelings and experiences of an American Jewess in the early 1800's, as well as an idea of her devotion to her people and the Jewish way of life. Rebecca died at the age of eighty-eight, a noble and honored woman.

This letter was written by Rebecca Gratz to her sister-in-law, Maria Gist Gratz (wife of her brother, Benjamin) with whom she corresponded regularly throughout her life. In it, she discusses the novel *Ivanhoe*, and the charming female character whom Scott had modelled after her. Her admiration and lively concern for this character and for the book itself, show a pride which would naturally follow that kind of flattery from a well-known author to a young woman. Rebecca was in her early thirties when the book was published.

Yet even with this unique excitement in her life, Rebecca still found time to inquire after her beloved brothers, and to be concerned with her many philanthropic and community activities such as the Deaf and Dumb Institution she mentions here.

TO MARIA GIST GRATZ—*May 10*

There is another novel just out by the Author of Ivanhoe, if it is as good, you shall see it—I am glad you admire Rebecca, for she is just such a representation of a good girl as I think human nature can reach—Ivanhoe's insensibility to her, you must recollect, may be accounted to his previous attachment—his prejudice was a characteristic of the age he lived in—he fought for Rebecca, tho' he despised her race—the veil that is drawn over his feelings was necessary to the fable, and the beautiful sensibility of hers, so regulated, yet so intense might show the triumph of faith over human affection. I have dwelt on this character as we sometimes do on an exquisite painting until the canvas seems to breathe and we believe it is life.

Jo & Jac (two of Rebecca's brothers) are managers of the Deaf & Dumb Institution—we are all much interested, you will be so too when you witness the expression of countenance every new idea lightens up in these poor little blanks—the Col. will tell you how capable they are of improvement and how happy they appear while receiving instruction—he and our Brothers have gone to take a ride this afternoon along the new canal at the Schuykill.

Give my best love to Dear Ben & Hyman, pray Maria

Rebecca Gratz, photo of Malbone miniature, from Leach's Philadelphia Portraits.

give Hyman charges in all his Sisters' names not to expose himself to an unhealthy climate in the approaching warm season—I have many apprehensions of his long journey & wish he was back again—Your husband is very much spoiled as a correspondent—do you require all his spare time—that he cannot give me any? Adieu, My dear Maria, May God bless You and him, prays your Most Affectionate RG. [18]

Rebecca was well acquainted with the writings of Grace Aguilar (see below), a woman whom she greatly admired. In this excerpt from a letter addressed to her sister-in-law Ann (Benjamin's second wife), Rebecca discusses one of Miss Aguilar's books, *Home Influence*, and sighs over the death of this "gifted author".

Sept. 15, 1848

I see they have just published a new novel, *Home Influence* by Grace Aguilar. I wish you would read it and give me your opinion of its merits, because I see many excellences in it, and found it deeply interesting—I know nothing as touching as the distresses and difficulties of childhood, and am glad to see them treated with consideration and sympathy by matured intellects ... it is to be lamented the gifted author did not live to complete her design of continuing her subject through another work... [19]

Rebecca Gratz was eighty-eight years old when she died on August 29, 1869. She was considered the foremost Jewish woman in America, and was admired by both Jew and Christian alike. Her last will and testament is a final proof of her devotion to her faith, as she concludes it with the *Sh'ma*, a statement taken from Deuteronomy (6:4-7) expressing the centrality of Judaism's belief in one God and the loyalty of Israel.

I Rebecca Gratz, of Philadelphia, being in sound health of body and mind, advanced in the vale of years, declare this to be my last will and testament. I commit my spirit to the God who gave it, relying on His mercy and redeeming love, and believing with a fine and perfect faith in the religion of my fathers, Hear, O Israel, the Lord our God is one Lord.[20]

Penina Moise

Devotion to Judaism was the moving force behind the lives of many Jewish women. Penina Moise is a forgotten bastion of that force in America. Although many Jews still sing her beautiful hymns, relatively few sing her praises. Yet Penina was one of the most prolific writers of poetry on Jewish themes that America has known. From the age of twelve, Penina wrote verses which were widely published in newspapers and magazines. She is the first Jew of either sex to publish a book of poetry in this country, and was one of the most popular poets in the South.[21]

Penina was born on April 23, 1797 in Charleston, South Carolina. Her father was a Sephardic Jew from Alsace who had settled in the West Indies and married a Jewish woman there. During the slave insurrection of 1791, the family, including four children, had fled to Charleston. Penina was one of many subsequent daughters and sons born in the United States, making a total of nine children.

When her father died, Penina, then twelve years old, assumed the difficult task of helping to care for her mother and siblings. Her parents, once rich and prosperous in business, had suffered a reversal, and there was little money left. In addition, Penina's mother was sick and could not care for the family alone.

Penina left school, and soon took charge of the entire household as well as complete care of her invalid mother, who ultimately became paralyzed. In spite of these burdens, the young woman found time to study and write on her own.

Penina published her first poems when she was very young. By the time she was thirty, she was widely known in publications throughout the country ranging from the *Boston Daily Times* to the *New Orleans Commercial Times,* to a current magazine called *Godey's Lady's Book.* In 1835, some of her verses were collected and published in a small volume entitled *Fancy's Sketch Book.* From that time on, Penina was included in literary circles and became friends with the cultural leaders of Charleston. Eventually, Penina's home became the center of a "literary salon" where writers and scholars met regularly.

The development of her status as a celebrity did not change Penina's commitment to Judaism. Unlike her well-known contemporaries of the German salons— women like Rachel Lewin, (Rahel von Varnhagen), Dorothea Mendelssohn, and Henrietta Herz, all of whom had turned their backs on their own tradition and culture[22]—Penina remained ever steadfast to Jewish life. Some of her poems were written on Jewish themes.

Penina Moise's life was not all pleasure and success. Beginning with her father's death and her mother's illness, she had more than a full share of troubles and hardships. Still, she never retreated from any job that had to be done. She nursed victims of a yellow fever epidemic which raged through South Carolina in 1854.

It was shortly before the Civil War that her eyesight began to fail. Despite the ultimate loss of her sight, Penina's writing continued throughout the War and afterwards. In fact, it was during this period that she wrote most of her beautiful hymns. These poems, set to music, are included in many collections in both the Conservative and Reform hymnals.[23] Penina was the author of most of the pieces which comprised the first collection of hymns used in the Charleston synagogue. Her work forms a large part of the collection in the Union Hymnal which is presently used by Reform Jews for services throughout America and the English speaking world.

When Penina died in 1880, never having married, she was eighty-three years old and by then, totally blind. This sad fact of her old age is reflected on her tombstone, where it is written:

> Lay no flowers on my grave.
> They are for those who live in the sun,
> And I have always lived in the shadow.[24]

The following poem was printed in the *Southern Patriot* in 1820. In subject matter, it very much resembles the poem "The New Colossus," which was written by Emma Lazarus more than fifty years later and subsequently engraved on the pedestal of the Statue of Liberty. It is entitled "To Persecuted Foreigners" and is an invitation for all those fleeing from oppression to come "to the homes and bosoms of the free." Although it would be difficult to determine whether Penina's poem had any influence on Emma Lazarus' later work, it is quite clear that these two women both had the same conception of their country. They enjoyed the freedom it offered, and were anxious to share it with all the oppressed of the world.

TO PERSECUTED FOREIGNERS

Fly from the soil whose desolating creed,
Outraging faith, makes human victims bleed,
Welcome! where every Muse has reared a shrine,
The respect of wild Freedom to refine. . . .
Rise then, elastic from Oppressions's tread,
Come and repose in Plenty's flowery bed.
Oh! not as Strangers shall welcome be
Come to the homes and bosoms of the free.[25]

Many of Penina's later works were in the form of hymns on Jewish themes. The two examples reprinted here are both included in the collection of the Union Hymnal used by the Congregation of Temple Emanu-El in New York City as well as by many other reform temples throughout the country. They have been set to music, some by several different songwriters. Her poem, "Aspiration," is presented in two musical versions in the Union Hymnal.

ASPIRATION

O God all gracious! In Thy gift
Though countless blessings lie,
My voice for one alone I lift,
In pray'r to Thee on high.

I ask but for the precious ore
Contained in virtue's mine;
And for her wreath that will endure
When diadems decline.

Let wisdom of the heart, O Lord!
Be now and ever mine;
Naught else is life's sublime reward,
We love Thy law divine.[26]

PRAISE YE THE LORD!

Praise ye the Lord! for it is good
His mighty acts to magnify,
And make those mercies understood,
His hand delights to multiply.
Praise ye the Lord! Praise ye the Lord!

Break forth O Israel, into song,
Let hymns ascend to heaven's vault;
No sweeter task has mortal tongue,
Than its Creator to exalt.
Praise ye the Lord! Praise ye the Lord!

Let hallelujah loudly rise!
Let hallelujah softly fall
Until on angel lips it dies,
As they unto each other call,

Praise ye the Lord! Praise ye the Lord![27]

Grace Aguilar

In each age there are outstanding persons whose merit lies not so much in the timeliness of what they say, but in its meaning for the future. Grace Aguilar is one of those persons. Her writing can stand today as a guide to women who are concerned with their status in the Jewish world. Unfortunately, Grace's name has been forgotten by the very people who repeat her words.

Grace Aguilar was a prominent woman writer of the modern age. A descendant of Marranos, she was born in Hackney, London, England in June 1816.[28] Like so many of the successful women of her era, she too, remained unmarried. Her life was devoted to literature and she had a broad and deep knowledge of Judaism and the Hebrew language — a knowledge that she consistently urged her fellow Jews, and especially the women, to embrace.

Most of her books were directed towards women, and her greatest work, *Women of Israel,* is a two-volume in-depth study of Biblical women.[29] In the preface to another of her books, *Spirit of Judaism,* Grace Aguilar stated:

The author of the following work . . . (hopes) that it may be permitted to find some response in the gentle minds of her own sex, to awaken one lethargic spirit to a consciousness of its own powers, its own duties. . .

She went on to say:

To the mothers and daughters in Israel it's (the book's) pages are particularly addressed: for to them is more especially entrusted the regeneration of Israel.

Despite her learning and her lofty goals for both women and men, Grace was an unpretentious soul. She hastened to add, in the same preface:

> When therefore the author looks to the support of her own sex for the support and countenance of her labours. . . . she ventures to hope that from all undue presumption her efforts may be absolved. Her aim is to *aid, not* to dictate; to *point* to the Fountain of Life, not presumptuously to *lead*; to waken the spirit to its healing influence, to rouse it to a sense of its own deep responsibilities, *not* to censure and judge.[30]

Grace Aguilar did not 'censure and judge" but despite her protestations, she did lead. Her leadership brought the Jewish women of England to the brink of the twentieth century more than fifty years before 1900 even arrived. She accomplished this by offering to them, through her writings, the gift of their own heritage and the understanding of their importance to it. Her fame even spread to America where several of her books were published. A library branch named for her still stands on 110th Street in New York City, in what was once a Jewish neighborhood.[31] It had been established in her name by Jacob Schiff, the noted Jewish philanthropist.

Unfortunately, this reluctant leader of England's Jewish women did not have enough time to continue her learning and writing, nor to continue to share her love of Judaism with her people. Grace had always been frail and sick, and at the age of 19, she became seriously ill and never completely recovered. More than ten years later, she was still not well and travelled to Frankfort, Germany to visit her sister in the hope of resting and achieving good health. This most unpretentious goal was never achieved, and she died in

Germany on September 16, 1847 when she was only thirty-one.

During her short life, Grace had managed to write and publish eight books and innumerable poems. A noted historian wrote about Grace:

> Her pen was dipped into the blood of her veins and the sap of her nerves; the sacred fire of the prophets burnt in her soul, and she was inspired by olden Jewish enthusiasm and devotion to a trust.[32]

This characterization is proven by her own last words. As Grace lay dying, no longer able to speak, she spelled out with her fingers the Biblical quotation: "Though He slay me, yet will I trust in Him." (Job 13:15)

On her gravestone is written the beautiful words from Proverbs: "Give her of the fruit of her hands, and let her works praise her in the gates." (Prov. 31:31) Grace's real epitaph, however, is a letter written to her and signed by more than a hundred Jewish women in England. The letter, which is included below following her poems, is a fine testimonial to her life and her accomplishments.

Women in Israel is considered to be Grace Aguilar's greatest work. In it, she sought to defend the role of women in the Jewish tradition. She was the first of several women in the nineteenth and twentieth centuries who undertook this defense. In 1891, a Jewish convert named Nahida Remy, wrote a book called *The Jewish Woman*.[33] It recounted the lives of many great women both from Biblical and more recent times. In 1932, Emily Solis-Cohen wrote a pamphlet in which

she sought to examine and defend the traditional
Jewish view of women.[34]

Grace's book on this subject is a full discussion on
all the Biblical women, from the Patriarch's wives,
Sarah, Rebecca, Leah and Rachel, to the women who
lived in the period of the Second Temple. Her final
chapter discusses women of Israel in the present, and
how they were influenced by the past. The following
are excerpts from this work:

> In Bible times the Hebrew females shared the holy
> privileges of the males; It was the falling off from
> spiritual Judaism . . . which degraded and blinded the
> Hebrews of the Babylonish captivity.

> We will return to the point whence we started and as-
> certain whether or not our venerable sages so com-
> pletely contradicted the spirit of the Law of Moses, as
> to ordain the degradation of the Hebrew female.

> Jewish degradation of woman, her abasement in the
> (English) social system, as a non-partaker of religious
> responsibility and immortality, if traced to its source
> will be found to have originated in blinded notions of
> the Jews of Barbary and other Eastern countries, in-
> fused unconsciously by the contempt for the sex pecul-
> iar to the Mohammedan inhabitants of those lands.

> We have gone further to draw forth every mention of
> our noble ancestors, that we might learn their domes-
> tic and social position at a time when inspired histo-
> rians were silent; we have scanned every statute, every
> law, alike in the words of Moses, and in their simplify-
> ing commentary by our elders, and the result of such
> examination has been, we trust, to convince every
> woman of Israel of her immortal destiny, her solemn

responsibility, and her elevated position, alike by the command of God, and the willing acquiescence of her brother man.[35]

The following excerpt from *The Wanderers*, written when Grace was twenty-two, immortalizes a Biblical story that has often been overlooked—the story of Hagar, Sarah's handmaiden, who was cast out of her home, together with her son, Ishmael. Sarah's decision to send Hagar away, in order to protect her son Isaac's position in the family, is recognized by the author to be based on the word of God. Yet Grace goes beyond this truth to describe the mother and son from a purely human point of view. Her description of the contrasting feelings of parent and child as they set out on their fateful journey into the wilderness is poignant and real. Hagar was one of the few women in the Bible to whom God communicated directly. Grace Aguilar, in a few skillful lines, transfers this meaningful event to the reader and brings to life the inherent drama of this biblical scene.

THE WANDERERS
Gen. xxi. 14-20

With a sadden'd heart and tearful eye the mother went her
     way,
The patriarch's mandate had gone forth, and Hagar must
     not stay.
Oh! who can tell the emotions deep that press'd on Ab-
     ra'am's heart,
As thus, obedient to God, from Ishmael call'd to part!

* * *

She lifted up her voice and wept—and o'er the lonely wild
"Let me not see his death!" was borne, "my Ishmael, my
     child!"

And silence came upon her then, her stricken soul to calm;
And suddenly and strange there fell a soft and soothing
balm;
And then a voice came stealing, on the still and fragrant
air—
A still small voice that would be heard, though solitude was
there.

"What aileth thee, oh Hagar?" thus it spoke: "fear not, for
God hath heard
The lad's voice where he is,—and thou, trust in thy Maker's
word!
Awake! arise! lift up the lad, and hold him in thine hand—
I will of him a nation make, before Me he shall stand."

It ceased, that voice; and silence now, as strangely soft and
still,
The boundless desert once again, with eloquence would fill;
And strength return'd to Hagar's frame, for God hath oped
her eyes—
And lo! amid the arid sands a well of water lies![36]

*   *   *   *

The following letter was written to Grace Aguilar
and signed by more than one hundred women who
had learned and benefited from her writings. It was
sent just before Grace's journey to Frankfort. Depite
the sincere attestations by these women that Miss
Aguilar had raised their Jewish self-awareness and
taught them to "appreciate their dignity," it is interesting to note the line: "Until you arose, it has in modern times, never been the case that a Woman in Israel
should stand forth the public advocate of the faith of
Israel." Apparently, and despite the fact that these
women were the enlightened and educated ones, they
still had no knowledge of women like the *firzogerins* of

past ages, Rebecca Tiktiner, Eva Bacharach, or Sarah Bat Tovim. Surely these women and many more like them, had also stood forth as "public advocates of the faith of Israel." Unfortunately, the silence of apathy had covered them over for several generations and Grace Aguilar had to break the same ground again in urging her sisters to reach out for "those higher motives. . . .which flow from the spirituality of our religion." This letter attests to her remarkable success.

> Dearest Sister—Our admiration of your talents, our veneration for your character, our gratitude for the eminent services your writings render our sex, our people, our faith, in which the sacred cause of true religion is embodied; all these motives combine to induce us to intrude on your presence, in order to give utterance to sentiments which we are happy to feel and delighted to express. Until you arose, it has, in modern times, never been the case that a Woman in Israel should stand forth the public advocate of the faith of Israel; that with the depth and purity of feelings which is the treasure of women, and with the strength of mind and extensive knowledge that form the pride of man, she should call on her own to cherish, on others to respect, the truth as it is in Israel.
>
> You, dearest Sister, have done this, and more. You have taught us to know and appreciate our dignity; to feel and to prove that no female character can be . . . more pure than that of the Jewish maiden, none more pious than that of the woman in Israel. You have vindicated our social and spiritual equality with our brethren in the faith; you have, by your own ex-

cellent example, triumphantly refuted the aspersion, that the Jewish religion leaves unmoved the heart of the Jewish woman. Your writings place within our reach those higher motives, those holier consolations, which flow from the spirituality of our religion, which urge the soul to commune with its Maker and direct it to His grace and His mercy as the best guide and protector here and hereafter.....[37]

Emma Lazarus

Emma Lazarus is one of the few Jewish women whose name immediately sparks recognition in the eyes of the most uninitiated students of Jewish women's history. It is a recognition that is well deserved.

Lazarus, born July 22, 1849, was the daughter of Portuguese Jews whose ancestors came to the New World in the sixteenth century. She was raised in the well-to-do Sephardic Jewish society of New York and given a private education which emphasized languages and the classics. One biography suggested that she never married because of the dominating influence of her father.[38]

The most famous of Emma's poems, "The New Colossus," which is engraved on the pedestal of the Statue of Liberty, is only one small contribution in a vast selection of excellent work. The earliest of her poetry, written in her teens, was first published in 1866 when she was only 17 years old. This was soon followed by other volumes of poetry as well as novels, many on Jewish topics.

Emma Lazarus' serious commitment to other Jews did not emerge until she had the opportunity to see the

Jewish refugees from the Russian pogroms of 1881 who were quarantined on Wards Island in New York harbor. This "wretched refuse" which Emma later immortalized in her well-known poem, touched her heart and convinced her that she had to help her people, which she did with both charitable and literary deeds. She organized groups to train Jews in industrial trades—a project which grew into the Hebrew Technical Institute.

This woman, who was admired by Ralph Waldo Emerson and his literary circle, began at the age of thirty to learn Hebrew—not at all the fashionable language of the time—and to translate the great poetry of her ancestors. Like Nina Davis Salaman who later did similar work in England, Emma became a foremost translator of the work of the great Spanish Jews, Solomon ibn Gabirol and Judah HaLevi. By her own initiative, she developed into one of the more learned Jewish scholars of her day.

Emma spoke for all Jews and especially for the downtrodden. Although she herself came from a comfortable, upper class family, her feeling for her fellow Jews was strong and unflagging. She constantly urged others of her class to help uplift their unfortunate sisters and brothers. As she eloquently pointed out: "Until we are all free, we are none of us free."[39]

Emma attended rallies for the destitute Russian Jewish immigrants and wrote poems and essays about their plight. Her work appeared in *The Jewish Messenger* and *The American Hebrew*, two widely-read Jewish periodicals of her time.

"The New Colossus," her short tribute to America and the immigrants who came to its "golden door," has been recited and repeated, set to music, and engraved in bronze. It was originally auctioned off for $1500 to raise money for the pedestal of the new

Statue of Liberty, a gift presented by the people of France to the United States of America in 1886. Unfortunately, Emma did not live to see it inscribed on the pedestal. After a painful illness, she died at the age of 38.

At her death, many noted poets rose up to mourn the loss of such a talented woman. One of them was John Greenleaf Whittier. His praise showed a sincere respect for Emma, but a woeful lack of knowledge of the history and accomplishments of Jewish women, when he wrote:

> Since Miriam sang of deliverance and triumph by the Red Sea, the Semitic race has had no braver singer....[40]

The year was 1887. The Civil War had been over for twenty two years. The United States was slowly mending and people from all over the world—the poor and neglected, the talented and ambitious, people of all nations—were finding their way past the Statue of Liberty into the arms of America. Among them came thousands of Jews who would hear of Emma Lazarus, read her words and stand a little straighter because of this noble Jewish woman.

Emma's first visit to the immigration centers of New York where the destitute Jews were pouring in from Eastern Europe, was her initiation into the experience of Jewish suffering and persecution. Thereafter, she was a champion of the cause of Jewish unity and also of Zionism. At a time when Zionism was not at all a popular cause, Emma proclaimed:

> I am fully persuaded that all suggested solutions

other than this (i.e., return to the homeland in Palestine) are but temporary palliatives.[41]

It was in the spirit of unity and early Zionistic fervor that Emma wrote this poem, recalling Israel's past glories and urging Jews to rise up again and defend their flag.

THE BANNER OF THE JEW

Wake, Israel, wake! Recall today
The glorious Maccabean rage

* * *

Oh, for Jerusalem's trumpets now
To blow a blast of shattering power,
To wake the sleepers high and low,
And rouse them to the urgent hour!

* * *

Oh, deem not dead that martial fire,
Say not the mystic flame is spent!
With Moses' law and David's lyre,
Your ancient strength remains unbent.
Let but an Ezra rise anew,
To lift the banner of the Jew!

A rag, a mock at first—erelong,
When men have bled and women wept,
To guard its precious folds from wrong,
Even they who shrank, even they who slept,
Shall leap to bless it and to save,
Strike! For the brave revere the brave![42]

One of America's most familiar poems, and the one that has made its author famous, is Emma Lazarus' sonnet, "The New Colossus." Here she compares the Statue of Liberty to the ancient Greek Colossus of Rhodes. Our statue, she says, is "not like the brazen giant of Greek fame," but it is "a mighty woman" whose "mild eyes" can "command." Perhaps these metaphors appealed to Emma, as they might appeal to any woman with the kind of aspiration and dreams Emma had come to possess.

Along with works by some of the most prominent writers of her time—Longfellow, Whitman, Bret Harte, and Mark Twain—Emma's work was sold at a fund-raising auction for the pedestal of the soon-to-be-delivered statue. It was then put aside and forgotten until 1903. In that year, Georgiana Schuyler, an admirer of Emma's, found the manuscript and arranged to have part of it inscribed on a bronze plaque and attached to the pedestal of the Statue of Liberty on Bedloe's Island. Ultimately, Emma Lazarus' poem was accepted by the American people as their own.

THE NEW COLOSSUS

Not like the brazen giant of Greek fame,
With conquering limbs astride from land to land;
Here at our sea-washed, sunset gates shall stand
A mighty woman with a torch, whose flame
Is the imprisoned lightning, and her name
Mother of Exiles. From her beacon-hand
Glows world-wide welcome; her mild eyes command
The air-bridged harbor that twin cities frame.
Keep, ancient lands, your storied pomp! cries she
With silent lips. "Give me your tired, your poor,
Your huddled masses yearning to breathe free,
The wretched refuse of your teeming shore.

Send these, the homeless, tempest-tost to me.
I lift my lamp beside the golden door.

The indignation that Emma felt against those "comfortable" Jews who would not hesitate to turn their backs on their poorer brothers and sisters, comes out in this work. In powerful words, Emma Lazarus challenged those Jews to acknowledge their kinship with the "caftaned wretch" who is also a part of their people. It is easy, she suggested, to honor and feel close to men like Moses ben Maimon, Judah HaLevi, Moses Mendelssohn, and others of their calibre. But those who have "faith in the fortune of Israel" must dare to unite with *all* Jews.

Emma Lazarus was one of the few who dared. While many in her own social circle turned their backs and worried about how these miserable refugees would affect their own status, she spoke out and wrote poems such as this one. Written a very short time before her death, it is the last poem on a Jewish theme that Emma ever wrote.

THE PROPHET

Moses Ben Maimon lifting his perpetual lamp over the path
  of the perplexed;
Halevi, the honey-tongued poet, wakening amid the silent
  ruins of Zion the sleeping lyre of David;
Moses, the wise son of Mendel, who made the Ghetto illustrious;
Abarbanel, the counselor of kings; Alcharisi, the exquisite
  singer; Ibn Ezra, the perfect old man; Gabirol, the
  tragic seer;
Heine, the enchanted magician, the heart-broken jester;

Yea, and the century-crowned patriarch whose bounty en-
girdles the globe;—

These need no wreath and no trumpet; like perennial as-
phodel blossoms, their fame, their glory resounds like
the brazen-throated cornet.

But thou—hast thou faith in the fortune of Israel? Wouldst
thou lighten the anguish of Jacob?

Then shalt thou take the hand of yonder caftaned wretch
with flowing curls and gold-pierced ears;

Who crawls blinking forth from the loathsome recesses of
the Jewry;

Nerveless his fingers, puny his frame; haunted by the bat-
like phantoms of superstition is his brain.

Thou shalt say to the bigot, "My Brother," and to the crea-
ture of darkness, "My Friend."

And thy heart shall spend itself in fountains of love upon
the ignorant, the coarse, and the abject.

Then in the obscurity thou shalt hear a rush of wings, thine
eyes shall be bitten with pungent smoke.

And close against thy quivering lips shall be pressed the live
coal wherewith the Seraphim brand the Prophets.[43]

The following excerpt from one of Emma Lazarus'
early poems effectively points out Emma's transforma-
tion from one who "dared not hope" to one who
eventually rallied her people to hopes of victory over
oppression. A biographer discussed this change with
the use of a Biblical comparison. He said:

It is as if a poor Ruth, a gleaner of the corn, had over-
night become a Deborah who had drunk of the wine
of victory and could move, dancing, at the head of a
people.[44]

Emma Lazarus had come to know, either through
knowledge of history or understanding of self, that

she had a great work to do and she could and would
accomplish it. In fact, she did "recite the dangers,
wounds, and triumphs of the fight," and coped effectively "with the world's strong-armed warriors." She
fought against apathy and indifference to the poor
and persecuted among her own people, and with her
pen, championed many Jewish causes. In these accomplishments, which she had once despaired of at-
taining, she followed in the footsteps of many sisters
of the past, and thereby broadened the pathways for
the many women who will continue to come after her.

> Late Born and woman-souled I dare not hope
> The freshness of the elder lays, the might
> Of manly, modern passion shall alight
> Upon my Muse's lips, nor may I cope
> (Who veiled and screened by womanhood must grope)
> With the world's strong-armed warriors and recite
> The dangers, wounds and triumphs of the fight...[45]

Rebekah Kohut

As Jewish-American society became more organized, a few women moved into the forefront of
Jewish life. Rebekah Kohut is one woman who effectively worked for universal causes within the
framework of Jewish women's organizations. She
became President of the World Congress of Jewish
Women, President of the New York Branch of the
National Council of Jewish Women, and, at the
time, the only female member of the New York
State Employment Committee.

Born into the Bettelheim family in 1864 in Hungary, Rebekah, one of six children, arrived in America at the age of two. Her father was a rabbi and a physician, a learned man whom she always loved and admired.

Although Rebekah's mother died when she was very young, she was a role model for her in her growing years. Rebekah knew that she had been "practically a revolutionary."

> She had become a school teacher—a job previously the monopoly of men. She was the first Jewess to become a school teacher in Hungary, and for this she was frowned upon and ostracized by various shocked members of the community. Her example inspired me, led me as a young girl to seek out all kinds of less sheltered activities, into which I entered with all the ardor of a cause, and I know I felt very brave and heroine-like to myself.[50]

So Rebekah followed in her mother's footsteps, was educated at the University of California in San Francisco where the family went to live in 1875, and plunged into an active and committed life.

Rebekah's husband, Alexander Kohut, a friend of her father's, was a widower rabbi from Hungary. Rebekah fell in love with him almost immediately after their first meeting and at the age of 24 settled down as his wife and "other mother" to his eight children, the oldest of whom was less than 12 years her junior. As she recalls in her own book *More Yesterdays*,[46] "...I was born for work and was unhappy unless I was getting more than my apportioned share of it. It must have been a contributing factor in my eagerness to marry Alexander Kohut.

Having been given eight children at once, I didn't have to look for work; I had it."

After only seven years of marriage, Alexander Kohut died and Rebekah was left as the sole support of his family. This became a major factor in her pursuit of a career as an educational and vocational expert. She writes in her memoirs, in a matter of fact style reminiscent of Glückel of Hameln (see Chapter XI):

> When my husband died I became, in addition to everything else, my family's chief breadwinner. I founded schools and camps, just as my son did later; and succeeded with both; and I managed also to find the time for a good deal of civic and national social work. As I look at it now, and consider all the different things I did, I don't know whether to be fascinated or appalled at my energy. But the sum of what I remember — and that includes all the worries and heartaches — is that it was wonderful.... [47]

In *More Yesterdays*, a sequel to her autobiography, *My Portion*, [48] Rebekah recalls her life and her accomplishments with both pride and humor. Speaking of her sensitivity to the miseries of European refugees after World War I she was aware that she was "looked upon by some as that ridiculous thing — a professional do-gooder. Oh, yes, I was the funny humanitarian type — just made for caricature and burlesque." At one point she felt she was "dying of too many committees" and decided to resign, but this decision was short-lived. As Rebekah recalls: "...I decided my revolt against committee-itis was causing me more pain and trouble than the malady."

Describing her work for the Council of Jewish

Women which she calls her "first love," Rebekah displays a healthy satisfaction with her work, a profound pleasure in her achievements as a woman, and the ability to overlook those subtleties and innuendoes of anti-feminism which were so prevalent in her day.

One of my fondest memories is a banquet which was given in my honor at the Hotel Commodore on the fiftieth anniversary of the founding of the Council. There were nine hundred guests, and among them some of the most distinguished people in American life. At this dinner I was presented with a check for fifty thousand dollars which I was free to apply to any good works I chose. In presenting the check the dinner chairman, Felix M. Warburg, said, "Now, mind, this is not for a mink coat."

One "mink coat" was the Council, to which I gave a check for ten thousand dollars the next day, and the other "coats" were accounted for by gifts to other organizations.

It is easy for the committee to be overdone. It is also a very easy thing to laugh at, and when I see those Helen Hokinson cartoons of committee-women in the *New Yorker,* I laugh too, as much as anyone. But the passion of women for serving on committees is a very understandable and laudable thing.

It was not so long ago that such activities were the exclusive prerogative of the male, and women are still intoxicated—and rightly so—with so-called equality, and take full advantage of it. And I am sure that when you compare their meetings to those of men, you will find that the ratio of nonsense to good sense in the course of an hour or two is not any higher.[49]

Rebekah's contemporaries form a Who's Who of Americans and Jews in the early twentieth century: from Solomon Schechter, the first Chancellor of the Jewish Theological Seminary of America, to Mrs. Sara Roosevelt (the mother of Franklin) to Julia Richman, the great American educator, Bertha Pappenheim of Germany, founder of the German Jewish Women's Organization, Lily Montagu, social worker, magistrate, and a pioneer of Liberal Judaism in England. Rebekah Kohut loved this commitment to work and service as well as to the human relationships. Her enthusiasm is evident in her narrative:

Apart from home and family, probably my most pleasant association of memory is my work in that splendid organization, the National Council of Jewish Women. Organizations are many and one gets quite used to them, but in this case the pull of nostalgia is especially strong. At the time the Council was founded, participation by women in public life was still a new thing, and there was an excitement, a heady sense of independence, a thrill, a feeling that one was taking part in the best kind of revolution, even if it involved nothing more at the moment than parliamentary debates about hot soup and recreation for school children.

At any rate, my introduction to the Council was a good one. We all continued to work harmoniously and well. The work that the Council had cut out for itself, in all its branches, was much needed. It established Americanization courses for immigrants, recreation rooms for children, work rooms in which people learned new trades, many cultural activities, and in particular the various Councils in their communities interested themselves in municipal health problems, playgrounds for children, milk stations, and general betterment. The Council acquired a national membership of six hundred thousand conscientious, public-spirited women devoted to their communities and co-operating fully with other public bodies. In the decades that followed it made a name for itself as an organization devoted on the highest plane to the Jews of each community and to that community in general.[51]

Rebekah Kohut died in 1951 at the age of 87, loved by her children and friends, and admired by the community as an educator, a vocational expert, and a leader. She had called herself "a matriarch who never had any children of her own" and yet her children and grandchildren came regularly to visit her during her later years of illness. She remembers with satisfaction being called "a Mother in Israel" as she was.

XV

From Foremothers
To Future Leaders

"She is clothed with strength and splendour,
She looketh to the future cheerfully."

PROVERBS 31:25

Re-examining the Past

Since our first journey into the past, more than ten years ago, we have continued our study of Jewish women. Gradually our research on individual women began to fall into place as part of general historical development, and to point to some common trends.

For example, we saw that in the 16th century, after the Italian Renaissance, activities by Jewish and Christian women outside the home seemed to increase. Their freedom to participate in cultural and communal areas followed new ideas about humanism and the beginning of the concept of individual rights.

In 18th century England, John Stuart Mill wrote his groundbreaking essay: "Declaration of the Rights of Man." Stirred by this, and the American Revolution, Mary Wollstonecraft outlined in "A Vindication of the Rights of Women" what she believed were *women's* rights.[1] These became the basis for later feminist goals.

We learned that a previous wave of American feminism, first organized in 1848, was a direct outgrowth of the early anti-slavery ideas of the abolitionists. Until women's suffrage was passed in 1920, the women's movement closely paralleled the fight for Black voting rights.

The women's movement as well as Jewish feminist concerns of the 1970's and 1980's had many of its roots in the civil rights movement of the 1960's. They were both part of the same historical development.

Placing our own generation within a broad framework of history allowed us to tentatively project trends for the future. Perhaps the development of an interest in feminist issues in Israel will require a serious increased sensitivity by an Israeli Jewish majority towards its own Jewish and Arab minorities.

The decisions and actions of Jewish people, in addition to being part of historical movements, also draw on their own legacy of culture and tradition. Therefore, a study of Jewish women's history not only reveals or reflects the growth of ideas and changes in society as a whole, but helps us to learn about individual lives and accomplishments, and teaches us about Jewish Law and general Jewish history.

Our continued study of Jewish women led to the development of several learning programs. The first, "Women Don't Have to be Footnotes," drew on information from this book combined with new material.

As part of that program, we expanded our pre-Biblical knowledge to include controversial, pre-patriarchal theories. These were drawn from archeological and anthropological sources, information on the ancient female goddesses, and the earlier religions which preceded Talmudic Judaism.[2] From there, we made an in-depth study of the women of the Hebrew Bible and the New Testament, exploring the still-living roots of western culture.

Jewish Law, although it was the basis for present-day assumptions of what traditional Jewish women lived by, was rarely understood by the average layperson. To help familiarize ourselves with this vital information, we developed a second learning program: "Life Stages of the Jewish Woman."

Laws of marriage and divorce, issues concerning birth control, abortion and rape, have all been re-examined over the last ten years,[3] revealing a considerable amount of legal leeway for women. The concern of contemporary women over these issues has led, in some cases, to new rabbinic rulings. (see Chap. XV part 2). Having women scholars and rabbis competent to interpret Jewish Law, has helped focus issues in creative and innovative ways.

In secular areas of Jewish life, we observed that twentieth century women seemed for the first time to be choosing the world of commerce or banking. However, we found within our heritage, Gracia Nasi, in the sixteenth century, managing her import-export network on an international scale. Esther Liebman took charge of the Austrian mint in the early eighteenth century. She was given the task as a partial payment for debts owed her by the royal family to whom she supplied jewelry after the death of her husband, Jost Liebman.[4] Although these women may have been the exceptions, they nevertheless created a precedent.

As for the supposed "new" political role of women, one could trace its beginning to the women of the Hebrew Bible. Rebecca's choice of one son over the other to be patriarch could be viewed as a political decision.[5] Deborah was an obvious national leader,[6] as was Athaliah, a ruthless queen mother who destroyed all the heirs to the throne so she could rule Judah alone in 841-835 B.C.E.[7]

In developing a third course which we named "Queens, Courtesans and Commoners," we included not only the wicked queen Athaliah, but also Queen Salome Alexandra, the Maccabean queen; Mariamne the Hasmonean princess who was married to Herod; and Doris, another of Herod's wives who unsuccessfully schemed to secure the throne for her son, Herod II.[8]

Berenice, a later princess of the Hasmonean line (b. 28 C.E.), married many times, each time using the political power she had gained. She eventually became the mistress of Titus, the Roman general who destroyed Jerusalem in 70 C.E., and thus ended by deserting the Jews.[9]

Like their non-Jewish counterparts, Jewish queens were often pawns in the shifting alliances of history. However, when they had power, they used it — sometimes for good and sometimes for evil.

Important work has been done in exploring the activities of Jewish women in antiquity. Not only Biblical and post-Biblical queens, but ordinary women's lives of the period have been examined. Bernadette Brooten, in her book *Women Leaders in the Ancient Synagogue: Inscriptional Evidence and Background Issue,*[10] discusses women who were prominent in early synagogues. By studying the inscriptions on remains of synagogue buildings and tombstones, Brooten revealed that Jewish women in Greek and Roman times often played active roles in the synagogue.

After the destruction of Jerusalem, the period known as the Diaspora began, when Jews scattered to the countries of Europe, Asia and Africa. The influence of individual women continued; not necessarily royal women, but women who possessed intelligence, daring and charisma. They are sometimes recorded as courtesans and mistresses of the powerful, and among them were Jewish women.

Pulcellina was the lover of Count Thibault of Blois, in northern France, during the late twelfth century.[11] When the Jews of Blois were falsely accused of blood libel, she tried to use her influence to intercede, unaware that she had fallen out of favor with the Count. Pulcellina was burned at the stake in 1171, together with thirty-one other Jews.

Another woman, Raquel, also known as "La Fermosa" or "The Jewess of Toledo," was the daughter of the Jewish Finance Minister to King Alphonso VIII of Castile.[12]

She became Alphonso's mistress during the late twelfth century. It was said of her that she exerted a positive influence on his policies toward the Jews, and that Alphonso was so beguiled by her beauty that for seven years he neglected his duties as King. A poet wrote of Raquel:

> For her the King forgot his Queen,
> His kingdom and his people. [13]

Her murder is often attributed to one of the King's courtiers, while others blame it on Queen Eleanor, Alphonso's wife.

A Polish-Jewish record concerns Esterka, the Jewish mistress of King Casimir III of Poland (1310-1370). [14] She was the daughter of a Jewish tailor from Opoczno when the King became infatuated with her. She bore him two sons, who were raised as Christians, and one daughter who retained her Jewish identity. The relationship of Esterka of Opoczno and Casimir III was the subject of many legends, and the King became known as a friend of Polish Jews.

In 1773, Eva Frank, the daughter of Jacob Frank, founder of the Frankists (a messianic movement which later separated from Judaism), became the co-leader of the sect together with her father. [15] At his death, she led it alone, and legitimizing her own position of leadership by rumors that she was really an illegitimate offspring of the Russian Romanovs, modeled her role on royalty. At her death in 1816, the movement dispersed. Eva Frank, however, continued to be revered, and pictures of her were often hung in the households of believers.

In the twentieth century Tehillah Lichtenstein was the founder and leader of Jewish Science in America, loosely modelled on the Christian Science movement. That organization was also conceived and led by a woman, Mary Baker Eddy. Jewish Science enjoyed wide acceptance in the early decades of our own century. (A book is presently being written about Lichtenstein by a noted scholar of religion, Dr. Ellen Umansky.)

In the preceding pages we mention some influential women whose lives may be unfamiliar, but who nevertheless give us examples of Jewish women who did not act in traditional ways. Wuhsha of Egypt (11th century) reminds us that some women rebelled against restrictions centuries before our own time. Esther Kiera (1530-1600) is an example of a woman who grasped at opportunities wherever she could, and used them to gain great power. Frumet Wolfe (d. 1849) points out that long before "freedom of the press" was an operative idea, women were writing dissident articles and speaking out on the issues of the time.

In more recent times Bertha Pappenheim, an early "modern" feminist (1859-1936), developed the German feminist movement and pioneered modern methods of social work.[16]

Flora Sassoon (1859-1936), a Jewish woman from India and a member of the noted Sassoon family, was a Hebrew scholar and businesswoman.[17] After her husband's death, she managed the family business in Bombay and continued with her Jewish studies. In 1924, at the age of 65, Flora Sassoon delivered a discourse on Talmud at Jews College in London. Six years later, at 71, she published an essay on Rashi.

From its early years in England and America the Jewish reform movement produced outstanding women. Lily H. Montagu (1873-1963) was one of the founders and leaders of liberal Judaism in England and played a major role in building the World Union for Progressive Judaism.[18] She conducted religious services and wrote many articles of Jewish interest.

Because so many American Jews have their roots in the culture of Central and Eastern European lands, new interest has been shown in the lives of Jewish women there. Important work on women in the early *shtetl* culture is being done by Chava Weissler of Princeton University.[19] She is presently exploring the varied forms of Jewish women's spiritual outlets in Eastern European Jewish communities of the late middle ages and early modern period. Research has revealed that Jewish women had their own prayers and customs, developed and used exclusively by and for women. These included not only special prayers for the holidays — for home and synagogue use — but traditions such as candle-making, cooking and preparing for Sabbath, etc. which women imbued with specific spiritual significance.

One of the purposes of a course called "From Shtetl to Suburbia," was to introduce portraits of Jewish women which would contrast with negative portrayals of the Jewish mother by male authors of the post-1960's. This stereotype, personified by Sophie Portnoy, Philip Roth's character in *Portnoy's Complaint,* was widely accepted as an accurate portrait rather than a grossly exaggerated caricature.

In our research we rediscovered Jewish women who had remained in Europe as well as those who left to help build new Jewish communities. Brave women like Hannah Senesh was only one of the more modern of these heroines.[20] Hannah was a young Hungarian Jew who returned to Hungary from Israel in June, 1944 to help rescue Hungarian Jews from the Germans. She died a martyr's death in a Nazi prison. Other women heroines of the Holocaust include Vitke Kempner, Zofia Yaika, Mala Zimetbaum, Rosa Robota, Niuta Teitelboim and Tzivia Lubetkin.[21]

Before World War II we learned about women like Sarah Schenirer, a Jewish seamstress from Cracow (1883-1938) who was committed to formal Jewish education for women. She founded the Beth Jacob school for girls in Poland.[22] Starting with just one school, the Beth Jacob schools grew and spread even beyond the Polish borders. This network of schools was later taken over by *Agudat Israel,* the ultra-right wing of orthodoxy.

Rosa Luxemburg (1871-1938) helped organize Socialist parties in Poland/Lithuania and Germany. In World War I, she worked to found the Communist Party of Germany.[23] Rosa rejected Jewish nationalism in favor of universal internationalism, but never denied her Jewish identity. Many women like her devoted themselves to the Socialist ideal, playing leading roles in the events that led to the overthrow of the Russian Czar.

It was during the late 1800's and the early 1900's that other Jewish women, socialists and committed Zionists, began to be counted among the early pioneers to Palestine. Among them were Sarah Malchin, the first woman to arrive (1901), Hannah Meisel, Rachel Yanait Ben-Zvi, Yael Gordon, Rachel Shazar Katznelson, Manya Shochat, and Ada Maimon.[24] These women served as role models for those who came later. They were involved in all aspects of the new country, from agriculture to construction, teaching, diplomacy, and unionization. Golda Myerson (Meir) (1898-1978), who later became a Prime Minister of Israel, was one of many Jewish women activists who originated from Eastern Europe, and helped create the modern state of Israel.[25] Except for a few books on pioneer women in recent years (now mostly out of print) there has not appeared a thorough history of women's involvement in building the state of Israel.[26]

A study of the Eastern European experience in America revealed active Jewish women who were leaders of the early labor movement of the 1900's. Theresa Malkiel, who began as a cloak maker, became prominent in the Socialist's Women's Society in New York, and ultimately found her role as a militant in the Women's Trade Union League. Although in 1909, Theresa Malkiel took a major role in the "women's strike," today she is virtually unknown.[27] Rose Schneiderman, one of the first trade union organizers; Mary Dreier, President of the New York Women's Trade Union League; Clara Lemlich, strike organizer, have also been largely overlooked for their historical importance until recently.[28]

Even the accomplishments of Emma Goldman, the radical and outspoken crusader for unions and for birth control are relatively forgotten.[29] Goldman was the first woman who dared to demonstrate the diaphragm contraceptive in public, to show other women that there was an alternative to having babies every year. For this, she was jailed and reviled in 1916. Three years later, Emma Goldman was deported because of her political activities. She lived in Europe for many years until finally, disillusioned by the failure of the socialist cause in the Spanish Civil War, she came to Canada where she died in 1940, forbidden to return to the United States.

Long forgotten Jewish women authors like Anzia Yezierska and Mary Antin, whose novels depicted the adaptation of the immigrant woman to American life, are now being acknowledged and reread with new recognition of their importance as social history.[30] They recreate a time and place which will soon slip completely beyond the realm of living memory.

Oral histories, portraying the lives of working class Russian and Polish women immigrants to America have also captured the thoughts and experiences of a recent generation of foremothers.[31] They, too, help to overcome the distorted images of the Eastern European Jewish mother.

American history offered a complex variety of Jewish women about whom we could learn, beginning with the first Sephardic Jewish settlers in the 17th century. These were followed by German Jewish immigrants, and then Russian and Polish Jews. Our course, "Revolutionaries, Rebels, Radicals and Reformers," studied the outstanding women from each of these groups (see Chap. XIV) and updated to the present time.

Investigations of the Jewish American club woman helped revise another negative stereotype. When the valued contributions of such women's groups as National Council of Jewish Women and Hadassah were retold, many new heroines were discovered. Under the direction of Hannah Solomon, Rebecca Kohut, and Sadie American, the women of the National Council are today perceived as innovators in helping immigrants adjust to new lives. With no professional training, they confronted such controversial problems as Jewish prostitution and juvenile delinquency, established homes and counseling centers, and provided aid to immigrants.[32]

Jewish women's contributions to social reform in America far exceeded their percentage in the population. From Rebecca Gratz (1789-1869), philanthropist and educator; to Ernestine Rose (1810-1892), abolitionist and activist in America who fought for the married women's property act of 1848;[33] to Lillian Wald (1867-1940) who is famous for her work with immigrants during the 1920's on the lower East Side of Manhattan,[34] our history is filled with dedicated and accomplished women.

Today, American-Jewish women like Bella Abzug, Aviva Cantor, Nora Ephron, Betty Friedan, Letty Cottin Pogrebin, Anne Roiphe and Susan Weidman Schneider continue to examine and confront women's issues. Gloria Steinem, whose father was Jewish, and whose Jewish grandmother Pauline Steinem was an early suffragist, is one of the leading Americans in the struggle for equal rights for women.*

*See Sondra Henry and Emily Taitz, One Woman's Power: *A Biography of Gloria Steinem.* (Minneapolis: Dillon Press, 1987)

Beginning with the earliest settlers to the New World, these women, each in her own way, have transformed their own dual identity as Jews and Americans into a dynamic and unique combination of Jewish-American values and culture.

Into the Future

In spite of progress—or because of it—the contemporary Jewish woman confronts new problems. Among them are: the real dilemma of the family versus the workplace; the sensitive issue of her status in Jewish Law within each of the major religious groups; and a problem of both self-image and perception by society.

Ideas and images about Jewish women have not always kept pace with the concrete advances made by women. Negative stereotypes of Jewish women, sometimes even among women themselves, persist. The cliche of the domineering, overprotective Jewish mother, obsessed with feeding her children, has been replaced by another, which, although opposite, is equally unfavorable. This is the image of the "Jewish American Princess" (JAP) a woman who is supposedly pampered, materialistic, vain, self-centered, and ambitious.

The JAP stereotype has again made Jewish women the target of vicious and unwarranted "humor." This phenomenon, which often masks anti-semitism, can be better understood with a background in Jewish women's history.

In the realm of Jewish Law, women have been extremely active over the past fifteen years. Their activity mirrors not only a general concern by women for taking charge of their own destiny. It is also part of an increased interest in Jewish Law among orthodox groups both in Israel and

America.

With Jews now ruling their own state in Israel, many aspects of Jewish Law, developed over centuries of Jewish statelessness, had to be re-evaluated and interpreted. For example, what is the responsibility of a modern Jewish political state to a woman whose husband refuses to grant her a divorce according to Jewish Law? How should a democratic state deal with intermarriage and what is the legal status of children from such a marriage?[35] Women's specific interest in re-examining and re-interpreting laws pertaining to their own status, fits into this wider Jewish concern.

In 1973, at an annual meeting of the Rabbinical Assembly, a group of educated and committed Jewish women came with demands for ritual equality, and forced a rethinking of many Jewish issues affecting women. They termed themselves *Ezrat Nashim*, the words originally designating the women's court in the ancient Temple, and now used to refer to the women's section of the synagogue. This group represented one of the signal efforts by Jewish women in the 1970's and is decribed by Anne Lapidus Lerner in her pamphlet *Who Hast Not Made Me A Man.*[36]

Since that breakthrough, more and more women have become visible in Jewish synagogue and ritual life. Beginning in 1972, when the Hebrew Union College in Cincinnati ordained the first woman Reform rabbi, Sally Priesand, women have entered the rabbinate in increasing numbers. Reform and Reconstructionist seminaries have been accepting women since that time, but new problems have arisen. Is a Jewish marriage performed by a female rabbi "Jewishly legal"? Can she preside over conversions, divorces and circumcisions? Can she be a witness in areas where women had *halachically* been considered improper witnesses? These questions are slowly being confronted and resolved by individual congregations.

In the Conservative movement change came more slowly. There, its rabbinical law committee had ruled in 1956 that women might be called up to recite a blessing on the Torah, but the use of that permission was at the discretion of the rabbi in each synagogue. Few had adopted the practice until 1973, when Jewish women began pressing for change. The pressure brought about serious discussions and several decisions.

There was a sharp difference of opinion between those who favored interpreting the Law to include Jewish women in the broadest possible capacity, and those who favored what they considered a traditionalist view. The more liberal scholars found precedents for women performing marriages, acting as public representatives of the community *(shaliah tzibbur)* and being counted in a minyan.[37] The traditionalists saw these concessions as a serious threat to Jewish family and community life.

Ultimately, the liberal group, representing a large part of the leadership of the Jewish Theological Seminary, won. In October, 1983 women were accepted as students in the Seminary's Rabbinical School, as candidates for degrees as rabbis and cantors. Rabbi Amy Eilberg, the first woman to be ordained as a Conservative rabbi, was graduated in 1985.

At the present time, the number of Conservative synagogues calling women for honors during the Torah service, and counting them in *minyans* is growing. The acceptance of women as lay leaders, board members, presidents of synagogues, etc. has been even more widespread in all the denominations except perhaps the extreme Orthodox.

Orthodox Jewish women face dilemmas concerning their participation in ritual. Many orthodox synagogues still insist on real separation of the sexes by use of a wall or a heavy curtain. A few urge the women not to sing too loudly, reminding them of the Talmudic injunction that "the voice of a woman is indecent" since it distracts a man from his own prayers. Jews who are more assimilated find it difficult to accept these concerns as legitimate. However, they are important issues for certain groups of Jews who believe that a commitment to Judaism equals a commitment to Jewish Law as it was traditionally practiced. Their intent is not to denigrate women, but to preserve the purity of Law.

Even among these groups, however, some movement can be seen in the direction of allowing women space for their own spirituality to develop. Although Orthodox synagogues rarely approve of a woman's *minyan,* they have acknowledged the legitimacy of women's communal prayer groups, on the grounds that they are as acceptable as women praying individually. Prayer has always been viewed as a positive commandment incumbent on women as well as men. Women's study groups are also acceptable.

There is presently a Woman's *Tefillah* Network which helps organize and encourage a variety of women's prayer groups within the traditional Jewish community, and maintains contact among them.

The most recent breakthrough in confronting the issues of women and Jewish Law was made in December, 1986 when a conference was convened in Jerusalem. The first of its kind, organized by Israeli feminist Pnina Peli, and sponsored by the Israel government's Ministry of Justice, it dealt with "*Halachah* and the Jewish Woman."

The conference was attended by hundreds of women and men from Israel and America, including lawyers and rabbis. Although no important conclusions were reached by the group and no consensus is near, the conference itself is evidence that this issue is becoming a major concern to all kinds of Jews.

Beyond questions of Jewish Law, change in Jewish women's roles has become more pronounced. Women are found in almost every profession: from law and politics, medicine, dentistry, and religion, to science, engineering, and space travel. Rosalyn Yalow, both a nuclear physicist and a traditional Jewish woman, shared the Nobel Prize for Medicine in 1977. Judith Resnik, the second female in space, and the first Jewish astronaut, was in the Challenger rocket which orbited the earth in 1984. She was killed with six other American astronauts when the spacecraft exploded in January, 1986.

In American politics, Jewish women have begun to be involved as professional workers as well as traditional volunteers, and some have become elected officials. Bella Abzug's name is well known as an advocate of women's rights in the House of Representatives for many years. In 1984 Madeline Kunin became the first Jewish woman governor in the state of Vermont. In the 1980's Jewish women established their own political action committee (PAC), to back issues and candidates of specific concern to them. This group, called JACPAC (Joint Action Committee PAC) has funded support to candidates who have favorable views on Israel.

As women have entered the arenas of money and power, they have also become philanthropists in increasing numbers. Peggy Tishman, who, only a few years ago commented that women volunteers did not gain top leadership positions in philanthropic Jewish organizations, is herself now President of UJA* Federation in New York. Elaine Winick and Sylvia Hassenfeld, both generous donors to Jewish philanthropic organizations, serve on the Executive Board of the Joint Distribution Committee. Ms. Winick is chairperson of the Public Information Committee and Ms. Hassenfeld heads the Resources and International Development Committee for JDC.

It is hoped that women's contributions to Jewish charities, and their leadership on institutional boards, will

*United Jewish Appeal

influence the choice of where and how this money will be spent. Issues which concern women specifically, such as Jewish day care services, Jewish education, abortion counseling, and changes in both secular and Jewish divorce law, may then receive a higher priority. With the double weapons of financial power and knowledge, women may be able to bring to these problems a Jewish and a female component, and to work towards change.

A recent book, *Jewish and Female,* by Susan Weidman Schneider,[38] explores the many different ways women live today, and how they have changed as a result of their feminist awareness. This encyclopedic work deals with such topics as the range of synagogue observances and women's participation in them; Jewish women within the family; their communal and personal rituals; marriage, intermarriage, and divorce. It guides Jewish women to a wide range of experiences and lifestyles, helping them to meet the needs of family, community, and self.

In the realm of developing rituals, *Miriam's Well* by Penina Adelman[39] also offers ideas for new traditions in women's life-cycle events and for the traditional holiday calendar. Feminists working in these areas have revived old traditions like immersion in the *mikvah* or *Rosh Hodesh* celebrations, and re-interpreted them to offer meaning to modern women.

Perhaps one of the most brilliant minds in the contemporary Jewish literary scene of the 1980's is Cynthia Ozick. In addition to several critically acclaimed novels, she has addressed women's issues in her excellent article "Notes Toward Finding the Right Question" where she claims that granting women equality within Jewish Law is not only "simple justice" for women, but "it is necessary for the sake of the Torah; to preserve and strengthen Torah itself."[40]

Other Jewish women writers today, like Rachel Biale, Blu Greenberg, Francine Klagsbrun, and Susannah Heschel have concentrated respectively on Jewish Law, sociology, and philosophy. *Lilith,* the periodical that addresses the concerns of Jewish feminists in America, contains timely articles on a variety of subjects.

Even with the profusion of writing and thinking in this field, Jewish women's equality remains a challenge. Jewish women's history, because it encompasses women's biographies, historical and sociological analyses and trends, and a variety of legal interpretations and precedents, remains the most effective weapon in meeting that challenge.

Henrietta Szold, in replying to a male friend who wanted to say *Kaddish* on her behalf on the occasion of Szold's mother's death in 1893, commented: Judaism ". . . permits women to take on new challenges in modern life" and ". . . rejoices in their opportunities."

A commitment to Judaism need not preclude a commitment to equal rights and equal recognition of women as a dynamic force in society and history. Jewish history confirms our right to take on this challenge, and gives us precedents to follow while at the same time it binds us more closely to our heritage.

BACKNOTES

INTRODUCTION

1. Israel Abrahams, *Jewish Life in the Middle Ages* (New York, Atheneum, 1975), p. 36.

I. *A TRADITION OF CHANGE:* An Overview

1. Gustav Karpeles, *Jewish Literature and Other Essays,* (Philadelphia, Jewish Publication Society of America, 1895), p. 110.
2. I. Epstein, 'The Jewish Woman in the Responsa: 900 C.E.-1500 C.E.' in *Response: The Jewish Woman — An Anthology,* Summer, 1973, Number 18, p. 23.
3. *Sotah* 20(a); *Kuddushin* 80(b) referring to *Tanna debe Eliyahu;* rabbinic comment that women are temperamentally lightheaded and unfit for study. *"Nashim daatan kalot."*
4. On polygamy see, Erich Brauer, "The Yemenite Jewish Woman," in *The Jewish Review,* London, No. iv., and Schifra Strizower, *Exotic Jewish Communities,* (London and New York, Thomas Yoseloff, 1962), pp. 31-32, 61.
5. *Baba Metzia* 74 (b); *Ketubot* 54(a); *Tannit* 24(a).
6. Israel Abrahams, *Hebrew Ethical Wills,* (Philadelphia, Jewish Publication Society, 1976), (first published in 1926).
7. *Tosefta Megillah,* Chapter 4, Mishna 11.
8. *Megillah* 23(a); Meir of Rothenburg, 108 (Prague).
9. *Berachot* 22(a) and *Hullin* 136(b), p. 782 for the Talmudic passage that the Torah, being a holy object in itself is unaffected by the impurity of contact is found in the Soncino Edition (English translation) of *the Talmud:* order Zera'im; tractate: Berachot, p. 131 and order; Ko'dashim, tractate: Hullin, p. 782.
10. Israel Abrahams, *Jewish Life in the Middle Ages.* (New York, Atheneum, 1975), pp. 25-26.

    'In the separation of the sexes, the synagogue only reflected their isolation in the social life outside. . . . If they did not pray together neither did they play together. The rigid separation of the sexes in prayer seems not to have been earlier, however, than the thirteenth century. The women had their own "court" in the Temple, yet it is not impossible that they prayed together with the men in Talmudic times. Possibly the rigid separation grew out of the medieval custom—more common as the thirteen the century advances—which induced men and women to spend the eve of the Great Fast in synagogue. By the end of the thirteenth century, and perhaps earlier, Jewish women had their own prayer-meetings....'

cf. Leonard Swidler, *Women in Judaism: The Status of Women in Formative Judaism*, (Metuchen, New Jersey. The Scarecrow Press, Inc., 1976), pp. 89-90, who suggests that the segregation of women began in Herod's Temple, 19 B.C.E.

11. e.g. Samuel ben Ali, Baghdad; Rashi, Troyes (France), both in the 11th-12th centuries.

12. *Mishna, Nedarim* IV:3 Judah the Pious, in the Middle Ages, wrote "Girls too should receive instruction in the Holy Law," quoted in J. H. Hertz (ed.), *Pentateuch and Haftorah*, (London, Soncino Press, 1960), p. 925.

13. *Kiddushin* I:7.

14. S. D. Goitein, "New Revelations from the Cairo Geniza: Jewish Women in the Middle Ages," in *Hadassah Magazine*, October, 1973, pp. 14-15, 38-39.
See also William Chomsky, "Jewish Education in the Medieval Period," in *Gratz College Annual of Jewish Studies*, (Philadelphia, 1975, Vol. IV), p. 37.

15. *Yad Melakhim* 1:16, for Maimonides on women and communal office; cf. Abrahams "Parnessa" (President), mater synagogae or pateressa, p. 54 and Meir of Rothenburg, 380 (Lemberg), communal funds were entrusted to women to administer and invest, cited in Epstein, "The Jewish Woman in the Responsa," pp. 24, 30.

16. *Yoma* 66(b), for Rabbi Eliezer's view that 'a woman should apply herself to spinning and not to Torah'.

17. *Kiddushin* 80(b), re 'lightminded'; *Kiddushin* 49(b), re "prone to gossip"; *Rosh Hashana* 22(a) and *Sotah* 47(b), re "inability to serve as witnesses in a Jewish Court *(Beth Din)."*

18. *Yevamot* 62(b), that a man should love his wife as himself and respect her more than himself.

19. Maimonides on wife-beating: *Yad Ishut* 21:3, 10.
"He can beat her with rods if the wife refuses to carry out the wifely duties of washing the husband's hands and feet or to serve him at the table."

20. Swidler, *op. cit.,* Chapter 4.

21. Articles by Paula E. Hyman, "Women in the Jewish Tradition," p. 67, Rachel Adler, "The Jew Who Wasn't There: Halacha and

the Jewish Woman"; p. 77, and Judith Hauptman, "Women in the Talmud," p. 161 in *Response: The Jewish Woman—An Anthology*, (Summer, 1973).

22. I. Epstein, *op. cit.*, "The Jewish Woman in the Responsa," p. 23 in *Response*.

II. *THE FIRST JEWISH HEROINES*

1. *Genesis 3:6* [all biblical quotations are from *The Holy Scriptures* (Philadelphia, Jewish Publication Society, 1957), unless otherwise indicated].

2. See explanation of wife-sister marriage in *The Anchor Bible: Genesis Translated* (introduction and notes by E. A. Speiser), (Garden City, N.Y., Doubleday and Co., 1964), p. 92.
   See also *Encyclopedia Judaica*, Vol. 12, Column 1288 (4) 'Nuzi' "When a Hurrian husband also adopted his wife as a sister, the marriage bonds were very difficult to break and punishment was much more severe than breach of a regular marriage."

3. *The Anchor Bible: op. cit. Genesis*, p. 120 discussing·original text from *Nuzi*.

4. *Genesis 16:1-4*.

5. *Genesis 21:1-4*.

6. See *Code of Hammurabi*, par. 146, referring only to priestesses of *Naditum* rank who were free to marry but not bear children, in James B. Pritchard (ed.), *Ancient Near Eastern Texts Relating to the Old Testament*, with supplement, third ed., (Princeton, Princeton University Press, 1969), and also, Speiser, *op. cit.*, p. 120.

7. Pritchard, *Code of Hammurabi*, pp. 138-167 and relevant paragraphs 117, 128, 129, 132, 133, 133a, 135, 138-141.

8. *Genesis 21:12*.

9. *Genesis 24:58*

10. *Genesis 25:22-23*

11. *Genesis 27:6-29*.

12. *The Anchor Bible: op. cit. Genesis*, p. 212 discusses *birthright* according to father's discretion and *Nuzi* document.

13. *Genesis 30:3*.

14. *Exodus 2:14*.

15. *Exodus 15:20*.

16. J. H. Hertz (ed.) *Pentateuch and Haftorah* (Hebrew Text, English Translation and Commentary), (London, Soncino Press, 1960, 2nd edition), p. 655.
    See also Louis Ginzburg, *Legends of the Jews*, Vol. I, (Philadelphia, The Jewish Publication Society, 1910).

17. *Numbers,* 12.
18. Hertz, *op. cit.,* p. 619, comment on verse 10.
19. *Micah* 6:4.
20. *Numbers* 20:1.
21. *I Samuel* 1:1-2.
22. *Berachot* 31(a).
23. *I Samuel* 1:11.
24. *II Kings* 22:14-20.
25. *Book of Ruth.*
26. *Book of Esther.*
27. *Judges* 4:4.
28. *Judges* 4:6-9.
29. *Judges* 4:17-22.
30. Anna Goldfeld, "Women as Sources of Torah," *Judaism,* Vol. 24, No. 2 (Spring 1975).
31. Hertz, *op. cit.,* p. 281 comment on Judges, 4.
32. *Judges* 5:1-13, 15-16, 19-21, 24-30, 31.

III. *BURIED TREASURES OF EGYPT AND GREECE*

1. *MIBTAHIAH*

1. A. E. Cowley, *Aramaic Papyri of the Fifth Century B.C.* (Oxford, 1923); and Emil G. Kraeling, *The Brooklyn Museum Aramaic Papyri* (New Haven, University Press, 1953).
2. Salo W. Baron, *A Social and Religious History of the Jews,* Vol. 1 (Philadelphia & New York, Columbia University Press and Jewish Publication Society, 1966), pp. 113-114.
3. John Bright, *A History of Israel,* (Philadelphia: Westminster Press, 2nd ed., 1974).
4. Bezalel Porten, *Archives from Elephantine: The Life of an Ancient Jewish Military Colony* (Berkeley and Los Angeles: University of California Press, 1968).
5. In the Elephantine Temple, sacrifices were made to the Jewish God and also the Egyptian gods. This was fairly common practice in Israel, also, and was a subject of distress often referred to by the prophets. See *Encyclopaedia Judaica* "Elephantine."
6. A. H. Sayce, and A. E. Cowley, *Aramaic Papyri Discovered at Assuan* (London, 1906), p. 10.
7. In the 11th century, Rabbi Gershom of Mayence issued a *takkanah* stating that women could not be divorced without their consent.

8. Sayce and Cowley, *op. cit.*
9. See Overview (Chapter I) for a full discussion on this.
10. Sayce and Cowley, Document G., p. 43.
11. *Ibid.*, Document E, p. 40.
12. *Ibid.*, Document F, p. 42.

2. *SAMBATHE*

1. The following are the main sources used in this chapter on the Sibylline Oracles.
   (1) Bate, H. N., *The Sibylline Oracles,* Books III-V, (New York: The MacMillan Co., 1918), reprint 1937.
   (2) Charles, R. H. (ed.), *The Apocrypha and Pseudepigrapha of the Old Testament,* 2 vols., (Oxford, Clarendon Press, 1913).
   (3) Terry, Milton S., *The Sibylline Oracles* (transl. from the Greek), (New York: Hunt and Eaton, 1890).
   (4) *Encyclopedia Judaica,* "Pseudepigrapha," p. 358.
2. Victor Tcherikover, *Hellenistic Civilization and the Jews,* (Philadelphia, Jewish Publication Society, 1959).
3. Seleucid was the first King of the northern Hellenic Empire.
4. Max Radin, *The Jews Among the Greeks and Romans,* (Philadelphia, Jewish Publication Society, 1915), p. 179.
5. Philo. Among Philo's many works are: *On the Decalogue; On the Special Laws: On the Virtues.*
6. Ralph Marcus, "Hellenistic Jewish Literature," in Louis Finkelstein (ed.), *The Jews: Their History, Culture and Religion,* (New York: Harper and Bros., 1955), Vol. II, pp. 764-65.
7. Terry, *op. cit., The Sibylline Oracles,* Book III, pp. 81-82, lines 255-289.
8. Simon Dubnow, *History of the Jews,* From the Beginning to Early Christianity (transl. from the Russian), (New York: Thomas Yoseloff, 1967).
9. *Ibid.*, p. 717.

IV. *DAUGHTERS OF THE LAW*

1. Jacob Neusner, *Invitation to the Talmud,* (New York, Harper and Row, 1973).
2. *Encyclopedia Judaica,* "Talmud," Vol. 15, Col. 750 "Mishna," Vol. 12, Col. 93 "Gemarra." Vol. 7, Col. 368 .
3. *Ibid.*, "Tosefta," Vol. 15, Col. 1283 "Baraita." Vol. 4, Col. 189. See also Philip Birnbaum, *A Book of Jewish Concepts,* (New York, Hebrew Publishing Co., 1975).

4. Neusner, *op. cit.*

5. *Eruvin* 53(b), and see *infra*, Section on Beruriah. The citations refer to the specific book and section of the Talmud and are uniform in every edition.

6. *Kiddushin* 80(b).

7. Leonard Swidler, *Women in Judaism*, (Metuchen, New Jersey, The Scarecrow Press, Inc., 1976), Chapter 4, "Women in Relation to Cult and Torah."

8. *Sotah* 20a.

9. *Yerushalmi Sotah* 3:4.

10. *Yoma* 66(b).

11. *Baba Metzia* 59(a) and (b), for discussion and explanation of Rabbi Eliezer's excommunication.

12. *Encyclopaedia Judaica*, "Imma Shalom." Vol. 8, col. 1298.

13. *Baba Metzia* 59(b); See Soncino edition, p. 354, fn. (4).

14. Swidler, *op. cit.*, pp. 97-104. See also Judith Hauptman, "Women in the Talmud," *Response* Magazine, Summer, 1973, No. 18, and Judith Hauptman, "Images of Women in the Talmud" in Rosemary Radford, *Religion and Sexism, Images of Women in the Jewish and Christian Traditions* (New York, 1974).

15. Swidler, *op. cit.*, p. 99; See also *Baba Metzia*, 1:6.

16. Rabbi Meir's tolerant attitude toward women's study was indicated by their admission to his lectures. Trude Weiss-Rosmarin, *Jewish Women Through the Ages*, (New York, The Jewish Book Club, 1940), pp. 33-34. On *Beruriah*, see also Nahida Remy, *The Jewish Woman*, (New York, Bloch Publishing Co., 1916), pp. 111-112. Remy states that Beruriah should not be mistaken for the convert Beturia, or Veluria, who converted to Judaism and became known as Sarah.

17. *Avodah Zarah* 18(b), Rashi ad locum.

18. Swidler, *op. cit.*, p. 101. For 'Status of Women in the World of the Talmud,' see Salo W. Baron, *A Social and Religious History of the Jews*, 15 vols. (New York, Columbia University Press, 1952), Vol. II, p. 235-241.

V. *POETS AND WARRIORS: OASES IN A DESERT*

1. Heinrich Graetz, *Popular History of the Jews*, (New York, Hebrew Publishing Co., 1937, 5th ed.), Vol. II, Chap. X, p. 488ff.

2. *Ibid.*

3. John Bright, *A History of Israel*, (Philadelphia, Westminster Press, 1964, 2nd ed.), and Solomon Grayzel, *A History of the Jews*, (Philadelphia, Jewish Publication Society, 1947) Chap. V, p. 245.

4. Graetz, *op. cit.,* p. 492, S. D. Goitein, *Jews and Arabs: Their Contacts Through the Ages.* (New York, Schocken Books, 1974, 3rd ed.), pp. 186, 203.

5. Professor Joanna Spector of the Jewish Theological Seminary, New York, has written on the oral folksongs of Jewish Yemenite women. On the vernacular poetry of these women, see Nissim Benjamin Gamieli, *Ahavat Teman,* (Tel Aviv, 1975).

6. Sham'ah, (which means candle) Shabazi was buried in a Tomb in Al-'udayn in Southern Yemen, a holy shrine for pilgrimages. Her own religious poetry may be immersed in the Shabazi family work, as suggested in correspondence with Professor S. D. Goitein.

7. Graetz, *op cit.,* pp. 495-498, On the Yemenite Jewish Kingdom, see also Schifra Strizower, *Exotic Jewish Communities,* (London, Thomas Yoseloff, 1962), Chapter I, 'The Yemenite Jews,' pp. 11-47.

8. For references to Sarah see David S. Margoliouth, *Relations Between Arabs and Israelites,* (London, Oxford University Press, 1924) and Meyer Waxman, *Blessed Is the Daughter,* (New York, Shengold Publishers, Inc., 1968), p. 39.

9. Waxman, *op. cit.,* p. 39.

10. The poem of Sarah, describing the downfall of the Quraiza tribe is found in: Kitab-l-Aghani,' The Book of Songs,' (Sarah's poem translated from the Arabic by Aliza Arzt), first published in German in Th. Noeldeke, *Beitrage zue Poesie der Alten Araber,* (Hannover, 1864), pp. 53, 54. (We wish to thank Dr. Israel O. Lehman, of the Hebrew Union College, Cincinnati, for locating this volume.)

11. Graetz, *op. cit.,* Vol. III, p. 67. The Graetz statement here is a conjecture, but appears to agree with the facts related in the sources given, supra footnote 10.

12. *Ibid,* p. 509-510.

13. Translated from *Kitab-l-Aghani* by Aliza Arzt. (The editor of *Kitab* is Abu al-Faraj al-Isbahani during the tenth century.

14. *Jewish Encyclopedia,* "Kahinah," Vol. 7. See also, under "Diah Cahena," in Solomon Grayzel, *A History of the Jews,* (Philadelphia, Jewish Publication Society, 1968), p. 233. (This edition, New American Library, Inc., Mentor PB.)

15. *Jewish Encyclopedia, op. cit.,* "Kahinah."

16. See also, *Sisters of Exile:* Sources on the Jewish Woman. (Pamphlet published by Ichud Habonim Labor Zionist Youth, 575 Sixth Avenue, New York, N.Y.)

17. *Jewish Encyclopedia* and *Sisters of Exile, op. cit.*

18. *Sisters of Exile, op. cit.,* p. 32.
19. Graetz, *op. cit.* p. 512.
20. Grayzel, *op. cit.* p. 233. See also Nahida Remy, *The Jewish Woman,* (New York, Bloch Publishing Co., 1916) p. 106.
21. See *al-Maqqari,* a late anthology on Arabic poetry. Kasmunah is also referred to as "Qasmuna" and "Xemona."
22. *Jewish Encyclopedia,* "Kasmunah." Vol. 7, p. 451.
23. Gustav Karpeles, "Women in Jewish Literature," in *Jewish Literature and Other Essays,* (Philadelphia, Jewish Publication Society, 1895) p. 118.
24. *Ibid.,* p. 118.
25. *Ibid.,* p. 118.

VI. *STOREHOUSE OF JEWISH WRITINGS*

1. For a major work on the Cairo Geniza, see: S. D. Goitein, *A Mediterranean Society: Volume I, Economic Foundations,* (Berkeley & Los Angeles, University of California Press, 1967) *A Mediterranean Society: Volume II, The Community,* Berkeley, Los Angeles and London, University of California Press, 1971).
2. "Solomon Schechter" Vol. 14, Col. 948 And "Geniza" Vol. 7 Col. 404, in *Encyclopaedia Judaica.*
3. Solomon Schechter, "A Hoard of Hebrew Manuscripts" in *Studies in Judaism,* (Philadelphia, Jewish Publication Society, 1938 (second series, 1908), pp. 2-30.
4. Jacob Mann, *Texts and Studies in Jewish History and Literature,* (Cincinnati, University of Cincinnati, 1932). Mann reprinted selections from Geniza documents with translations.
5. S. D. Goitein, *Jews and Arabs, Their Contacts Through the Ages,* (New York, Schocken Books, (3rd ed.), 1974), pp. 92-95.
6. Solomon Grayzel, *A History of the Jews,* (Philadelphia, Jewish Publication Society, 1968 (Mentor PB), pp. 246-68, 250-55.
7. Rabbi Gershom of Mayence was also referred to as "The Light of the Exile," and the traditional scholarly title of "Rav," teacher, was changed to "Rabbenu," our teacher. This was a token of love and esteem.
8. Rashi's father and teacher had been a student of Rabbenu Gershom in his Academy at Mayence.
9. Before this, Jewish men, according to Biblical Law, were permitted more than one wife. Although European Jewish men rarely took more than one wife, this decree of Gershom's was nevertheless considered an important step for the Jewish community, and especially for women. Rabbenu's second *takkanah,*

that a woman's consent be obtained before a divorce was granted also protected women.

10. *Mishneh Torah*, R. Moses ben Maimon (Maimonides), 14 Volumes, completed in 1180.

11. Grayzel, *op. cit.*, p. 234.

12. *Ibid.* pp. 312-13. The exception to the ruling regarding the wearing of the "badge" by the Jews occurred in Christian Spain where Jews were, at that time, very prosperous and powerful, and were therefore exempt from the Church's decree.

13. S. D. Goitein, *op. cit.*, Vol. I, Chapter on "Professions of Women," pp. 127.130.

14. S. D. Goitein, "The Jewish Family in the Days of Moses Maimonides," in *Conservative Judaism*, Vol. XXIX, Number I Fall, 1974, pp. 25-36 ©1975 by Rabbinical Assembly. Reprinted by permission of Rabbinical Assembly.

15. S. D. Goitein, "Messianic Troubles in Baghdad"; in *Jewish Quarterly Review*, Vol. 1952-53, pp. 57-76.

16. S. D. Goitein, "New Revelations from the Cairo Geniza: Jewish Women in the Middle Ages," *Hadassah Magazine*, October, 1973 pp.14-15, 38-39. Reprinted by permisssion of Hadassah Magazine.

17. *Ibid.* p. 15, 38-39.

18. See also, S. D. Goitein, "A Jewish Businesswoman of the Eleventh Century," the 75th anniversary volume of the *Jewish Quarterly Review*, (Philadelphia, 1967) pp. 225-242.

19. S. D. Goitein points out in "The Jewish Family in the Time of Moses Maimonides," supra fn. 14, that some of the so-called "Jewish Virtues" with regard to family, children, education, care of parents, etc., are dictated by, and due to the framework of Jewish Law.

20. S. D. Goitein, "New Revelations from the Cairo Geniza"; *op. cit.*

21. *Ibid.*

22. In the 10th and 11th centuries, the Jews of Fostat often had to ransom Jews captured in war, or by pirates, and was the duty of the nearest community, rather than (distant) relatives, to raise such money.

23. Goitein, S. D., "New Revelations from the Cairo Geniza," *op. cit.*, and *A Mediterranean Society — Foundations, op. cit.*, volume III of *The Family*.

VII. *SISTERS IN EXILE*

1. Jacob R. Marcus, *The New in the Medieval World: A Source Book 315-1791* (New York, Atheneum, 1974) pp. 273, 415, 432.

2. Israel Abrahams, *Jewish Life in the Middle Ages* (New York, Atheneum, 1975) p. 54. See also Epstein, "The Jewish Woman in the Responsa", in *Response, The Jewish Woman: An Anthology,* Summer, 1973, pp. 23-31.

3. The daughter of Samuel ben Ali was described in the travel diary of Rabbi Petachiach of Regensburg, *Sibuv HaRav Rabbi Petahiah miRegensburg,* Dr. L. Grunhut (ed.), (Jerusalem, 1967) pp. 9-10.

4. *Ibid.* See also Trude Weiss-Rosmarin, *Jewish Women Through the Ages,* (New York, Jewish Book Club, 1940), pp. 63-64. Reference to Bat HaLevi, daughter of Rabbi Samuel ben Ali, in Baghdad in: Gustav Karpeles, *Jewish Literature and Other Essays,* (Philadelphia, Jewish Publication Society, 1895), in the essay on "Women in Jewish Literature," pp. 106-144, and p. 117. See also A. Posner, "Literature for Jewish Women" in Leo Jung (ed.), *The Jewish Library,* Vol. 3, *The Jewish Woman* (New York, 1934), pp. 63-83.

5. Karpeles, *op. cit.,* p. 117, See also M. Kayserling, *Die Jüdischen Frauen en der Geschichte Literatur und Kunst,* (Leipzig, 1879), and Nahida Remy, *The Jewish Woman,* transl. by Louise Mannheimer, (New York, Bloch Publishing Co., 1916) pp. 114, 168.

6. Dulcie of Worms, sometimes also referred to as *Dolca,* was the wife of Rabbi Eleazer of Worms, author of *Rokeach,* a study of the dietary laws. The date of Dulcie's martyr death is given as 1213 C.E. by Karpeles and Weiss-Rosmarin. But cf. Israel Zinberg, *A History of Jewish Literature,* transl. and edit. by Bernard Martin, (New York, K'tav, 1975), Vol. VII, p. 23, which gives the date as 1196 and quotes Rabbi Eleazer praising her.

7. Zinberg, *op. cit.,* p. 23.

8. On the role of the *firzogerin,* or foresayer, see Zinberg, *op. cit.,* pp. 23, 29. The word *foresayer* is translated from the Yiddish and variously spelled *vorsugerin* (A woman reader) and *woilkenivdicke.* See Solomon Schechter, *Studies in Judaism,* First series, 1911, "Women in Temple and Synagogue," Chap. xiii, *vorsugerin* was "one who translated prayers into the vernacular for the less learned women, and (she) was found in every synagogue in Poland and known in London".

9. Zinberg, *op. cit.,* Vol VII, p. 23, refers to Marat Guta Bat R. Nathan, (died 1308) as another *firzogerin* of the Middle Ages whose name has been preserved.

10. Leo Jung (ed.), *The Jewish Library:* Woman, Vol. 3, (New York, Soncino Press, 1970), pp. 76-77, or an earlier edition, *The Jewish*

Library: The Jewish Woman (New York, 1934), p. 233 on Rashi's daughters.

11. *Ibid.* Rashi's daughters are also referred to in Karpeles, *op. cit.,* p. 118 and Weiss-Rosmarin, *op. cit.,* p. 63. See also *Jewish Encyclopedia* and *Encyclopaedia Judaica,* under heading "Rashi, Solomon bar Isaac, of Troyes, France (1040-1105)."

12. On the medieval Jewish businesswoman of England, and particularly Norwich, see, Vivian D. Lipman, *The Jewish Woman in Medieval England,* delivered as a Presidential Address on November 19, 1934 before the Jewish Historical Society of England, 1967).

13. *Ibid.,* Lipman, *The Jewish Woman in Medieval England.*

14. Zinberg, *op. cit.* Vol. VII, pp. 241-242. See also, Meyer Waxman, *A History of Jewish Literature,* (New York, Bloch Publishing Co., 1938-1941), Vol. II, chap. xii.

15. Muriel Jay Hughes, *Women Healers in the Middle Ages,* (New York, Kings Crown Press, 1943).

16. *Jewish Encyclopedia,* Article on "Alchemy," Vol I, for information on "Maria Hebrea."

17. Zinberg, *op. cit.,* p. 108.

18. *Ibid.* See reference to Bibliographer Johann Christoph Wolf, p. 368. See also Karpeles, *op. cit.,* p. 119: "In the sixteenth century their names (women) reappear on the records, not only as Talmudic scholars, but also as writers of history in the German language. Litte of Ratisbon composed a history of King David in the celebrated Book of Samuel, a poem...."

19. Solomon B. Freehof, *The Responsa Literature* and *A Treasury of Responsa,* (New York, K'tav, 1973). Re Eva Bacharach and her grandson Jair Hayyim, who wrote *Havot Ja'ir,* "His book of responsa is named in reference to his grandmother Eva Bacharach, who interestingly enough, was herself famous as a rabbinic scholar. The title *Havot Ja'ir* means "The Tents of Ja'ir" (son of Menassah) from Deut. 3:14; but the first word *Havot* sounds like his grandmother's name Hava, or Eva, and hence the title." p. 85.

20. On Rebecca Tiktiner, see Zinberg, *op. cit.* pp. 241, 285, and Remy, *op. cit.* pp. 114, 168. Remy, herself a convert to Judaism, states that Rebecca "Held the position of Preacher and gained a special distinction by writing for women. She lived in Poland around 1520 and published *Duties for Women.*" Karpeles, *op. cit.* pp. 119-120 refers to the literary language of Jewish women during the 16th-17th centuries as *Jüdendeutsch* or *Altweiberdeutsch* (Old Women's German).

21. The *Schulchan Aruch* was written by Joseph Caro, a Sephardic Jew in 1564 and first printed in Venice. Moses Isserles, a Polish rabbi, made the code applicable to Ashkenazi Jews also.

22. YIVO Institute for Jewish Research, 1048 Fifth Avenue, New York, N.Y.

23. The YIVO librarian Zalman Alpert referred us to the Jewish Theological Seminary for the rare book *Meneket Rivkah* and the article on *Meneket Rivkah*.

24. *The Bulletin of the Library of the Jewish Theological Seminary,* Column by Dr. Menahem Schmelzer, Library Newsletter, Spring, 1974.

25. *Meneket Rivkah,* Courtesy of the Jewish Theological Seminary Library, Tiktiner, Rebecca bat Meir, *Meneket Rivkah,* Cracow, 1618.

26. Gustav Zeltner (1672-1738), *De Rebecca Polona,* (Rostock, 1719)

27. *Meneket Rivkah, op. cit.*

28. *Ibid.*

29. "Simhat Torah" Poem from *Tehinnah Imahot Gedolah,* translated in Zinberg, *op. cit.,* p. 285.

30. Law of Divorce: Deuteronomy 24:1-4. On the *Agunah,* see *Ruth* 1:13, and in the *Talmud, Yevamot* 122 (b), and Maimonides, *Yad Gerushim* 13:29.

31. Franz Kobler, (ed.), *A Treasury of Jewish Letters,* 2 volumes, Vol. I, (New York, East and West Library, Farrar Strauss and Young, 1952), "Letter of Donna Sarah."

32. *Encyclopaedia Judaica,* "Byzantine Empire," Vol. 4, p. 1554.

33. *I Samuel* 14:3. See also *Exodus* 28:28-31, for a description of the "Breastplate of Judgment" which was used for a "lot" oracle by the High Priest, and also the explanation given by J. H. Hertz (ed.) *Pentateuch and Haftorahs,* (London, Socino Press, 1960), p 342.

34. Kobler, *op. cit.,* Vol. I. "Letter of Lady Maliha."

35. S. D. Goitein, *Jews and Arabs; Their Contacts Through the Ages,* (New York, Schocken Books, 3rd ed., 1974) p. 186. Photograph of the Rebbetzin Mizrachi manuscript, Courtesy of Hebrew Union College, Cincinnati, and the assistance of Dr. Israel O. Lehman, Hebrew Union College Library.

36. For information on the Kurdish women and their prominence in tribal leadership see *Encyclopaedia Brittanica.* "Kurdistan," and "Kurds," Vol. 13.

37. *Encyclopaedia Judaica,* "Kurdistan," Vol. 10, p. 1298.

38. For information on the Aramaic language of the Jewish community in Kurdistan see *Encyclopaedia Judaica,* "Amadiya," Vol. 2, p. 786.

39. Jacob Mann, *Texts and Studies in Jewish History and Literature.* (Cincinnati, Hebrew Union College, 1932), p. 483. The letter of the Rebbetzin Mizrachi is printed in Hebrew in *Texts and Studies,* translated in this work by Isaac Taitz.
40. *Ibid.*

VIII. *SCRIBES AND PRINTERS*

1. Solomon Schechter, *Studies in Judaism,* First series, 1911, "Women in Temple and Synagogue," Chap. xiii, p. 264.
2. S. D. Goitein, *Jews and Arabs: Their Contact Through the Ages,* (New York, Schocken Books, 3rd. ed., 1974), p. 186. See also: *Encyclopaedia Judaica,* "Benayah," Vol. 4, and Jacob Saphir, *Maasei le-Teman,* (ed., A. Yaari, 1951), pp. 173-174. Saphir visited Yemen in 1859 and describes the Pentateuch that Miriam copied.
3. Gustav Karpeles, *Jewish Literature and Other Essays* (Philadelphia, Jewish Publication Society, 1895), in the essay "Women in Jewish Literature," p. 117, and Leo Jung (ed.) *The Jewish Library: The Jewish Woman* (New York, 1934), p. 233. Breslau (Wroclaw) is now in Poland, on the Polish-German border.
4. See Zotenberg, *Catalogue des Manuscrits Hebreux de la Biblioteque Imperial,* 1866, p. 55, #408.
5. David Amram, *Makers of Hebrew Books in Italy.* (Philadelphia, Julius Greenstone, 1909), p. 32.
6. Amram, *op. cit.,* p. 32 for reference to Estellina Conat.
7. *Ibid.*
8. *Jewish Encyclopedia,* "Typographers," Vol. 12.
9. Israel Zinberg, A History of Jewish Literature, transl. and edit. by Bernard Martin, (New York K'tav, 1975), Vol. VII, p. 242, See also Jung, *op. cit.,* (3rd series, 1970), p. 68.
10. Zinberg, *op cit.,* p. 242.
11. *Jewish Encyclopedia,* "Typographers," Vol. 12.
12. Zinberg, *op. cit.,* p. 242.
13. Ella of Dessau, 1696, prayer book page. Courtesy of Jewish Theological Seminary Library, librarians Anna Kleban and Susan Young.
14. Cecil Roth, *The House of Nasi: Donna Gracia* (Philadelphia, Jewish Publication Society, 1948).
15. *Ibid.*
16. Zinberg, *op. cit.,* p. 242.

IX. *LIBERATED WOMEN: RENAISSANCE STYLE*

1. Solomon Grayzel, *A History of the Jews,* (Philadelphia, Jewish Publication Society of America, 1968), p. 249 (New American Library Mentor PB).
2. *Ibid.,* p. 412.
3. *Ibid.,* p. 415.
4. Cecil Roth, *The Jews in the Renaissance,* (Philadelphia, Jewish Publication Society of America, 1959), p. 54. Women physicians in Italy most likely attended only women.
5. *Ibid.,* p. 300. Andrea Calmo wrote of the Venetian Jewess Madonna Bellina in the 16th century Lettere Piacevoli (ii. 33).
6. *Ibid.,* p. 285.
7. *Ibid.,* p. 50.
8. See infra, Chapter X. Benvenida Abrabanel, in Ferrara, Italy was the tutor to Leonora, daughter of the Spanish Viceroy.
9. Women as ritual slaughterers, See Salo W. Baron, *A Social and Religious History of the Jews,* (New York, Columbia University Press, 1937, 2nd ed., 1952) Vol XII (1200-1650), p. 88. Women by then were not ritual slaughterers, except in Italy, where they were permitted as shochetot and there are licenses existing from that time. See also S. D. Goitein, *Jews and Arabs: Their Contacts Through the Ages,* (New York, Schocken Books, 3rd ed., 1964), p. 187, that women officiated as shochetot or ritual slaughterers, and that there is nothing in Jewish Law against it.
10. Roth, *op cit.,* p. 51.
11. Cecil Roth, *The Jews of Venice,* (Philadelphia, Jewish Publication Society of America, 1930), p. 237 and see also, Nathaniel Kravitz, *3000 Years of Hebrew Literature,* (Chicago, Swallow Press 1972) pp. 399-400.
12. *Jewish Encyclopedia,* "Ascarelli, Deborah," Vol. 2.
13. Nahida Remy, *The Jewish Woman,* translated by Louise Mannheimer, (New York, Bloch Publishing Co., 1916), p. 140.
14. *Devora Ascarelli,* Sindacato Italiano Arti, (Roma, published by Pellegrino Ascarelli, 1925). Other copies of her work exist on microfilm in the Biblioteca Angelica, Rome, Italy.
15. The Apocrypha, a Greek word meaning "Hidden," is the collection of ancient writings which were not included in the Bible. See *Introduction to The Apocrypha,* (New Hyde Park, N.Y., University Books, Inc., 1962).
16. *The Apocrypha,* a facsimile of the famous Nonesuch edition of 1924, reprinted according to the authorized version of 1611,

(New Hyde Park, N.Y., University Books, Inc.) p. 165, The History of Susanna.

17. *Devora Ascarelli* (Roma, 1925), pp. 5, 6.
18. Krafitz, *op. cit.,* p. 400. On Sara Sullam see also, Remy, *op. cit.,* pp. 140-152. Remy refers to two biographies of Sullam, by E. David, and Leone di Modena, (Paris, 1877).
19. *Manifesto* of Sara Coppia Sullam, against Baldassare Bonifaccio Venice, 1621. See also Remy, *op. cit.,* pp. 148-151.
20. Franz Kobler, (ed.), *A Treasury of Jewish Letters,* (New York, Farrar, Strauss and Young, Inc., 1952), Vol. II, pp. 442-447.

X. *WOMEN OF INFLUENCE*

1. *Encyclopaedia Britannica,* "Byzantine Empire," Vol. 4, p. 518 and "Turkey," Vol. 22.
2. Solomon Grayzel, *A History of the Jews,* (New York, Mentor-New American Library PB, 1968), pp. 375-378.
3. *Encyclopaedia Judaica,* "Abrabanel," Vol. 3.
4. *Jewish Encyclopedia,* "Benvenida Abravanel," Vol. I, and see also Salo W. Baron, *A Social and Religious History of the Jews,* 12 vols. (New York, Columbia University Press, 2nd ed., 1952), Vol. XII.
5. Cecil Roth, *The House of Nasi: Dona Gracia* (Philadelphia, The Jewish Publication Society of America, 1947), pp. 61-67, 570-579.
6. Roth, *op. cit.,* p. 68, quoting a contemporary chronicler Imanuel Aboab.
7. *Ibid.,* pp. 17-20, on Beatrice de Luna's family and nephew.
8. *Ibid.,* pp. 13-14.
9. *Ibid.,* pp. 21-49, on thue Nasi-Mendes family in Antwerp.
10. *Ibid.,* pp. 50-64 on the Nasi-Mendes family in Venice. Grayzel, *op. cit.,* p. 412 on the origin of the word *ghetto,* from the Italian word "geto," iron foundry, first used in 1516.
11. Roth, op. cit., pp. 60-63.
12. The name *Hannah* is derived from the Hebrew word "Chen," for Grace.
13. Roth, *op. cit.,* pp. 73-74 on the dedication of the Ferrara Bible, translated from Hebrew into Spanish and signed "Yom Tob Athias and Abraham Usque."
14. *Ibid.,* pp. 112-113.
15. Cecil Roth, *The House of Nasi: Joseph, Duke of Naxos,* (Philadelphia, The Jewish Publication Society, 1948).

16. Roth, *op. cit., Dona Gracia,* p. 133, quoting Samuel Usque.
17. *Ibid., Dona Gracia,* p. 132, quoting Rabbi Moses Almosnino of Salonica.
18. *Ibid., Dona Gracia,* p. 133.
19. The original letter from "Anna the Hebrew" to Caterina Sforza can be found in, Pier Desiderio Pasolini, *Caterina Sforza,* Rome, 1893, III, pp. 608-609. A translation of the letter in Jacob R. Marcus, *The Jew in the Medieval World,* A Source Book: 315-1791, (New York, Atheneum, 1974), pp. 399-400. Jewish women in Italy who were expert cosmeticians, and excerpts from Anna's letter in Cecil Roth, *The Jews in the Renaissance,* (Philadelphia, The Jewish Publication Society of America, 1959), p. 48.
20. Marcus, *op. cit.,* p. 399.
21. Roth, *op. cit.,* p. 48.
22. Marcus, *op. cit.,* p. 399-400.
23. *Jewish Encyclopedia,* "Kiera, (Esther)." Vol. 7. p. 487.
24. Roth, *op. cit.,* pp. 105-107; Grayzel, *op. cit.,* p. 402.
25. *Encyclopaedia Britannica,* "Turkish History," Vol. 22.
26. *Jewish Encyclopedia,* "Kiera, (Esther)," Vol. 7, p. 487.
27. Roth, *op. cit.,* p. 106. For other reference to Esther Kiera see a monograph by Abraham Galante, (Constantinople, 1926) and a study by J. H. Mordtmann, *Die Jüdischen Kira im Serai der Sultane* (Mittelungen des Seminars fur Orientalische Sprachen XXXII, ii).
28. *Jewish Encyclopedia,* "Kiera," Vol. 7, p. 487.
29. *Encyclopaedia Britannica,* "Turkey," Vol. 22.
30. Roth, *op. cit.,* p. 105.
31. Cecil Roth, *The House of Nasi: Joseph, Duke of Naxos,* (Philadelphia, The Jewish Publication Society of America, 1949). Samuel Shulan published a chronicle, *Yuasin,* by Zacuto, at her expense.
32. *Jewish Encyclopedia,* "Kiera," Vol. 7. Refers to several books in European languages in which Esther Kiera figured as the heroine.
33. See Chapter VII, "Sisters in Exile."
34. The original letter of Esperanza Malchi to Queen Elizabeth in Ellis, *Original Letters Illustrative of English History,* III, 53-5. The letter is dated November 16, 1599. See also Franz Kobler, *A Treasury of Jewish Letters* (New York, Farrar, Strauss and Young, 1952), Vol. II, pp. 391 and Roth, *op. cit., Dona Gracia,* pp. 107-108.

XI. *VOICES FROM THE GHETTO*

1. *The Jews of Czechoslovakia.* Historical Studies and Surveys, Volume I. (New York, Jewish Publication Society of America, Philadelphia Society for the History of Czechoslovak Jews, 1968).

2. C. V. Wedgewood, *The Thirty Years War*, (New Haven, Yale University Press, 1939).

3. Franz Kobler (ed.), *A Treasury of Jewish Letters*, 2 vols. (New York, Farrar, Strauss and Young, Inc., 1952), pp. 449-450, Vol. II, #66, "Private Letters from the Ghetto of Prague, Written on the Threshold of the Thirty Years War."

4. *Ibid.*

5. *Ibid.*, p. 464.

6. *Ibid.*, p. 479, footnote #47.

7. *Ibid.*, p. 479, footnote #49.

8. Alfred Landau and Bernard Wachstein, *Jüdische Privatbriefe aus dem Jahre 1619 — Nach den Originalen des K.O.K. Haus.* (Wien, 1911). (Research from the Germany by Alice Morawetz).

9. Kobler, *op. cit.*, p. 479, footnote #58.

10. *Ibid.*, pp. 470-472 (Henele's letter).

11. *Ibid.*, pp. 472-473 (Resel Landau's letter).

12. *Ibid.*, pp. 474, (Freidel's letter).

13. Wedgewood, *op. cit.*

14. Solomon Grayzel, A History of the Jews, (Philadelphia, The Jewish Publication Society of America, 1966), Chapter V, part 2.

15. *Ibid.*, Chap. V, part 3. As a result of this "announcement" pronouncing the name of God as it is written (something never done by Jews since the destruction of the Temple and before then only by the High Priest on special occasions), Sabbatai Zvi was excommunicated by the leaders of the Smyrna Jewish Community.

16. *The Memoirs of Glückel of Hameln, (1646-1724)* written by Herself. Translated from the original Yiddish and edited by Beth Zion Abrahams. (New York; Thomas Yoseloff, 1962), Book V, pp. 125-126. The *Memoirs of Glückel of Hameln* in original Yiddish published by David Kaufmann with introduction in German, in 1896. In 1910, Bertha Pappenheim published a complete German translation. A Hebrew version, by A. Z. Rabinovitz in 1929. An English version, *The Memoirs of Glückel of Hameln* was

translated by Marvin Lowenthal. (New York, Harper and Bros. [Behrman Book House] 1932). *YIVO-Bleter*, VI (1934), pp. 138-144, provides a bibliography on Glückel, by J. Shatzky. (YIVO Institute for Jewish Research).

17. Solomon, Schechter, *Studies in Judaism* (Philadelphia, Jewish Publication Society, 1908), p. 128.

18. *Memoirs, op. cit.*, Book I, pp. 7-8.

19. *Ibid.*, Book II, p. 13.

20. *Hedler* — a Hebrew word meaning literally "room" was used in Yiddish to mean *school* where the children received a religious education.

21. *Memoirs, op. cit.*, Book II, p. 13.

22. *Ibid.*, pp. 13-14.

23. *Ibid.*, Book II, pp. 32-33.

24. *Ibid.*, Book III, pp. 45-46.

25. *Ibid.*, Book V, p. 110.

26. The Jews traditionally observe seven days *(Shiva,* Hebrew word for seven) of mourning in their home immediately following the death of a close relative.

27. *Memoirs, op. cit.*, Book V, pp. 109-110.

XII. *ONE STEP AHEAD — HASIDIC WOMEN*

1. Harry M. Rabinowicz, *The World of Hasidism,* (London, Hartford House, 1970), Chap. 21, "Lady Rabbis and Rabbinic Daughters," pp. 202-210.

2. Milton Aron, *Ideas and Ideals of the Hasidim,* (New York, The Citadel Press, Inc., 1964), Chap. X, "The Worlds of Six Hassidic Masters," pp. 33, 84, 144, 290. Eli Wiesel, *Four Hasidic Masters and Their Struggle Against Melancholy,* (Notre Dame, London, Univ. of Notre Dame Press, 1978), "Rebbe Barukh of Medzebozh," pp. 33-36.

3. Dan Ben Amos and Jerome R. Mintz (eds.), *In Praise of the Baal Shem Tov.* (Bloomington, London, Univ. of Indiana Press, 1970), "The Interruption of the Besht's Vision," #114, p. 136.

4. Meyer Levin, *Hassidic Stories* (Tel Aviv, Greenfield Ltd., 1932), "Rabbi Israel's Daughter," p. 113.

5. Dan Ben Amos and Jerome R. Mintz, *op. cit.,* #222, p. 223. See also Elie Wiesel, *op. cit.,* for another version of this tale.

6. *Encyclopaedia Judaica*, Vol. II, "Adel."

7. Jacob S. Minkin, *The Romance of Hassidism,* (New York, Thomas

Yoseloff, 1955), pp. 233, 345-46. See also, Aron, *op. cit.,* pp. 33, 85, 144.

8. Rabinowicz, re *Mitnagdim,* pp. 57-58, 66.
9. Charles Raddock, *Portrait of a People,* (New York, Judaica Press, 1965), Vol. II, pp. 256, on women's place in religious activities.
10. S. A. Horodezky, "The Jewish Woman in Hassidism," in *Ha-Hassiduth,* Vol. IV, pp. 68-71; Rabinowicz, p. 205.
11. Aron, *op. cit.,* pp. 110-13.
12. In most synagogues the name of a person being given a special *Mi Sheberach* prayer, ("He that Blessed Abraham Isaac and Jacob Bless. . ."—insert the name of the person to be blessed) for illness, for example, is always referred to as the son or daughter of the mother.
13. Minkin, *op. cit.,* pp. 343, 346.
14. Rabinowicz, *op. cit.,* p. 204.
15. Aron, *op. cit.,* pp. 190, 193-94.
16. Rabinowicz, *op. cit.,* p. 204.
17. Rabinowicz, *op. cit.,* p. 203; Aron, pp. 110-13.
18. Rabinowicz, *op. cit.,* p. 204.
19. Charles Raddock, "Once There Was a Female Hassidic Rabbi," in *The Jewish Digest,* December, 1967, pp. 20-21.
20. I. B. Singer, *Shosha,* (New York, Fawcett, 1978).
21. *Encyclopaedia Judaica,* "Ludomir, Maid of," Vol. XI, p. 554.

XIII. *THE THREE PORTALS*

1. *Encyclopaedia Britannica,* "Yiddish Language," Vol. 23; Charles Madison, *Yiddish Literature: Its Scope and Major Writers,* (New York: Shocken Books, 1971), p. 2.
2. Israel Zinberg, *A History of Jewish Literature,* translated and edited by Bernard Martin, (New York, K'tav, 1975), Vol. VII, pp. 124-125, "Old Yiddish Literature from Its Origins to the Haskalah Period."
3. Zinberg, *op. cit.,* pp. 252-256; *Encyclopaedia Judaica,* "Bas-Tovim," Vol. 4, p. 318; See also, *Jewish Encyclopedia, "Devotional Literature,"* Vol. 4.
4. H. Schauss, *Guide to the Jewish Holy Days,* (New York, Schocken Books, 1969), pp. 273-275.
5. *Shloysha Sheorim,* translated from the Yiddish by Joseph Adler. Prayer pamphlet. Courtesy of YIVO Institute for Jewish Research.

6. Zinberg, *op. cit.*, pp. 256-257. See also, Meyer Waxman, *A History of Jewish Literature*, (New York, Bloch Publishers, 1938-41), pp. 618, 623, 642; N. B. Minkoff, "Old Yiddish Literature," in *The Jewish People: Past and Present*, 3 Vols. (New York, Jewish Encyclopedia Handbooks, CYCO, 1946-1952) Vol. III, pp. 145-164; Yudel Mark, "Yiddish Literature" in Louis Finkelstein (ed.), *The Jews: Their History, Culture and Religion*, (New York, Schocken Books, 1973), pp. 417-468.

7. See Chapter VII, "Sisters in Exile."

8. Zinberg, *op. cit.*, pp. 254-256.

9. Translated from the Yiddish by Joseph Adler.

10. *Ibid.*

11. See Chapter III, "Daughters of the Law," for allusion to this quotation by Ima Shalom.

12. *Techinah of the Matriarchs for Rosh Hodesh Elul,* by Serel Segal Rapoport. An early edition, Frankfort, 1783, is referred to by M. Steinschneider, the bibliographer. Quoted in *The Jewish People: Past and Present*, Vol. III, and Zinberg, *op. cit.*, p. 257.

13. Zinberg, *op. cit.*, pp. 257-259.

14. Solomon Freehof, *Devotional Literature in the Vernacular;* in *Yearbook of the Central Conference of American Rabbis*, Vol XXXIII (1923).

15. Solomon Grayzel, *A History of the Jews*, (Philadelphia, The Jewish Publication Society of America, Mentor PB, 1968), pp. 468-471.

16. Frank Kobler, (ed.), *Her Children Call Her Blessed* (New York, Stephen Daye Press, 1955), pp. 143-144. "Excerpts from the Will of Frau Frumet (Fani) Wolf" reprinted here courtesy of Frederich Ungar Publishing Co. Kobler refers to Frau Wolf's controversial pamphlet, but without further sources.

17. Kobler, *op. cit.*, p. 143.

18. *Ibid.*, pp. 143-144.

19. Sonia L. Lipman, "Judith Montefiore—First Lady of Anglo-Jewry," in *The Jewish Historical Society of England, Transactions*, Sessions, 1962-67, Vol. XXI, p. 287.

20. Quotations from the diary of Lady Judith Montefiore by Sonia L. Lipman, whose cited source is Louis Loewe, Diaries of Sir Moses and Lady Montefiore, Vols. I and II.

21. Lipman points out the accepted date of 1784, but it may have been later.

22. This synagogue was located in the center of London and attended by many prominent Jews.

23. See *supra*, p. 192, re Sarah Bat Tovim.

24. From Judith Montefiore's diary.

25. Lipman, *op. cit.*, p. 289.
26. *Ibid.*, pp. 301-302.
27. *Encyclopaedia Judaica.* "Trieste," Vol. 15, for basic information on the Jewish Community of Trieste.
28. This was a very popular book, written in the 11th century C.E., by Bahya ibn Pakuda, a Spanish Jew. It was translated into Yiddish by Rebecca Tiktiner. See Chap. VII, *"Sisters in Exile."*
29. *Jewish Encyclopedia,* "Rachel Morpurgo," Vol. 9.
30. Vittorio Castiglioni (ed.), *Ugasv Rahel,* new ed., Y. Zmora (1943).
31. Dora Kobler, *Four Rachels,* (London, 1945). (Pamphlet available YIVO Institute for Jewish Research, reference library).
32. For other sources on Rachel Morpurgo, see Nina Davis Salaman, *Rachel Morpurgo and Contemporary Hebrew Poets in Italy,* (London, 1924), p. 47; Henry Samuel Morais, *Italian Hebrew Literature* (1926); Gustav Karpeles, "Women in Jewish Literature," pp. 106-144, in *Jewish Literature and Other Essays,* (Philadelphia, Jewish Publication Society, 1895). Nathaniel Kravitz, *3000 Years of Hebrew Literature,* (Chicago, Swallow Press, Inc., 1972), pp. 448-449; Trude Weiss-Rosmarin, *Jewish Women Through the Ages,* (New York, Jewish Book Club, 1945), p. 87.
33. Schauss, *op. cit.*, pp. 273-275.
34. Castiglioni, *Ugav Rahel,* Forward. (Translated from the Hebrew by Elisa Blankstein).
35. *Ibid.*
36. Grayzel, *op. cit.*, *A History of the Jews,* pp. 593-594.
37. Nahum Slouschz, *The Renascence of Hebrew Literature,* (Philadelphia, Jewish Publication Society, 1909), pp. 82-84, translated from the French and Hebrew by Henrietta Szold.
38. Translated from the Hebrew poems of Rachel Morpurgo in Castiglioni, *Ugar Rahel* (Rachel's Harp), by Elisa Blankstein.
39. *Ibid.*
40. Slouschz, *op. cit.*, p. 84. Translated into verse by Nina Davis Salaman in the following anthologies: Nathaniel Kravitz (ed.), *3000 Years of Hebrew Literature,* (Chicago, Swallow Press, Inc. 1972) p. 595; Leo W. Schwarz (ed.), *A Golden Treasury of Jewish Literature,* (New York, Rinehart & Company, 1937), p. 595.
41. Castiglioni, *Ugav Rahel.*

XIV. *OPENING DOORS*

1. Nahida Remy, *The Jewish Woman,* translated by Louise Mannheimer, (New York, Bloch Publishing Co., 1916), p. 108.

2. Charlotte Baum, "What Made Yetta Work? The Economic Role of Eastern European Jewish Women in the Family," in *Response: The Jewish Woman — An Anthology*, Number 18, Summer, 1973, pp. 22-38.
3. Jacob R. Marcus, *The Jew in the Medieval World: A Source Book: 1315-1791*, (New York, Atheneum, 1974), pp. xiii-xiv, p. 209.
4. Mark Zborowski and Elizabeth Herzog, *Life is With People: The Culture of the Shtetl*, (New York, Schocken, 1974), p. 215, and re: women, pp. 128-132, 138-141, 361-376. In earlier times, the Jewish leaders dealt with the State as representatives of the Jewish community. They were responsible for collecting taxes, which were paid by the Jewish people as a whole to the state.
5. See Chapter XIII, "The Three Portals."
6. See Chapter XII, "One Step Ahead."
7. See Chapter XIII, "The Three Portals."
8. Hannah G. Solomon, *Fabric of My Life: Autobiography of a Social Pioneer*, (New York, Bloch, 1946).
9. Anita Libeson, *Recall to Life: The Jewish Woman in America*, (New York, Thomas Yoseloff, 1970), pp. 228-230.
10. Nina Davis Salaman, *Rachel Morpurgo and Contemporary Hebrew Poets in Italy*, (London, 1924). Salaman has also written: *Songs of Exile, Voices of the Rivers, Apples and Honey, Songs of Many Days*, and the *Poems of Yehudah Halevi*, translated into English.
11. Leo Jung (ed.) *The Jewish Library, Volume 3: The Jewish Woman*, 3rd series (New York, Jewish Library Publishing Co., 1934).
12. Stephen Birmingham, *The Grandees*, (New York, Harper & Row, 1971), Chap. 11, p. 158; see also Jacob Rader Marcus, *The American Jewish Woman, 1654-1980*, (New York, K'tav, 1981).
13. Stephen Birmingham, *op cit.*, Chap. 11, pp. 159-160.
14. Anita Libeson, *op. cit.*, Chap. 3
15. Anita Libeson, *op. cit.*, and *Jewish Pioneers in America, 1492-1848*, (New York, Behrman, 1931).
16. Sidney M. Fish, "The Problem of Intermarriage in Early America," in *Gratz College Annual of Jewish Studies*, Vol. IV, (Philadelphia, 1975), pp. 85-95.
17. David Philipson, *Letters of Rebecca Gratz*, (Philadelphia, Jewish Publication Society, 1929).
18. *Ibid.*, pp. 30-32.
19. *Ibid.*, p. 351.
20. Philipson, *op. cit.*, p. xxiv.
21. Tina Levitan, *Jews in American Life, From 1492 to the Space Age*, (New York, Hebrew Publishing Co., 1969) pp. 190-191.

22. Remy, *op. cit.*, on "Apostates," pp. 178-191. On women of the Berlin Salon, see *Sisters in Exile: Sources on the Jewish Woman* (New York, Ichud Habonim Labor Zionist Youth, 1973).

23. Union Hymnal (New York, The Central Conference of American Rabbis, 1948), p. V, hymn numbers 8, 45, 50, 55, 65, 73, 93, 140, 156, 157, 209, 212, 219.

24. Levitan, *op. cit.*, pp. 190-191.

25. Louis Harap, *Image of the Jew in American Literature, From Early Republic to Mass Immigration,* (Philadelphia, Jewish Publication Society, 1974), p. 261.

26. Union Hymnal, *op. cit.*, pp. 49, 53.

27. *Ibid.*, p. 66.

28. Remy, *op. cit.*, pp. 217-219.

29. Grace Aguilar, *Women of Israel,* 2 volumes, (New York, D. Appleton & Co., 1854).

30. Grade Aguilar, *Spirit of Judaism,* (Cincinnati, Bloch, 1842), pp. 10-11.

31. *Jewish Encyclopedia,* "Grace Aguilar" Vol. 1, p. 274.

32. Gustav Karpeles, *Jewish Literature and Other Essays,* (Philadelphia, Jewish Publication Society, 1895), essay on "Women in Jewish Literature."

33. Nahida Remy, *The Jewish Woman,* translated by Louise Mannheimer, (New York, Bloch, 1916).

34. Emily Solis-Cohen, *Status of Women in Jewish Law and the Bible.* (New York, Jewish Welfare Board, 1932).

35. Grace Aguilar, *Women of Israel, op. cit.*

36. Grace Aguilar, "The Wanderers," in *Spirit of Judaism, op. cit.,* p. 245.

37. Karpeles, *op. cit.*, "Women in Jewish Literature."

38. H. E. Jacob, *The World of Emma Lazarus,* (New York, Schocken, 1949), pp. 27-29, 217.

39. Charlotte Baum, Paula Hyman, Sonya Michel, *The Jewish Woman in America,* (New York, Dial Press, 1976), p. 39.

40. "Since Miriam sang of Deliverance". . . . quoting John Greenleaf Wittier in Jacob, *op. cit.,* p. 204.

41. *The Poems of Emma Lazarus,* (Boston and New York, Houghton, Mifflin and Co., 1889) p. 27. See also Morris U. Schappes, ed., *Emma Lazarus: Selections from her Poetry and Prose,* (New York, Cooperative Book League, 1944), pp. 197-198.

42. "The Banner of the Jew" quoted in Jacob, *op. cit.,* p. 92.

43. "The Prophet" quoted in Jacob, *op. cit.,* pp. 197.

44. Jacob, *op. cit.*

45. *The Poems of Emma Lazarus, op. cit.,* p. 201.
46. Rebekah Kohut, *More Yesterdays: An Autobiography (1925-1949),* (New York, Bloch, 1950), p. 14.
47. *Ibid.,* p. 13.
48. Rebekah Kohut, *My Portion,* (New York, Albert & Charles Boni, 1927).
49. Rebekah Kohut, *More Yesterdays, op. cit.,* p. 35-36.
50. *Ibid.,* p. 30.
51. *Ibid.,* p. 123.

XV. FOREMOTHERS TO FUTURE LEADERS

1. Mary Wollstonecraft, "A Vindication of the Rights of Women." (1792).
2. The most recent of these is Gerda Lerner, *The Creation of Patriarchy.* (New York and London: Oxford University Press, 1986). Others include: Erich Neuman, *The Great Mother; An Analysis of the Prototype.* (Princeton: Princeton University Press, 1963), translated from German by Ralph Manheim; Raphael Patai, *The Hebrew Goddess.* (New York: KTAV Publishers, 1967); Evelyn Reed, *Women's Evolution: From Matriarchal Clan to Patriarchal Family.* (New York: Pathfinder Press, 1975); Merlin Stone, *When God Was A Woman,* (New York: Dial Press, 1976).
3. Rachel Biale, *Women and Jewish Law.* (New York: Schocken, 1984); David Feldman, *Marital Relations, Birth Control and Abortion in Jewish Law.* (New York: NYU Press, 1969; Schocken, 1974); Blu Greenberg, *On Women and Judaism: A View from Tradition.* (Philadelphia: Jewish Publication Society, 1982), and *How to Run a Traditional Jewish Household.* (New York: Simon & Schuster, 1983); Judith Hauptman, "Women and Change in Jewish Law." *Conservative Judaism* (Fall, 1974). M. Meiselman, *The Jewish Woman in Jewish Law.* (New York: KTAV, 1979).
4. Selma Stern, *The Court Jew.* (Philadelphia: Jewish Publication Society, 1950).
5. Genesis 27:1-29.
6. Judges 4 & 5.
7. II Kings, 11.
8. Salome Alexandra lived from 139-67 B.C.E. and ruled Judea from 76-67 B.C.E. Mariamne lived from approximately 60 B.C.E. to 20 B.C.E. She was King Herod's second wife. Doris of Jerusalem was Herod's first wife. The dates and details of her early life are unknown. She married Herod in 45 B.C.E., before he became king. Herod dismissed her to marry Mariamne, but she was later recalled to his palace and his favor. For reference to these women see Josephus, *Wars* and *Antiquities.*

9. Berenice was born in 28 C.E. The date of her death is not confirmed. Several novels have been written about her life, including L. Kalb, *Princess of Judea* and Lion Feuchtwanger, *Josephus: A Trilogy.*

10. Bernadette Brooten, *Women Leaders in the Ancient Synagogue: Inscriptional Evidence and Background Issue.* (Chico, Ca.: Scholars Press, 1982).

11. The documents referring to Pulcellina can be found in A. Haberman, *Sefer Gezerot Ashkenaz v'Tzarfat.* (Jerusalem: 1945). pp. 141-146.

12. For references to Raquel of Toledo see Salo Baron, *A Social and Religious History of the Jews,* 2nd ed. Vol. IV. (New York & London: Columbia University Press; Philadelphia: Jewish Publication Society, 1957; 4th reprint, 1971). p. 37 and fn. p. 252. Heinrich Graetz, *Popular History of the Jews,* Vol. III. (New York: Hebrew Publishing Co., 1937). p. 386.

13. Lion Feuchtwanger, *Raquel: Jewess of Toledo.* (New York: Julian Messner Inc., 1954). Feuchtwanger cites *Chronica General of Alfonso el Sabio,* c. 1270 as the source of these lines.

14. Graetz, *op.cit.* Vol. IV, p. 112.

15. Eva Frank is referred to in the following general histories: Max Dimont, *Jews, God and History.* (New York: Signet Books, 1964). Solomon Grayzel, *A History of the Jews.* (Philadelphia: Jewish Publication Society, 1970). See also *Encyclopedia Judaica* "Frank, Jacob and the Frankists." Vol. 7, p. 55.

16. Marian A. Kaplan, *The Jewish Feminist Movement in Germany: The Campaigns of the Judischer Frauenbund, 1904-1938.* (Westport, Conn.: Greenwood Press, 1979).

17. S. Jackson, *The Sassoons.* (New York: Dutton, 1968). Cecil Roth, *Sassoon Dynasty.* (New York: Ryerson Press; England: R. Hale, 1941).

18. Ellen Umansky, *Lily Montagu and the Advancement of Liberal Judaism: From Vision to Vocation.* (Lewiston, N.Y.: Edwin Mellen Press, 1983). Ellen Umansky, ed. *Lily Montagu: Sermons, Addresses, Letters and Prayers.* (Lewiston, N.Y.: Edwin Mellen Press, 1985).

19. Chava Weissler, "Voices from the Heart: Women's Devotional Prayers," in *The Jewish Almanac,* eds. R. Siegel and C. Rheins. (New York: Bantam, 1980):541-545. "Women in Paradise." *Tikkun* 2:2 (1987):43-46. "The Traditional Piety of Ashkenazi Women," in *History of Jewish Spirituality,* Vol. II. ed. Arthur Green. (New York: Crossroads Press, forthcoming).

20. Anthony Masters, *The Summer that Bled: the Biography of Hannah Senesh.* (New York: St. Martin's Press, 1972). Hannah Senesh, *Letters, Diary, Poems.* (New York: Herzl Press, 1972). Marie Syrkin, *Blessed is the Match.* (Philadelphia: Jewish Publication Society, 1974; reprint 1977).

21. Yuri Suhl, *They Fought Back.* (New York: Crown, 1967); Aviva Cantor, "She Fought Back—An Interview with Vilna Partisan Vitke Kempner." *Lilith* (Spring, 1987):20-24.

22. Deborah Weissman, "Bais Yaakov: A Historical Model for Jewish Feminism," in Elizabeth Koltun, ed. *The Jewish Woman: New Perspectives.* (New York: Schocken, 1976).

23. P. Froelich, *Rosa Luxemburg.* (England: Gollancz; New York: Ryerson Press, 1940). Rosa Luxemburg, *Comrade and Lover: Letters to Leo Jogiches.* (Boston: M.I.T. Press, 1981). J.P. Nettl, *Rosa Luxemburg.* 2 vols. (England: Oxford University Press, 1966).

24. Ada Maimon, *Women Build a Land.* (New York: Herzl Press, 1962); Rachel Shazar (Katznelson), ed. *The Plough Woman.* (New York: Herzl Press, 1975).

25. Golda Meir, *My Life.* (New York: Dell, 1975).

26. Leslie Hazelton, *Israeli Women: The Reality Behind the Myths.* (New York: Simon & Schuster, 1978) explores the changes in Israeli women's self-image and lifestyles since those early pioneer days, and some of the reasons for those changes.

27. Mari Jo Buhle, *Women and American Socialism: 1790-1920.* (Urbana, Ill.: University of Illinois Press, 1983). p. 176-179.

28. For brief biographies on Jewish women in the labor movement, see: Baum, Hyman and Michel, *The Jewish Woman in America. op.cit.;* Carol Hymowitz, Michele Weissman, *A History of Women in America.* (New York: Bantam, 1978). Also Rose Schneiderman and Lucy Goldthwaite, *All for One.* (Middlebury, Vt.: Paul S. Erickson, 1967).

29. Richard Drinnon, *Rebel in Paradise: A Biography of Emma Goldman.* (Chicago: University of Chicago Press, 1961); Emma Goldman, *Living My Life,* 2 vols. (New York: Dover, 1971).

30. Mary Antin, *The Promised Land.* (Boston: Houghton-Mifflin, 1969; reprint). Anzia Yezierska, *Bread Givers.* (New York: Persea Books, 1978; reprint); *The Open Cage.* (New York: Persea Books, 1979; reprint). Yezierska has also written *Hungry Hearts* (1902), *Children of Loneliness* (1923), *Salome of the Tenements* (1922), *All I Could Ever Be* (1932) and *Red Ribbon on a White Horse* (1950).

31. Sydelle Kramer and Jenny Masur, eds. *Jewish Grandmothers.* *(Boston: Beacon Press, 1976).*

32. *Rebekah Kohut, My Portion.* (New York: Albert & Charles Boni, 1925); *More Yesterdays.* (New York: Bloch, 1950); Hannah G. Solomon, *Fabric of My Life.* (New York: Bloch/National Council of Jewish Women, 1946; reprint, 1974). See also June Sochen, *Consecrate Every Day: The Public Lives of American Jewish Women, 1880-1890.* (Albany, N.Y.: SUNY Press, 1981).

33. Yuri Suhl, *Ernestine Rose and the Battle for Human Rights.* New York: Reynal & Hitchcock, 1959).

34. Irving Bloch, *Neighbor to the World.* (World Press, 1969); Lillian Wald, *House on Henry Street.* (New York: Henry Holt & Co., 1915).

35. At the present time in Israel, Jewish men may be jailed for refusing to give a wife a Jewish divorce, but the state will not force him to issue the divorce, nor act for him. Intermarriage is presently not possible in Israel, since civil marriage is not available. Children of these marriages (performed outside of Israel) often have questionable status if the non-Jewish spouse is the woman, and must undergo official conversion to Judaism.

36. Ann Lapidus Lerner, "Who Hast Not Made Me A Man: The Movement for Equal Rights for Women in American Jewry." Pamphlet, AJC.; reprinted from *American Jewish Year Book* (1977).

37. See for example Joel Roth, "Ordination of Women: An *Halachic* Analysis." *Judaism* (Winter, 1984):70-78.

38. Susan Weidman Schneider, *Jewish and Female: Choices and Changes in our Lives Today.* (New York: Simon & Schuster, 1984).

39. Penina Adelman, *Miriam's Well.* (Fresh Meadows, N.Y.: Biblio Press, 1986).

40. Cynthia Ozick, "Notes toward Finding the Right Question." *On Being a Jewish Feminist* by Susannah Heschel. (New York: Schocken Books, 1983) pp. 120-152.

BIBLIOGRAPHY

The following were used as general source references:

Encyclopaedia Britannica, 23 volumes and index. Chicago, London, Willaim Benton, 1969

Encyclopaedia Judaica, 16 volumes, Jerusalem, Israel, Keter Publishing House Ltd., 1972

Jewish Encyclopedia, 12 volumes, New York, K'tav Publishing House, Inc. 1901 (reprint)

TEXTS:

Abrahams, Israel, *Hebrew Ethical Wills,* Philadelphia, The Jewish Publication Society, 1976

Abrahams, Israel, *Jewish Life in the Middle Ages,* New York, Atheneum, 1975 (first edition, 1896, 2nd edition edited by Cecil Roth, 1932)

Aguilar, Grace, *Spirit of Judaism,* Cincinnati, Bloch Publishing Co., 1842.

Aguilar, Grace, *Women of Israel,* 2 volumes, New York, D. Appleton & Co., 1854; London, G. Routledge and Sons, 1888

Aron, Milton, *Ideas and Ideals of the Hasidim,* New York, The Citadel Press, Inc., 1964

Ascarelli, Devora, *Sindacato Italiano Arti,* Roma, published by Pellegrino Ascarelli, 1925 (Italian)

Baron, Salo Whitmayer, *A Social and Religious History of the Jews,* 12 volumes, New York, Columbia University Press, 1952

Bate, H. N., *The Sibylline Oracles, Books III-V,* New York, The Macmillan Co., 1918, (reprint 1937)

Baum, Charlotte, Paula Hyman, and Sonya Michel, *The Jewish Woman in America,* New York, Dial Press, 1976

Birmingham, Stephen, *The Grandees,* New York, Harper & Row, 1971

Birnbaum, Philip, *A Book of Jewish Concepts,* New York, Hebrew Publishing Co., 1975

Bright, John, *A History of Israel,* Philadelphia, Westminster Press, 1964, 2nd edition

Cantor, Aviva, *The Jewish Woman: 1900-1980,* Bibliography, 2nd edition and Supplement, New York, Biblio Press, 1982

Castiglioni, Vittorius (ed.) *Ugav Rahel* (new edition), Y. Zmora, 1943 (Italian and Hebrew)

Charles, R. H. (ed.), *The Apocrypha and Pseudepigrapha of the Old Testament,* 2 volumes, Oxford, Clarendon Press, 1913

Cowley, Arthur, *Aramaic Papyri of the Fifth Century B.C.*, Oxford, 1923

Dash, Jean, *Summoned to Jerusalem: The Life of Henrietta Szold,* New York, Harper & Row, 1979

Dubnow, Simon, *History of the Jews From the Beginning to Early Christianity* (translated from the Russian) New York, Thomas Yoseloff, 1967

Edinger, Dora, *Bertha Pappenheim: Freud's Anna O.,* Highland Park, Ill., Cong. Solel, 1968

Feuchtwanger, Lion, *Raquel, Jewess of Toldeo,* New York, Julian Messner Inc., 1954

Finkelstein, Louis (ed.), *The Jews: Their History, Culture and Religion,* New York, Harper and Bros. 1955

Ginsberg, Louis, *Legends of the Jews,* 7 volumes, translated from the German manuscript by Henrietta Szold, Philadelphia, Jewish Publication Society, 1910

The Memoirs of Glückel of Hameln (1646-1724) written by Herself, translated from the original Yiddish and edited by Beth-Zion Abrahams, New York, Thomas Yoseloff, 1962

Goitein, S.D., *Jews and Arabs: Their Contacts Through the Ages,* New York, Schocken Books, 1974

Goitein, S.D., *A Mediterranean Society, Volume I, Economic Foundations,* Berkeley and Los Angeles, University of California Press, 1967; *Volume II, The Community,* Berkeley, Los Angeles and London, University of California Press, 1971

Gore, Norman C. *Tzenah U-Re'enah, A Jewish Commentary on the Book of Exodus,* New York, Vantage Press, 1965

Graetz, Heinrich, *Popular History of the Jews,* New York, Hebrew Publishing Co., 1937, 5th edition (first edition in German, 1887-1889)

Grayzel, Solomon, *A History of the Jews,* Philadelphia, Jewish Publication Society, 1970 (Mentor PB, 1968)

Greenberg, Blu, *On Women and Judaism: A View from Tradition,* Philadelphia, Jewish Publication Society, 1982

Haberman, A., *Sefer Gezerot Ashkenaz v'Zarfat,* Jerusalem, 1945, (Hebrew)

Harap, Louis, *Image of the Jew in American Literature from Early Republic to Mass Immigration,* Philadelphia, Jewish Publication Society, 1974

Hertz, J. H. (ed.), *Pentateuch and Haftorah* (Hebrew Text, English Translation and Commentary), London, Soncino Press, 1960, 2nd edition (first edition, 1937)

Introduction to the Apocrypha, New Hyde Park, N.Y., University Books, Inc.

Jacob, H. E., *The World of Emma Lazarus,* New York, Schocken Books, 1949

Jung, Leo (ed.), *The Jewish Library: Volume 3: The Jewish Woman,* (3rd series) New York, Jewish Library Publishing Co., 1934

Kayserling, M. *Die Judischen Frauen en der Geschichte Literatur und Kunst,* Leipzig, 1879 (German)

Karpeles, Gustav, *Jewish Literature and Other Essays,* Philadelphia, Jewish Publication Society, 1895

Kitab-l-Aghani, Abu al-Faraj al-Isbahani (Arabic)

Kobler, Dora, *Four Rachels,* London, 1945

Kobler, Franz (ed.), *Her Children Call Her Blessed,* New York, Stephen Daye Press, 1955

Kobler, Franz, (ed.), *A Treasury of Jewish Letters,* 2 volumes, New York, Farrar, Strauss and Young, Inc., 1952

Kohut, Rebekah, *My Portion,* New York, Boni & Livright, 1925

Kohut, Rebekah, *More Yesterdays,* New York, Bloch Publishing Co., 1950

Kolton, Elizabeth (ed.), *The Jewish Woman: New Perspectives,* New York, Schocken, 1976

Kraeling, Emil, *The Brooklyn Museum Aramaic Papyri,* New Haven, Conn., Yale University press, 1953

Kramer, Cydelle and Jenny Masur (eds.), *Jewish Grandmothers,* Boston, Beacon Press, 1976

Kravitz, Nathaniel, *Three Thousand Years of Hebrew Literature,* Chicago, Swallow Press, 1972

Lacks, Roslyn, *Women in Judaism: Myth, History and Struggle,* New York, Doubleday, 1980

Landau, Alfred and Bernard Wachstein, *Judische Privatbriefe aus dem Jahre 1619,* Vienna, 1911

Lerner, Anne Lapidus, "Who Has Not Made Me a Man: The Movement for Equal Rights for Women in American Jewry," Pamphlet, AJC. (Reprinted from 1977 American Jewish Year Book)

Levitan, Tina, *Jews in American Life: From 1492 to the Space Age,* New York, Hebrew Publishing Co., 1969

Libeson, Anita, *Recall to Life: the Jewish Woman in America,* New York, Thomas Yoseloff, 1970

Libeson, Anita, *Jewish Pioneers in America: 1492-1848,* New York, Behrman, 1931

Maimon, Ada, *Women Build A Land,* New York, Herzl Press, 1962

Mann, Jacob, *Texts and Studies in Jewish History and Literature,* Cincinnati, University of Cincinnati, 1932

Marcus, Jacob R., *The Jew in the Medieval World: A Source Book, 1315-1791,* New York, Atheneum, 1974 (first edition, 1938)

Marcus, Jacob R., *The American Jewish Woman: A Documentary History,* New York, K'tav Publishing, 1981

Marcus, Jacob R., *The Jew in the Medieval World: A Source Book, 1315-1791,* New York, Atheneum, 1974 (first edition, 1938)

Margoliouth, David S., *Relations Between Arabs and Israelites,* London, Oxford University Press, 1924

Meir, Golda, *My Life,* New York, Dell, 1975

Minkin, Jacob S., *The Romance of Hassidism,* New York, Thomas Yoseloff, 1955

Neusner, Jacob, *Invitation to the Talmud,* New York, Harper & Row, 1973

Noeldeke, Theodore, *Beitrage zur Poesie der Alten Araber,* Hanover, 1864 (German)

Philipson, David, (ed.), *Letters of Rebecca Gratz,* Philadelphia, Jewish Publication Society, 1929

The Poems of Emma Lazarus, Boston and New York, Houghton, Mifflin and Co., 1889

Porten, Bezalel, *Archives from Elephantine: The Life of an Ancient Jewish Military Colony,* University of California Press, 1968

Pomeroy, Sarah B., *Goddesses, Whores, Wives and Slaves,* New York, Schocken, 1975

Pritchard, James B. (ed.), *The Ancient Near East: An Anthology of Texts and Pictures,* Princeton University Press, 1958

Rabinowicz, Harry M., *The World of Hasidism,* London, Hartford House, 1970

Radin, Max, *The Jews Among the Greeks and Romans,* Philadelphia, Jewish Publication Society, 1915

Raddock, Charles, *Portrait of a People,* 3 volumes, New York, Judaica Press, 1965

Remy, Nahida, *The Jewish Woman,* translated by Louise Mannheimer, New York, Bloch Publishing Co., 1916

Response, The Jewish Woman: an Anthology, Summer, 1973

Reuther, Rosemary (Radford), *Religion and Sexism: Images of Women in the Jewish and Christian Tradition,* Harper & Row, New York, 1974

Roth, Cecil, *The Jews in the Renaissance,* Philadelphia, Jewish Publication Society, 1959

Roth, Cecil, *The Jews of Venice,* Philadelphia, Jewish Publication Society, 1930

Roth, Cecil, *The House of Nasi: Dona Gracia,* Philadelphia, Jewish Publication Society, 1947

Roth, Cecil, *The House of Nasi: Joseph, Duke of Naxos,* Philadelphia, Jewish Publication Society, 1948

Sayce, A.H. and A.E. Cowley, *Aramaic Papyri Discovered at Assuan,* London, 1906

Salaman, Nina Davis, *Rachel Morpurgo and Contemporary Hebrew Poets in Italy,* London, 1924

Schappes, Morris U. (ed.), *Emma Lazarus: Selections from Her Poetry and Prose,* New York, Cooperative Book League, 1944

Schechter, Solomon, *Studies in Judaism,* Philadelphia, Jewish Publication Society, 1938

Shazar, Rachel (Katznelson) (ed.), *The Plough Woman,* New York, Herzl Press, 1975

Sisters in Exile: Sources on the Jewish Woman, New York, Ichud Habonim Labor Zionist Youth, 1973

Solomon, Hannah G., *Fabric of My Life,* New York, Bloch Publishing Co./National Council of Jewish Women, 1946 (reprint 1974)

Speiser, E. A., *The Anchor Bible: Genesis* translation, introduction and notes by E. A. Speiser, Garden City, New York, Doubleday & Co., 1964

Stern, Selma, *The Court Jew*, Philadelphia, Jewish Publication Society, 1950

Strizower, Schifra, *Exotic Jewish Communities*, London and New York, Thomas Yoseloff, 1962

Suhl, Yuri, *Ernestine Rose and the Battle for Human Rights*, New York, Reynal and Hitchcock, 1959

Swidler, Leonard, *Women in Judaism: the Status of Women in Formative Judaism*, Metuchen, New Jersey, Scarecrow Press, 1976

Tcherikover, Victor, *Hellenistic Civilization and the Jews*, Philadelphia, Jewish Publication Society, 1959

Terry, Milton S., *The Sibylline Oracles* (translated from the Greek), New York, Hunt and Eaton, 1890

Wald, Lillian, *House on Henry Street*, New York, Henry Holt & Co., 1915

Waxman, Meyer, *Blessed Is the Daughter*, New York, Shengold Publishers, Inc., 1968

Waxman, Meyer, *A History of Jewish Literature, from the Close of the Bible to Our Own Days*, 6 volumes, New York, Bloch Publishing, 1938-1941

Wedgewood, C. V. *The Thirty Years War*, New Haven, Yale University Press, 1939

Weiss Rosmarin, Trude, *Jewish Women Through The Ages*, New York, The Jewish Book Club, 1940

Zbrowski, Mark and Elizabeth Herzog, *Life Is With People: The Culture of the Shtetl*, New York, Schocken Books, 1974

Zinberg, Israel, *A History of Jewish Literature*, translated and edited by Bernard Martin, New York, K'tav, 1975 (first edition in German, 1929-1937)

Zotenberg, *Catalogue des Manuscrits Hebreux de la Bibliotèque Impérial*, 1866, p. 55, #408 (French)

299

INDEX

Abrabanel, Benvenida 137-139, 143
Abzug, Bella 255
Adultery 3
Aguilar, Grace 229-236
Agunah 102
Alexandria 38-40
Aliya (women) 6
American, Sadie 254
Anna, The Hebrew 143-145
Antin, Mary 254
Aramaic Papyri 30-37
Arwyller, Frommet (of) 115-117
Ascarelli, Devora 14, 127-130
Ashkenazi, Hannah 90
Athaliah, Queen 250
Austrian Empire 152-155, 205
Babylonia 16, 30-31, 45-46, 59
Babylonian Exile 30-31
Bacharach, Eva 90-91, 235
Banu (B'Nai) Quraiza, 59-64
Baraita 45
Barak 24-29
Bat HaLevi 2, 9, 86
Bat Sheba (Verona) 118
Bellina, Madonna 126
Benayahu, Miriam 115
Ben Zvi, Rachel Yaanit 253
Beruriah 9, 44-47, 54-58
Bible 3-7, 15, 33, 38, 93, 105, 185-187, 231
Black Plague 83-84
Businesswomen 75, 86, 88, 119, 165
Castiglioni, Vittorio 201, 202
Characteristics of Women (Talmud) 9, 47, 55-56
Chassen, Bella Hurwitz 90, 118
Chmelnitzki 166, 175, 186
Commandments (see Mitzvot) 5-9, 86-87, 184-193
Conat, Estellina 117-118
Constantinople 104, 119, 136, 146
Cosmeticians 143, 145-147
Crusades 83, 87
Dahiyah Kahinah (see Kahinah, Dayiyah Bint Thabitah Ibn Tifan) 14, 65-67, 69
Daughter of Joseph 76
Deborah (Judge and Prophetess) 2, 24-29, 67

Divorce 3, 32-37
Doctors 89-90, 124-126
Dreier, Mary 254
Dulcie of Worms 87
Education, Italy 87, 125
Education of Women 79, 123-125, 169, 176, 202, 205
Elephantine Colony 30-37
Eliezer ben Hyrcanus 9, 48-53
Elis bat Mordechai of Slutzk 118
Elizabeth, Queen (England) 150-151
Ella of Dessau 119-120
England 13, 72, 84, 88-89, 91, 201-203, 229-230
Entertainers 126
Ephron, Nora 255
Esterka (Opoczno, Poland) 252
Esther, Queen of Persia 23
Ethical Will 192-194
Europa, Madama 126
Eve 15
Ferrara Bible 141-142
Fishels, Roizl 118
Foresayers *(Firzogerin)* 87, 187-188, 189, 234
Fostat 71-72
Frank, Eva 252
Franks, Abigail Levy 215
Friedan, Betty 255
Gamaliel (Rabban) 48-49, 52-53
Gela 121
Gemarra 45
Geniza (Cairo) 71-82, 100
German Salon women 225
Germany 165-173, 185, 197, 205
Gershom (Rabbenu) of Mayence 4, 73-74
Ghetto 92, 124, 126, 141, 152-164, 165, 205, 217
Glückel of Hameln 165-173
Goitein, S.D. 72
Golden Age of Spain 68, 73, 124, 137
Goldman, Emma 254
Gordon, Ya-el 253
Gracia Nasi (See Nasi, Dona Gracia)
Gratz, Rebecca 218-224, 255
Gutman, Sarel 152-159

Hagar 16, 233-234
Hamerschlag, Friedel 163-164
Hannah 21-23, 195
Haran 16
Hasidic women, 175-183; Udel (Edel) 177; Feige, 178; Malkah, 179; Eidele, 179; Soreh, 211; Sarah, 181; Perele, 181; Malkele, 181.
Hasidism 175-183, 197
Hayes, Esther Etting 215-216
Hellenization of Jews 38-43
Heller, Henele 159-161
Herz, Henrietta de Lemos 255
Huldah 26
Hungary (Eisenstadt) 197
Hurrians 16
Hurwitz, Bella Chassen (see Chassen)
Ima Shalom 14, 44, 47-53
Inheritance (women) 5, 33
Inquisition 137-141
Italy 123-135, 205-207
Jerusalem 45
Jewish Theological Seminary 72, 93
Judah HaNasi 45
Judels, Rachel & Rebecca 118
Judith 67
Kahinah, Dahiyah 14, 65-67, 69
Kairouan 79-80
Karaites 73
Kashrut (dietary laws) 12, 191
Kasmunah 68-70
Katznelson, Rachel Shazar 253
Kiera, Esther 14, 138, 146-149, 252
Kohen, Gutel 118
Kohut, Rebekah Bettelheim 243-252
Kurdistan 14, 91, 108-109
Landau, Resel 161-163
Lazarus, Emma 236-243
Leah (wife of Jacob) 18-19
Lemlich, Clara (Shavelson) 254
Leonora, Dutchess of Tuscany 138
Lerner, Anne Lapidus 255
Lewin, Rachel (Varnhagen) 225
Licoricia of Winchester 88
Liebman, Esther 250
Lita (Litte) of Regensburg 90
Ludomir, Maid of (Hannah Rachel Werbermacher) 11, 182-183

Luna, Beatrice de (see Dona Gracia Nasi)
Luria, Miriam Shapira 87
Luxemburg, Rosa 253
Maimon, Ada 253
Maimonides, Moses 8-9, 74-75, 86, 241
Malchi, Esperanza 11, 150-151
Malchin, Sarah 253
Maliha, Lady 104-107
Mansi, Paula dei 115
Mann, Jacob 72
Marat Guta 87
Maria Hebrea 90
Mariamne (Queen) 250
Marranos 136, 139-141, 229
Matriarchs (Biblical) 15-19, 185, 187, 193, 232
Mediterranean Society 71-72, 74
Meir, Rabbi 9, 54-58
Mendelssohn, Moses 197, 241
Mendelssohn, Dorothea (Schlegel) 225
Mendes, Edel 90
Meneket Rivka 92-99, 190
Menstruation (see Niddah) 5-7, 12
Messiah 209
Messiahs 76
Mibtahiah 10, 30-37
Middle Ages 91
Mikveh 6
Minis, Abigail 215
Miriam 19-21, 238
Mishna 45, 49
Mitnagdim 178, 197
Mitzvot (commandments) 7-9, 81, 176, 184
Mizrachi, Rebbetzin 2, 14, 108-113
Modena, Bathsheba (Fioretta) 126
Modena, Pomona 126
Moise, Penina 224-228
Montagu, Lillian 247
Montefiore, Judith (Lady) 201-204, 214
Montefiore, Moses (Sir) 201, 203
Morpurgo, Rachel 204-211, 214
Moses 19-21
Nasi, Dona Gracia Mendes (Beatrice de Luna) 11, 119, 136, 139-143, 149
Nasi, Reyna 139-142

Nasi, Joseph (Joao), Duke of
    Naxos 139-142
'New Colossus' 236-237, 240
Niddah (laws of purity) 5-7, 12,
    188
North Africa 59-61, 65-67
Occupations of women 75-76,
    89-91, 114-119
Osnath 108
Ottoman Empire (Turkey) 108,
    136, 137, 138
Pappenheim, Bertha 247, 252
Patroness 86, 90, 138, 141, 148
Perna of Fano 124
Persia 31-32
Philanthropy 119, 142
Philo 39
Physicians 89-90, 124
Poetry 60-64, 67-70, 109, 128-130,
    132, 208-211, 215, 227-228,
    233-234, 239-243
Pogrebin, Letty Cottin 255
Poland 85, 89, 92
Politics 142-143, 146-149
Polygamy 4, 73-74
Portugal 139-141
Prague 89, 92, 94, 152-154
Prayers (see *techinah*) 87, 100
Printers 85, 117-122
Rabbanot (women rabbis) 176-183
Rachel (wife of Jacob) 18-19, 21
Rapoport, Serel Segal 193
Raquel of Toledo 251
Rashi's daughters, granddaughters
    12, 88
Rebecca (Isaac's wife) 18
Rebecca (Ivanhoe) 220
Redemption of captives 81-82, 141
Remy, Nahida 231
Renaissance, Italy 123-135
Richman, Julia 247
Roles of women 1-3, 75-76
Rose, Ernestine 255
Salaman, Nina (Davis) 214-215,
    237
Salome Alexandra (Queen) 2, 250
Sambathe (Sabbe) 38-43
Sarah (Abraham's wife) 2, 15-17
Sarah (Arabic poet) 62-64
Sarah, Donna 102
Sassoon, Flora 252-253
Schechter, Solomon 72, 168

Schenirer, Sarah 253
Schneiderman, Rose 254
Scholars 44, 47, 54, 85, 108-113
Scribes 75, 114-115
Separation in synagogues
    (mehitza) 10
Sex, in Bible 3; in Talmud 46
Sforza, Catherine 143-145
Sham'ah Shabazi 61
Shmuel Buch 90
Shochtot, ritual meat slaughterers
    128
Sibylline Oracles 38-43
Solis-Cohen, Emily 231
Solomon, Hannah G. 254
Sonneschein, Rosa 214
Spahis (Turkey) 148
Steinem, Gloria 255
Sullam, Sara Coppia 130-132
Sultana Baffa (Turkey) 146-149
Susannah and the Elders 128-130
Szold, Henrietta 256
Talmud 44-58, 59, 73, 87, 109, 169
Teachers 54, 75, 85
Techinah (prayers) 87, 100,
    186-196
Thirty-Years War 152-153, 165
Tiktiner, Rebecca, 11, 88, 89,
    92-100, 235
Tosefta 45
Tovim, Sarah Bat 11, 184-193
Translators 115, 127, 187, 237
Turkey 104, 119, 136, 146
Tzena Urena 186
Varnhagen (See Levin, R.)
Venice 147
Wald, Lillian 255
Werbermacher, Hannah Rachel
    11, 182-183
Witnesses in court 77
Wolf, Frau Frumet (Fani) 197-200
Wuhsha 10, 77-78
Ya-El 25-29, 67
Yemen 60-62
Yemenite poetry 60
Yezierska, Anzia 254
Yiddish 87, 118-119, 154, 185, 196
YIVO (Institute for Jewish
    Research) 93
Zaynab 67
Zelophehad, Daughters of 5, 33
Zvi, Sabbatai 166, 171-172